What people are say

No Justice, No I

"Globally, there are increasing concerns about police use of force within both democratic nation-states and authoritarian regimes. This is combined with a growing awareness of the fact that criminal justice systems are institutionally racist. This book does an admirable job of drawing together these issues and asking urgent questions: what is the role of the police; what could justice be in the 21st century; do black lives really matter? The book will be invaluable for all students interested in justice, equality and rights in the age of Black Lives Matter."

David Baker, University of Liverpool, author of: *Deaths after Police Contact: Constructing Accountability in the 21st century* (2016, Palgrave-Macmillan), *"We Are Not the Enemy": Police Related Deaths in the United States"* (2021, Lexington Books)

"This timely edited volume exposes a threatening dialectic manoeuvre: the 21st century is returning to the situation present within the origins of capitalist society when the military was in charge of public surveillance, but now it does so in a more egregious manner: through militarized policing. However, the book does not leave us without hope. Instead, it is a call to build upon a worldwide social movement demanding the defunding of the police and proposing a transformative way of dealing with crime and punishment."

Valeria Vegh Weis, Professor of Criminology, Universidad de Buenos Aires; Researcher, Konstanz Universität, Germany; author of *Marxism and Criminology* (2018, Haymarket)

"This collective volume edited by Matt Clement achieves something few of us might have anticipated. Setting off with

analyses of struggles for justice, through to re-discussions of 'policing the crisis' and the return of colonial models of policing, the book lands on the terrain of what criminologists identify as abolitionism. A refreshing journey that successfully crosses several areas of the social sciences."
Professor Vincenzo Ruggiero, Middlesex University, London

No Justice, No Police?

The Politics of Protest
and Social Change

No Justice, No Police?

The Politics of Protest and Social Change

Matt Clement

Winchester, UK
Washington, USA

JOHN HUNT PUBLISHING

First published by Zero Books, 2023
Zero Books is an imprint of John Hunt Publishing Ltd., No. 3 East St., Alresford,
Hampshire SO24 9EE, UK
office@jhpbooks.com
www.johnhuntpublishing.com
www.zero-books.net

For distributor details and how to order please visit the 'Ordering' section on our website.

Text copyright: Matt Clement 2022

ISBN: 978 1 78904 945 9
978 1 78904 946 6 (ebook)
Library of Congress Control Number: 2022935493

All rights reserved. Except for brief quotations in critical articles or reviews, no part of this
book may be reproduced in any manner without prior written permission from the publishers.

The rights of Matt Clement as author have been asserted in accordance with the Copyright,
Designs and Patents Act 1988.

A CIP catalogue record for this book is available from the British Library.

Design: Matthew Greenfield

UK: Printed and bound by CPI Group (UK) Ltd, Croydon, CR0 4YY
Printed in North America by CPI GPS partners

We operate a distinctive and ethical publishing philosophy in
all areas of our business, from our global network of authors to
production and worldwide distribution.

Contents

Abstracts and Contributor Details

Jeff Ferrell is Visiting Professor of Criminology at the University of Kent, UK, and Emeritus Professor of Sociology at Texas Christian University, USA. He is author of *Drift (2018), Crimes of Style, Tearing Down the Streets* & *Empire of Scrounge*. He is co-editor of the books *Cultural Criminology, Ethnography at the Edge, Making Trouble, Cultural Criminology Unleashed,* and *Cultural Criminology: Theories of Crime*

Chapter 1: What Is to Be Done About the Police?

It is worth remembering that the police were first introduced into industrializing societies like Britain in order to replace the military, who were judged to be too blunt an instrument for effective social control in the new era of mass public demonstrations, as proven by the traumatic events of the 1819 Peterloo Massacre in Manchester. Through their role of regular public surveillance they were to build up a closer relationship with communities that allowed them to disperse crowds effectively without resort to armed force.

This methodology is now in a crisis due to the police adopting the same militarized demeanor as the forces they once replaced, with predictably counter-productive results. In the US the police's institutionalized racism has reached unprecedented levels of street violence, echoed in many other nations from Brazil to France and the UK. At the same time, some of the states that command them are showing increasing tendencies toward relying upon police violence to control political opposition on the streets, from Belarus to Hong Kong, from Thailand to Nigeria. Public calls for abolition and reform of the police in some states are mirrored by struggles to defend democracy and win civil rights in others. Old criminological discourses described as forms of "realism" appear increasingly utopian and raise questions about the kind of social movements needed to recapture popular power from the institutions of social control. **Matt Clement (Senior Lecturer in Criminology, Royal Holloway University of London)**

Chapter 2: Do Black Lives Really Matter?

Feminists have argued that prison does not work for women, as it was designed for men by men. If we apply this logic to institutions such as the police and justice system, one can argue that these institutions were not built with BAME communities in mind and, therefore, cannot respond to the multiplicity of needs this group presents. The argument throughout this chapter will be that institutional racism can only be addressed properly if we first unpick the collective term "BAME", and recognize that the discrimination and oppression faced by each group within this broad category is fundamentally different. Second, it will suggest that the police and justice system must understand and acknowledge the foundations of the discriminative bias within their institutions to develop change from an informed perspective.

In doing so, they can work in consultation with the communities that are most affected by their institutional racism. There will be focus on how policing in black communities can be reformed, while also considering how the justice system contributes to their experiences. This chapter recognizes that minority groups are seeking radical changes, and have grown exhausted of light touch approaches to change.

Nicole Nyamwiza: Lecturer in Criminology, University of Kingston, UK

Chapter 3: "Fund the People Not Police!": The Movement to Defund Law Enforcement

In 2014, the United States witnessed the rise of Black Lives Matter (BLM) protests, triggered by the police killings of numerous black, brown and indigenous people. In the streets, people cried out "No justice, no peace, fuck the police!"; "The whole damn system is guilty as hell!"; "If we don't get it [justice], shut it down!" and "No more killer cops!" These uncompromising positions were amplified by grassroots collectives that advanced demands of local and state governments regarding law enforcement. These demands ranged from police reform to community control to calls for the total abolition of the institution of policing. In 2020, following the killing of George Floyd at the knee of a Minneapolis police officer, the country erupted, with uprisings across the country. These demonstrations were more militant and more sustained than in 2014, stretching for more than 100 days of continuous protest. Building on 2014 efforts to "disarm, disempower, and dismantle" policing, calls to "defund the police" went mainstream. Government officials have been forced to take police abolitionist claims more seriously.

This chapter examines the implementation of abolitionist demands to transform and ultimately eliminate the function of police in US society. Specifically, drawing on our own experience working on defunding campaigns, we critically analyze this strategy, examining the possibilities and potential pitfalls of this effort. We will also reflect on the promise of police abolition more broadly, particularly its potential for challenging racial capitalism and related forms of domination.

Meghan G. McDowell, Ph.D. is an Assistant Professor of Criminology and Criminal Justice at Northern Arizona University. Meghan's research and organizing is focused on building a world where punishment, prisons, and police power are unthinkable. Her recent work can be found in *Critical Criminology, Theoretical Criminology, and Social Justice: A Journal of Crime, Conflict, and World Order.*

Dr Luis A. Fernandez is a professor in, and chair of, the Department of Criminology and Criminal Justice at Northern Arizona University. He served as the President

of the Society for the Study of Social Problems in 2017-18 and is currently the co-editor of *Critical Issues in Crime and Society*, Rutgers University Press. He has worked in various community-based efforts related to immigration and policing. He is the author and editor of several books, including *Policing Dissent*, *Shutting Down the Streets* and *Alternatives to Policing*. His most recent research focuses on understanding the claims and consequences of police defunding and abolitionist practice.

Laura Rethmann is a student-activist with a bachelor's degree in sociology from Northland College and is a graduate student at Northern Arizona University studying applied criminology. Laura continues to work toward a future in which police are made obsolete and all communities have the resources needed to thrive.

Brooklyn Rincones is a graduate student in the applied criminology program at Northern Arizona University. When she is not in the classroom, Brooklyn is out making a difference in the community. Brooklyn began researching the movement to defund the police in the spring of 2021 and has been working on that ever since.

Chapter 4: Resistant Imagery in Struggles for Justice

Migrant Media is a collective of migrant, black and refugee film activists established in 1991. The struggles of race and class are at the core of their resistance-based documentary film-making and a dominant thread in their work is around campaigns for justice by the families of people killed by the police in the UK. They employ the techniques of *Third Cinema* to incite political change through a provocative strategy of deconstructing established narratives. As Getino and Solanas (1971) state: "Every image that documents, bears witness to, refutes or deepens the truth of a situation is something more than a film image or purely artistic fact; it becomes something which the system finds indigestible." In this spirit Migrant Media challenges conventional documentary, adopting a position of the filmmakers as the gatherers of resistant imagery. This documentary practice is a radical approach in confronting dominant media and state narratives. Resistance, from a community perspective, is documented over 3 decades, employing a "documentary of force" research method.

Ken Fero is Director of Migrant Media

Contact and more information www.ultraviolencefilm.com https://vimeo.com/migrantmedia Instagram: @migrantmedia

Chapter 5: Riots as the Language of the Unheard

In the late 1960s and early 1970s prominent political theorists such as Hannah Arendt, John Rawls and Michael Walzer began to reflect on the implications of the tumultuous 1960s. They quickly reached a consensus that the non-violent direct political action of Martin Luther King was a legitimate form of political protest and that riots were illegitimate. Curiously King himself refused to condemn the urban US riots of the late 1960s, describing riots as the "language of the unheard." This chapter exams how mainstream political theorists appropriated Kings political strategy to delegitimize rioting. By tracing how riots have been delegitimized in liberal political theory discourse over the last 50 years, we can better understand recent responses to riots and mass political protest.

Jonathan Havercroft is Associate Professor of Politics and International Relations at the University of Southampton, and was awarded the 2020 British Academy Brian Barry Prize in Political Science for a "highly original" essay presenting a theoretical framework for the permissibility of rioting against injustice.

Chapter 6: Policing the Crisis – the Criminalization of Racial Minorities

Policing the Crisis (1978) examined how in a period of crisis a racially focused establishment culture came to target Britain's black population. It investigated the new, racialized crime of "mugging"– the only distinctive aspect of which was that it was presented as being particularly committed by young black men. The book expanded into a study of a historical political shift in what Antonio Gramsci called the hegemonic consensus, through the decline of Britain's post-war settlement. Arguments about how black people and anti-racists should respond to such criminalization were further developed by Paul Gilroy, A Sivanandan and others. This chapter will examine how these arguments can help create a political response to an increasingly racialized politics in a different period of crisis. For a time after the Macpherson Report, the police reluctantly accepted and challenged institutional racism. However, the government's "hostile environment" has seen a return to the targeting of specific communities. Race is again at the center of ideas about law and order – with the criminalization of refugees arriving in Britain in small boats, the deportation of black British citizens in the "Windrush scandal" and the prime minister dismissing Black Lives Matter protests.

Ken Olende is co-author of *Does Privilege Explain Racism?* (2020) and is currently researching a PhD in Rethinking "black" as a racial identity at the University of Brighton.

Chapter 7: "A Momentary Brotherhood of Uncomfortable White Men, Trying to Figure Stuff Out": Cultural Unity, Political Divisiveness and the Black Lives Matter Protests

A survey of cities and towns that experienced unrest during the summer of 2020 revealed that in these protests there was a marked turn away from the kinds of destructive and deadly violence characteristic of racial protests and disorder in nineteenth- and twentieth-century America. Contemporary Americans have reintroduced *civility* to their public confrontations, showing greater temperance than expected and little inclination to kill other persons or destroy their property. The reasons for this return to a more "social" kind of unrest show us that all kinds of Americans today are able to share the rights and privileges as well as the duties and obligations that come with being accepted as members in good standing in the communities where they live and work.

Professor Daniel J. Monti, PhD, Saint Louis University Department of Sociology, author of various books on gangs and US cities.

Chapter 8: Searching for Justice in the Twenty-first Century

The first 2 decades of the twenty-first century have seen the emergence of a number of key, transnational, social movements which have galvanized significant numbers on protest and resistance to the status quo. The global anti-capitalist movement in the early years of the century, the growth of Occupy after the financial collapse and the introduction of austerity, Climate Change activism and school strikes and more recently the explosion of the social movement Black Lives Matter which took to the streets across the world even in a time of extreme stress and pandemic. They have called for new forms of justice which are environmental, social, economic, political and cultural. Each has demonstrated alternative forms of social organization and created new sets of demands which contain within them the seeds of how a newly emerged post-capitalist society might look (Webb 2019). Calls for fair and equitable distribution of the world's resources, the common ownership of land, the adoption of sustainable consumption and the defunding of the carceral state (Davis 2016) have been a few of their most prominent and revolutionary demands. There is a great deal of work to be done, however, to envisage what progressive forms of "justice" might look like in an alternative society and there is currently little consensus emerging. This chapter asks whether the social movements of today can help us to envisage what the "justice" of tomorrow might become.

Karen Evans, Senior Lecturer in Criminology University of Liverpool, most recently co-author of *Zero Tolerance or Community Tolerance?* **(2019) with Sandra Walklate.**

Chapter 9: A History and Analysis of Police in the United States: The Need for Community Control of Budget and Public Safety

Born under a centrist black president, the movement for black lives reached a zenith under a blatantly right-wing racist one. Under the fog of a crippling pandemic in the summer of 2020, millions of Americans took to the streets for weeks in a multi-racial fusion that covered every nook and cranny of the country. This massive force came together protesting the endless police murders of black people. Statues representing slave traders were toppled in its wake. Schools, towns and states restructured their police departments and reallocated those departments' budgets instead to priorities like mental health support and early education and intervention programs. Yet as Joe Biden was lifted to victory by the votes of activists who had a couple of months prior been marching in the streets to defund the police and demanding that black lives matter, Biden distanced himself from the movement and argued that police forces should be given an additional $300 million. The path forward for Americans who want to dismantle racism remains the same under Biden as it was under Trump. For black lives to matter, capitalism itself must be dismantled.

Virginia Rodino is United Against Hate and Fascism:

Convenor; Coalition of Labor Union Women, AFL-CIO: Executive Director; Asian Pacific American Labor Alliance, AFL-CIO: National Executive Board; National Writers Union, IFJ: member; Marx 21: member

Chapter 10: Why Defund the Police?

"We're all in it together" was the oft repeated mantra of Prime Minister Boris Johnson at the outbreak of the coronavirus pandemic in Britain. This was seemingly confirmed when he, Prince Charles and Health Secretary Matt Hancock all contracted the virus. It has since been revealed that Charles's son and heir Prince William was also struck down in those early months.

It soon became apparent, however, that the pandemic was disproportionately affecting people from Black, Asian and Minority Ethnic (BAME) backgrounds. A great proportion were becoming critically ill and dying, a consequence of the inequality which made them less able to work from home, self-isolate and maintain social distance. Since then it has become increasingly clear that people from BAME backgrounds have also been adversely affected by the restrictions that have been imposed, such as the Coronavirus Act 2020. In addition, they continue to suffer as a result of pre-existing provisions such as s60 of the Criminal Justice and Public Order Act 1994. The new provisions have added to the inequality identified in reports such as the 2017 *Lammy Review* and Dame Elish Angiolini's study into deaths and serious incidents in custody.

The year 2020 was dominated by Covid–19, but another defining feature was the dramatic resurgence of the Black Lives Matter movement (BLM) last seen in 2016. Sparked by the police killing of George Floyd in Minneapolis, Minnesota, BLM has mobilized millions of people across the globe and raised profound questions about structural racism and the nature and role of policing in modern, multicultural societies. This contribution will consider these issues and examine the arguments associated with the rallying calls by BLM activists to defund the police.

Brian Richardson is a criminal barrister at Nexus, the Chambers of Michael Mansfield QC and editor of *Say it Loud! Marxism and the fight against Racism (2013).*

Chapter 11: Emerging Intersections in Appalachia: #BLM, Police Abolition and Anti-capitalist Social Movements

Police brutality and racially motivated violence against black people have generated an organized #BLM movement in the US and other geographies. Rural Appalachian communities (across 13 US states and comprising 25 million inhabitants) are not often seen as allies to #BLM, but have joined anti-policing social movement campaigns across the region with little notice. The newfound focus of Appalachians on #BLM is creating an opportunity for coalition-building. Groups from across this cultural region continue to shoulder a long tradition of anti-capitalist and anti-carceral resistance, which emerged in the late 1800s in a fight against exploitation by extractive industries. Appalachian resistance to class oppression intersects with the #BLM goal of ending police oppression. Fostering this intersectional awareness and calling for coalition-building around it presents abolitionists with an opportunity to explore what police abolition means in these communities. Analyzing the literature of Appalachian social movements and surveying current events in Appalachia through an ethnographic lens (film, news reports, activist spaces and social media), this chapter uses intersectionality theory to identify how the identities of #BLM and of traditional Appalachian social movements can highlight discrimination, oppression, and the colonialist, white supremacist and racial capitalist abuses of state and corporate power.

Keywords: Police Abolition, Appalachia, #BLM, Social

Movements, Intersectionality, Coalition Building

Michael J. Coyle, PhD is Professor, Department of Political Science and "Criminal" Justice, California State University, Chico. Works include *The International Handbook of Penal Abolition* **(Routledge 2020), and the forthcoming** *Seeing Crime: Penal Abolition as the End of Utopian Criminal Justice* **(University of California Press).**

Stephen T. Young is an Assistant Professor in Criminal Justice and Criminology at Marshall University in Huntington, West Virginia. His primary areas of concentration include rural criminology and carceral studies. His most recent research has appeared in *Social Justice, Critical Criminology*, **and** *The Howard Journal of Criminal Justice*.

Chapter 12: Black Lives Matter and Police Reform: Global Echoes of an American Social Movement

The Black Lives Matter (BLM) movement began in the US and was primarily focused on protesting police excesses and agitating for reform of law enforcement practices and routines. This has historical antecedents and is rooted in slavery, segregationist and discriminatory practices against African Americans. The philosophy underlying and tactics employed by the BLM movement have been adopted and adapted by residents of many countries around the world. This chapter surveys BLM-inspired movements in 12 countries, namely Australia, Brazil, Canada, Denmark, France, India, Italy, Israel, Japan, New Zealand, Nigeria and the United Kingdom. I discuss these efforts in terms of their successes, if any, in reforming the police and focus on related questions pertaining to democracy, the police and the plight of subjugated groups.

N. Prabha Unnithan was born and brought up in Malaysia. He studied criminology in India and, after moving to the US, received a PhD in sociology from the University of

Nebraska-Lincoln. He has been a member of the faculty of the Department of Sociology at Colorado State University since 1987 and was named a John N. Stern Distinguished Professor in 2019. Unnithan was President of the Western Social Science Association in 2014-15 and President of the Academy of Criminal Justice Sciences in 2019-20. He has served as editor of the *Journal of Criminal Justice Education* and the *Social Science Journal* as well as co-editor of *The Sociological Quarterly*.

Chapter 13: #EndSARS: The Struggle against Police Brutality in Nigeria

Tens of thousands of young people took to the streets to protest police brutality across the Nigerian federation in October 2020. The EndSARS revolt started as a demand for scrapping the Special Anti-Robbery Squad (SARS), an elite police unit notorious for extortion, brutality and extrajudicial killings.

This youth rebellion will serve as the chapter's point of departure for a historical materialist analysis of policing and police brutality in the country. Starting as a force to maintain colonial law-and-order, the evolution of the Nigeria Police Force and manifestations of its brutality have been shaped by the changing global order, and dynamics of the local ruling class.

The chapter will look at how the structural adjustment program from the 1980s sowed the seed for SARS to supplant the anti-riot mobile police (MOPOL) as the primary face of police brutality since 1992 and particularly so in the twenty-first century. The forms of resistance, including how international events have inspired some of its strategy and tactics, will also be examined.

The EndSARS movement's liberal wing's argument for increased police funding as a solution to police brutality will be critically appraised. And the chapter will conclude with perspectives on the interconnectedness of the struggle for system change and against police brutality within the Nigerian context.

Baba Aye: Co-convener, Coalition for Revolution (CORE,

Nigeria); Contributing editor; Review of African Political Economy (RoAPE), and author of *Era of Crisis and Revolts* (2012).

Chapter 14: Formed from the Colonial Model: Prospects for Reforming the Mexican Police

The Mexican police has earned a negative reputation for three main aspects: its double articulation between federal- and state-based prevents an effectiveness of its action. Its endemic corruption, due to low wages, sees police forces subjugated by criminal organizations. Its violent approach to demonstrators and citizens makes it responsible for such atrocities as extrajudicial executions and mass killings, like the case of Ayotzinapa. The relations between Mexican police forces and the public are heavily strained, with the wealthiest groups of Mexican society relying upon private security and the lower-middle classes suffering all the discriminatory practices and the brutalities which might be connected to the colonial model of police analyzed by Mike Brogden (1987). This paper, starting from the colonial aspects of Mexican policing, will eventually move to discuss possible models of development of an alternative policing involving the direct participation of the public and bridging the social and cultural rifts of Mexican society.

Fernando Tenorio Tagle – Professor of Law at UAM, Mexico City and author of *The Criminal Justice System in Mexico City*.

Vincenzo Scalia – Associate Professor in Criminology at the University of Florence, Italy and author of *Crime, Networks and Power* (2017).

Chapter 15: The Police in Neoliberal Greece: Toward a Radical Confrontation?

The neoliberal restructuring of Greek society since the 1990s and particularly since the intensification of the process after the implementation of the economic adjustment memoranda and brutal austerity in the 2010s has also entailed a repositioning of the police apparatus in the country's public life. Organizational and other strategic restructuring of the police has meant that confrontations of the police with protesters and other political "undesirables" has escalated since. The years of coalition government under Syriza were no exception despite the fact that SYRIZA's manifesto did promise a radical reform of the police. This chapter takes stock of the key aspects and manifestations of the repositioning of the police as a tool for repression and key lever in Greece's neoliberal restructuring. It also considers, in the context of evolving social and political struggles in Greece, the prospects for a modest or radical reform of the police, also in light of older and contemporary movements (such as defund).

Georgios Papanikolaou and Stratos Georgoulas both teach at the University of the Aegean, Mytilene, Greece.

Foreword to No Justice, No Police
Jeff Ferrell

Around the world, the police have their knees on more necks than we can know. As circumstances get worse and resources for survival scarcer, the police will surely find more necks for more knees, aggressively guarding what remains in the interests of those elites who guide and benefit from their actions. As the sickness of white power and white privilege spreads, and as ethnic conflict continues to erupt around the globe, the police will continue to serve on the side of dominant groups and dominant ideologies. For those who would work to interrupt this downward trajectory, to create a more just and sustainable world, the militarized policing of protests and social movements will also recur. In such a world, a sad question has arisen for many of us already: If you haven't been confronted by the police lately – warned, ticketed, surveilled, followed home, arrested, beaten, shot, killed – well, what sort of privilege is protecting you, in a way unavailable to so many millions of others?

It is for these reasons and in this context that something must be done – now. Abolish the police, defund the police, disarm the police – call it what you like, but this hyper-policing of our everyday lives, this state-sanctioned violence and state-funded protection of the privileged, has to stop. We need more protests, more community solidarity, more neighborhoods dedicated to mutual coexistence without the presence of the police. We need to act locally and globally at the same time; recognizing and confronting the particulars of police abuse while also situating such abuse in global trajectories; we can find ways to connect our local struggles against the police to transnational activism against policing. And we need books like this one – books crafted by those equally committed to scholarship and to activism, books critically engaged with deep structures of social control and contemporary controversies alike, books that can speak to varying audiences across the globe and in doing so help bring them together.

As to the scope of the problem, let's be honest: the police are the most dangerous and potent of street gangs, spreading fear and violence wherever they operate. They function as a concierge service for the privileged, shooing away undesirables and looking after personal property, and as an occupying army for the rest of us. They spawn a police culture of clannish closure, toxic masculinity and ritualized violence – a culture that sees everyday people as masses to be herded or threats to be extinguished. With neoliberal reductions in city budgets and tax revenues diverted to the wealthy, the police also increasingly operate as a revenue source founded in excessive ticketing and exorbitant fines, a daily drama of shakedowns and takedowns designed to prop up the crumbling economies of local governance. In the realms of ideology and perception, police-led charity drives and mediated performances of police community engagement help to normalize everyday policing, masking the pervasiveness of police misconduct and legitimating both the police and the violent state apparatus of which they are part.

So pervasive is contemporary policing and its harms – so wide the net and thin the mesh, to paraphrase Stan Cohen – that yet another question emerges: these days, who exactly *isn't* the police, and what *isn't* policing? Each new law passed further criminalizes everyday life and invites the police into one more area of social interaction; likewise, the stationing of police officers inside public schools has the effect of turning youthful disobedience into police matters of apprehension and arrest. Each new or emerging technology soon enough becomes a tool for policing and social control: facial recognition programs, digital searches, data bases, surveillance cameras on the streets, tracking cameras in the shops, motion sensors, listening devices, military hardware and software – all coalesce into a ghostly network of round-the-clock policing and police surveillance. Now this network is increasingly augmented by e-carceration technologies that track and confine those accused of crime, pre-trial and post-trial, while creating a vast digital prison where the police not only kneel on your neck but stay locked around your ankle. The ongoing privatization of public space closes such space to civic engagement but invites into that space both private security forces and state-sanctioned policing, mixing CPTED spatial controls with the policing of leisure and consumption. Daily media reporting casts cops as problem-solvers and protectors, an image echoed in countless televised police dramas, "real crime" shows, and law-and-order films. All of this suggests the degree to which police and policing saturate contemporary society – and more than this, the degree to which police and policing are endemic and essential to the existing social order. Because of this, to confront the police is to confront the limits of our own lives, to confront the myriad interwoven mechanisms of social and legal control that shape our lives, and to attempt a revolution of everyday life. To confront the police is to confront injustice – not only the injustices of everyday policing, but the structural injustice of the world the police are paid to protect. In this confrontation, modest goals won't matter, modest reforms won't work, because contemporary policing is itself no modest exercise, but instead an immodest, militarized enterprise designed to permeate social life and protect those who benefit from it.

But how do we undertake this revolution, and from what angles can we gain the leverage to pull it off? As this volume so insightfully demonstrates, there are a plethora of critical perspectives available, and a multitude of strategies and tactics that can be of use. As chapter after chapter in this volume also show, though, there is one perspective in particular that is essential to any critical confrontation with policing: an understanding of the historical and contemporary role of policing in repressing people of color. Emerging from slave patrols in North America, and more broadly from colonial domination of indigenous populations worldwide, contemporary policing remains inextricably intertwined with the development of racist ideologies and ethnic domination. Likewise, throughout the history of capitalism, local and state policing has been used to restrict the movement of low-end workers, and to assault those who would dare to organize or strike – with special police brutality reserved for the ethnic minorities who often led such strikes and organizing efforts. Today, of course, this pattern perpetuates itself; it is certainly no accident that contemporary condemnations of police violence have emerged from the Black Lives Matter movement as it originated in the United States. The top-down policing of ethnicity and social class is at the root of policing's history and at the heart of its present operations; because of this, any call for the abolition of policing must be at the same time a commitment to ethnic liberation and a dedication to broad redistributions of power. Put bluntly: the police have long operated on the wrong side of history. That history must change now.

I'd add two further perspectives that I find particularly useful in critically confronting police and policing. The first is provided by the interactionist approach in sociology – sometimes denoted as "labeling theory" in the areas of crime and deviance. This approach teaches us that acts matter less than the meanings that are assigned to them via social interaction – especially when those meanings are assigned and enforced by those in power. A moment of interpersonal conflict, for example, can come to be labeled as domestic violence, assault, intimidation, playful hijinks, a needed comeuppance, or an incident not worth remembering at all, depending on who has the power to define and label it. Once a definition is decided and meaning assigned, this in turn sets in motion social processes – selective perception, group exclusion, collective remembrance – that seem to confirm the initial definition, and in so doing construct it as real. In this context we begin to understand the terrible power that the police are granted: the power to decide meaning in everyday life, to determine via biased perception and selective enforcement what constitutes crime and what does not, to sort people and their actions into meaningful, consequential categories of criminal and non-criminal. A second perspective – this one provided by anarchist critiques of authority -- takes these interactionist insights a step further. Anarchists understand the state to be an assemblage of external, hierarchical power that unjustly controls people and their localized interactions. This control rests in the state's institutionalized legal authority, which not only encodes historical privilege and domination, but sets a rigid legal system over and against what should be fluid, community-level negotiations of human issues. In this sense, to call the police into a situation is to invite the overwhelming authority of the state into that situation as well, and to transform an episode of human interaction into a matter of state jurisdiction and state violence. As opposed to the myth that the state empowers its citizens, then, an anarchist view sees each encounter with state authority as a disempowering of individual autonomy and community-level problem-solving. Over time, this dynamic reifies state authority and cripples the ability of people to determine their own lives. In the end, petitioning the state for help mostly just helps the state.

Together, these two perspectives constitute a damning indictment of police and policing. State law and the policing agencies that enforce it create the very categories of crime and criminality they claim to abhor; it might even be said that legal and policing institutions conspire to construct and promote criminality as a social reality. For their part the police manufacture a steady stream of trouble by selectively but prolifically defining human events as criminal, and by enforcing these definitions through ongoing state violence. These processes spawn a host of negative dynamics for those caught up in them – social stigma, job loss, interpersonal anger and isolation, violent victimization – that in turn promote further cycles of violence, destruction…and policing. Criminologists have various terms for this social acceleration – the dramatization of evil, the deviancy amplification spiral – but whatever the terminology, the lessons are clear: reliance on the police to control everyday life makes everyday life more dangerous, more unequal and more susceptible to violence and police abuse. Policing creates the need and justification for policing. By the very existence of the police we lose the possibility of a peaceful and just society; the only question, day to day, is how badly we will lose and by how much. The one way out of this vast, destructive self-fulfilling prophecy is the abolition of the institution on which it rests.

Then again, you don't need a degree in interactionist theory or anarchist criminology to figure this out; plenty of folks on the streets understand all too well how the police create crime and perpetuate violence. Resistance to this cycle occurs every day, around the globe; in their own ways, people steadily work to subvert the police and to abolish the harsh policing of their own lives. Some attempt to misdirect or undermine police investigations, or refuse to cooperate with police inquiries entirely; a too-easy rhyme, and hardly a full-blown formula for a better world, "snitches get stitches" nonetheless embodies this understanding that working with the police generally means working against one's community. Knowing how quickly and predictably policing situations can go bad, others take care to record even routine police encounters and traffic stops, often putting themselves at risk in doing so. As contributors to this book point out, landmark cases like that of George Floyd would hardly exist without such on-the-spot recordings – a fact that the Pulitzer Prize committee recognized in presenting Darnella Frazier, the teenager who recorded Floyd's knee-on-the-neck murder, a special journalism award. Still others organize various forms of self-protection and community protection from the crimes committed by the police and other intruders, while the families of police violence victims dedicate themselves to campaigns for social and legal justice. For reasons of survival many folks may sing under their breath now and then, but they sure as hell harmonize with NWA on "Fuck Tha Police."

As this volume carefully documents, when broader social movements against police and policing emerge from such efforts, they take a variety of forms. Legal and political activism, street actions and public confrontations, community organizing and neighborhood empowerment, alternative media development – all these and more are appropriately part of the push to abolish the police. To the extent that policing is expansive and pervasive – to the extent that the police are everywhere – then our response can and should come from everywhere as well. Of course, it's all but inevitable that aggressive policing will in turn be deployed against our responses – and yet, in organizing against the police and defending against police aggression, we can't let ourselves become them. The underlying logic of policing is after all one of external, top-down control over those deemed deviant or dangerous, and a legitimization of such control via fixed and enforceable regulations. Opposing policing means not only denying its legitimacy and resisting its authority, but declining to reproduce its logic in our own activism. This is why many of the newer sorts of abolitionist social movements – often anarchic and anti-authoritarian, and mixing ephemerality with endurance – provide such hope: in their battle against policing they at the same time sketch the dynamics of a world liberated from policing and its logic. Such social movements also tend to subvert the logic of policing by being open and invitational, adept at communication and coalition-building across borders, and rhizomatic in their use of non-hierarchical networks. A look at this volume's chapters suggests the power of this approach, documenting as they do a decentralized movement that is both local and global, stretching from US urban centers to Appalachian highlands, and from the US to Mexico, Nigeria, Greece, and beyond.

As the chapters in this volume also show, the movement to abolish the police must in turn be a movement to wipe away the sheen of legitimacy and inevitability that has been constructed around policing. We need to craft alternative histories of policing that dismantle the myth of policing as public protection and resituate it in the historical trajectories of racism, colonialism and servitude – and in fact a number of chapters here do just that. We need to understand that policing operates as public performance, a daily ritual of state legitimacy and ready violence; in response, we need to invent disruptions of this performance and to organize demonstrations of policing's failures, all while staging our own public stories of community solidarity, celebration and police-free self-determination. The police, and the state and corporate powers they serve, are already caught in a legitimation crisis in which more and more people question their validity; our job is to accelerate that crisis by revealing the police to be the dangerous fools they actually are. Rallies, speeches, theater productions, books, podcasts, websites, public art – all of these and more are part of the abolitionist project, all part of demonstrating by word and deed the incompatibility of policing with any vibrant and inclusive social world.

In all this we'd do well to remember Bakunin's dictum: "The destructive urge is a creative urge, too." In battling to abolish the police we also battle to create – to create open spaces in which alternatives to policing can flourish, in which communities of trust and cooperation can emerge, in which a better world can be imagined and begun. This isn't easy work; an essential part of contemporary policing is the manufactured myth that no social world and no social order can exist without policing, and that because of this another world is not possible, not desirable...not imaginable. There's a partial truth to this, of course; we in fact *can't* imagine every contour of a non-policed future world, can't answer every question such a world will raise, from inside the present hyper-policed historical moment. But we can continue to confront the police, to open and defend non-policed spaces, and in those spaces to engage in the sorts of collective actions that over time accumulate into new ways of organizing and caring for a better world. Contemporary policing is a condemned building, endangering everyone in it; we have the right and the duty to run from that building, and to help others escape it, even if we haven't completed blueprints for safer shelter. But the more we carry each other from that condemned place, the more we stand together to confront the violence that is policing – the more we work together to get their knees off our necks – the more that new shelter takes shape.

Introduction

Sparked by the particularly brutal nature of the police murder of George Floyd, the "second wave" of the #blacklivesmatter protest movement has surged across over 100 US cities in 2020, spilling over into Brazil, South Africa, Paris and London – to name just a few of the primary sites of active resistance. Moreover, it is a movement that is deep as well as broad. Perhaps because the causes and the realities never really went away after the initial explosion in Ferguson, New York and Baltimore in 2014-15, activists are intent on going beyond street protests at police violence and are following in the tracks laid out by Black Power activists in the 1960s who first coined the term "institutional racism" to describe the systematic nature of the oppression that confronts BAME communities.

As Gary Younge recently summarized, these events:

> offered evidence of both an ideology (white supremacy) and the system that sustains it (racism) at their most fundamental level: state murder. In the following months it sparked debate not just about policing in America, but school curricula in Britain, the repotoire of the Paris Opera, St Nicholas's assistant Zwarte Piet in the Netherlands, and racial disparities in Covid deathrates across the West.[1]

Ideas and solutions about how to combat police racism and brutality now tend to delve deeper into the means by which injustice is manufactured, and how property rights confer the legacy of imperialism and racism by diverting wealth into the hands of a minority who feel sanctified in their possession of so much that the poorest lack – shaping ruling bodies to legitimize their hegemony. So rather than calls to equip the police with body cameras, or measures to enhance diversity in recruitment, a far more radical agenda of police reform and even abolition is being advocated. Moreover, the new deadly dimension of racism revealed in pandemic mortality rates has injected a fearlessness and urgency into the movement: One which is encompassing far wider swathes of the population than are traditionally associated with political activism. This is a new movement, with a disproportionately large section of young people – black and white – using language and tactics of their own devizing to fundamentally challenge the whole range of racist institutions that govern our globalized world.

This collection aims to capture something of the range and diversity of themes being thrown up in the course of acts of protest, focusing in particular on the role that the use of state violence plays in their provocation. As Jeff Ferrell outlines above, these social movements are often anarchic and non-hierarchical. They tend to represent popular resistance from below against the harms inflicted by imperialism, institutionalized racism and the whole capitalist system; with demands and debates emerging around decolonizing, abolitionism, for equality and against economic and political privilege. Socialists have also pointed to "the revitalization of Marxism as a research program and the growth of its audience in the wake of the revival of anti-capitalist contestation since the Seattle protests of November 1999... reaffirmed by the development in 2007-8 of the greatest systemic crisis that capitalism has experienced since the 1930s."[2] This can include the injustice of incarcerating or otherwise punishing those challenging and exposing the state and its agents of social control. Exposing these social harms can be a reaction to contemporary events such as a police shooting, or historic – such as the ongoing campaigns to release Julian Assange or Mumia Abu-Jamal. Protests can challenge centuries-old injustices: For example, in January 2022, four protesters appeared in court charged with offenses related to the pulling down of the statue of slave merchant Edward Colston during a Black Lives Matter

(BLM) protest of over 10,000 in Bristol, UK in June 2020. All BLM protests are, of course, a reaction against police violence, but the nature of the crowd's action in "rolling" Colston's statue into the city dock points to the way in which many aspects of protest at institutional racism are coming together. The racist legacy bequeathed by the slave trade scars both the US and the UK, hence the targeting of statues erected to honor the heritage of slavery and empire on both sides of the Atlantic.[3] The strength of public opinion against racism and the burden of shame felt over Britain's pioneering role in the once "respectable trade" of slavery led the defense lawyers for the "Colston Four" to argue that the real criminal in this scenario were not the protesters but Colston himself. The jury agreed and they were acquitted of charges of criminal damage to his statue.

However, the fact that many of these symbols of imperial racism and cruelty still stand points to the endurance of racism and a society unwilling to come to terms with its past. As if to prove the point, the contemporary form of this institutional racism is starkly illustrated by the disproportionate exposure of black people to Covid–19. Therefore, protests sparked by the police killing of George Floyd have become anti-racist movements, highlighting the systematic nature in which capitalism divides and discriminates along vectors of race, while also focusing on other divisions such as gender and class. When even as divisive a figure as George W. Bush acknowledges the US has a problem of "systemic racism," the depth of institutional anomie becomes apparent. Societies create and maintain institutions in order to govern. In a democracy, they gain public consent to the extent that they appear to meet the needs of the people. Often they will start to lose that consent when they fail, leading to disillusionment, cynicism and – sometimes – protest. A crisis in housing or education can expose institutional failure and generate initial protest waves, as occurred in London following the 2017 Grenfell fire, or the

2020 A level grading fiasco, but these may not be sustained. With policing, in some ways the most overt instrument of social control, the degree of institutional failure and the manner of its manifestation may ensure the protest continues. When the police mission to "serve and protect" is carried out by inflicting stigmatization, surveillance and violence upon a section of the community that it has criminalized, the victims have arguably no choice but to resist.

This is undoubtedly the case with what has become the largest ever street-based social movement to emerge across the cities of the world's most powerful state, with the *New York Times* estimating over 26 million BLM participants by July 2020. The crisis for the US police is therefore especially deep, leading to calls for more fundamental reform than had previously been contemplated. However, the crisis of policing institutions is international for a variety of reasons which will be explored by the contributors below. Since 2019, we have witnessed a surge in street-based protest movements which often demand regime change in very large numbers. Unpopular rulers inevitably call upon their armed forces in the police and the army to buttress their position. Some leaders have been deposed, such as the presidents of Sudan and Algeria in 2019 or Peru in 2020. Some have clung on to power relying on police batons, flash grenades and sometimes even bullets to quell the opposition, while augmenting the popular bitterness and sense of injustice; think of the case of Lukashenko in Belarus, the monarchy in Thailand, the Myanmar military or the Chinese regime in Hong Kong.

Such repression takes our liberties: For example, contributors who chronicled the 2018-19 struggle for social justice in Hong Kong had to withdraw from contributing to this book because of fear of the consequences. In other states, such as France, the government has faced smaller but determined social movements such as the *gilets jaunes* or "Yellow Vests" who sustained their actions over long periods. Police repression with so-called "flashball" grenades has blinded several protesters, only exacerbating the mood of resistance, so much so that in 2021 President Macron introduced a new Security Law: Anyone publishing images of a public event including police agents in a way that could "harm the agent's physical or psychological well-being" faces one year in jail and a €45,000 fine! When the proportion of the population protesting is significant then the crisis also becomes one of "democracy." Opposition movements can claim a popular mandate and point to a crisis of legitimacy for the government concerned. This can, of course, take progressive or reactionary forms, as Trump's followers showed with their march on the Capitol in January 2021; another case where criminal selectivity in policing was apparent. Police failure to protect other citizens from right-wing violence illustrated which side they favor.

Looking back through time, the first police forces were created to maintain public order when rulers realized the dangers of using their armies to maintain social control. For example, repressing riots and demonstrations with armed troops led to a series of bloody massacres in England in the late 1700s and early 1800s. To continue on this path risked provoking a popular uprising. Indeed, the principal idea behind the formation of the "new police" was that an institution created from among the general population and carrying out the fight against crime in the day to day would be more likely to gain popular consent, and thus able to maintain public order when crowds gathered at less risk of provoking mass retaliation.[4]

This did not just apply in Victorian Britain, but also to examples like the post-Pinochet regime in Chile in the 1990s and 2000s, where an alternative to the brutality of the army was valued by a population that had suffered mass military bloodshed under the rule of the general. Although it is important to recognize that, in times of greater social consensus, in certain countries it has been possible for police forces to gain majority public acceptance of their function by promoting an image of "community policing" or the "bobby on the beat," there always remained several "over-criminalized" groups within the general population who bore the brunt of violent and discriminatory policing and resented the injustice of their treatment. Nowadays, the proportion of the population questioning police legitimacy is far broader, especially among younger people raised in the post-2008 years of austerity and racism. Clement examines the lessons of history for what is to be done about the police today. The focus of this study is that, increasingly, policing and protest cannot be studied separately. The movements of protest are pointing out that the solutions to the problem of policing and social control require questioning the possibility of piecemeal reform. "Do black lives really matter?" to the institutions of criminal justice asks Nyamwiza, inviting the reader to consider more fundamental change. From here, McDowell, Fernandez *et al* also debate the pros and cons of the defunding/abolition debate. Police violence has all too often been the source of resistance movements as film director Ken Fero has chronicled in a remarkable account of the perils of putting state violence on screen.

When protests take the form of riots, they have often been delegitimized not only by the state, but also by liberal thinking that underplays the police role in fomenting violence, as Havercroft explores. Today, that majority sentiment favoring unquestioning acceptance of policing no longer exists. Arguably it began to fracture from the end of the 1970s as neoliberalism ascended. States have become accustomed to using the power of the police to control mass demonstrations and riots, developing a more militaristic style of control tactics and extensive surveillance, enhanced equipment and the repressive behavior that goes with it. Olende charts the UK's journey from the blatant police racism and criminalization of black people in the 1970s, its brief retreat in the early 2000s due to the official acknowledgment of the police's institutional racism, and the current anti-liberal backlash spearheaded by Metropolitan Police chief Cressida Dick – which has finally led to her resignation as public concern mounted over the methods and behavior of the officers she led. Monti argues this movement for diversity is a "civilizing process" which swept across the US, but looked rather different in smaller towns than in big cities; while the critical consciousness generated by rising levels of anti-racist activism can relate to other threatening social justice issues such as climate change and the pandemic as discussed by Evans. Rodino charts the explosion of defunding actions across the US, seeing this as a revolutionary challenge to the state's institutions of social control. Richardson discusses the legal and political issues raised and their social consequences within the context of 50 years of anti-racist struggle in Britain. A regional case-study of how BLM relates to the history of social movements in Appalachia is presented by Coyle and Young. The explosive impact of the 2020 second wave of BLM is testament to the rising levels of solidarity across ever-broader layers of the public committed to acting together to demonstrate their intolerance of police racism. Several contributions consider how the policing and protest dialectic is playing out around the globe in a section introduced by Unnithan: Aye's account relates how the Nigerian government has used the police to violently repress popular unrest in 2020. Tagle and Scalia discuss the case of Mexico, where criminal collusion by police has had violent and tragic consequences. In this case, and that of Greece, the scale of opposition to police violence and authoritarianism is rising, as discussed by Papanikolaou and Georgoulas.

Chapter 1

What Is to Be Done About the Police?
Matt Clement

Over the course of history, maintaining and manufacturing stability has underpinned the process of government, often termed social control. Ruling institutions are constantly assessed by their subjects as to how well their living conditions, their physical and mental health are being provided for. Of course, this extends beyond Maslow's paradigm of food, clothes and shelter. People measure the quality of their housing, the suitability of their education and overall sense of well-being in relation to the safety and security of their communities and the sustainability of economic arrangements.

Acts of protest – riots, strikes, marches and demonstrations – are the methods, the means of communicating popular discontent. They are designed to alert our rulers to the need for change. Managing these conflicts requires a complex combination of repression and concessions. The creation of special agencies of social control has often come about when rulers discover that armies deployed to combat large crowds of protesters cannot be relied upon: Recruited from the general population, their loyalty to their officers can be put under strain, or their ready resort to arms can be too blunt an instrument. If the protesting people themselves turn to arms, as has been happening in Myanmar in 2021, then revolution beckons.

Alternatively, generals can lead their armies in a *coup d'état,* a "blow against the state." Virtually all existing governments can claim a heritage that evolved either from a coup or revolution. Maintaining control dictates that what state rulers require are special bodies equipped with the capacity to enforce order who are neither just "called up" from the general population, nor generally isolated in barracks and therefore so cut off from the everyday life of the people as to make it hard to be credible enforcers, other than through brutal bouts of repression which can cause alienation and further resistance. The solution often resorted to is replacing public deployment of the army with a police force: A specialized body with a legal monopoly of the use of violence, distinguished from the army by their uniform and special training.

Unlike armies, which are confined to barracks or fighting in foreign territory, the police carry out their public order role actively on the streets throughout the year, developing a more symbiotic relationship with "their" community through a regular presence. Active surveillance also generates localized knowledge, facilitating an informed methodology for "keeping things under control" that is likely to gain greater public consent through a judicious balance of the twin elements sometimes described as the "iron fist and the velvet glove."[1] For most citizens most of the time, the police have become the public face of society's mechanisms and institutions of control. Over the last 2 centuries, as part of the state, policing has advanced and globalized,[2] hand-in-hand with the corporations of capitalism as was explained by US scholar Sidney Harring in his classic 1970s account *Policing a Class Society*, "the rise of full-time, permanent forces capable of continuously asserting the power of the capitalist state up and down every street in every city represents an enormous extension of the power of the bourgeoisie, and one that is absolutely necessary."[3]

This study focuses on a broader grouping, or figuration, the political police. A definition of which was provided by the founder of the UK's state research group, Tony Bunyan, over 40 years ago: "Those state institutions which operate primarily through the actual, or potential, use of coercive sanctions and repression (including physical force). These institutions include the military, the police, the prisons, the courts of law, the government (the exercise of executive power, i.e. PM and cabinet) and the state administration."[4] Not many would quibble with this statement as it appears to point to the necessary functions of any state if the society in question is to function effectively and maintain social control. However, Bunyan adds a further caveat which points to fundamental problems with this model in terms of delivering justice to all, stating "these institutions should be seen not as subservient to government, as the liberal-democratic notion suggests, but rather as interdependent centers of state power."[5] If he is correct, then society faces the problem that the bodies they elect do not simply direct the state to do their bidding. Rather, those institutions develop their own agendas and opinions about alleged threats to what they often call national security. History shows this can lead them off down all kinds of paths that frequently defy or undermine governments – and seek to justify the use of their powers to coerce and suppress individuals and groups whom they regard as "the enemy of the people."[6]

Some may object to this characterization of the machinery of the state. Surely it is there to serve society as a whole rather than take the part of one section against another. Is this a case of criminological paranoia? Harring epitomizes the Marxist critique of the benevolent view of the state with this incisive summary of the process of social control: "The ruling class institutes disorder when it imposes its power over others...to which the bourgeoisie respond by creating new social institutions. These institutions, in effect, help to legitimate the new social order by rendering a valued 'service' to all classes in society."[7] The idea that the state is neutral – i.e. standing above distinct class interests and arbitrating for society as a whole – came about during the modernizing period of Enlightenment Europe between 1730 and 1830, when a body was needed to negotiate between the claims of the old forms of merchant capitalism and the new era of industrialization. This was "less for reasons of democracy than as a means of arbitrating between the warring capitalist factions and combatting working class demands."[8]

Historically, police forces often evolved from earlier institutions rooted in communities such as constables appointed by landowners, who themselves often "made law" through sitting in judgment on their tenants, and organized them to raise a posse to pursue lawbreakers. As Reiner describes "communal policing forms are converted in incremental stages to state-dominated ones, which begin to function as agents of class control in addition to general social control."[9] A brief history of British policing below tracks the path from coercion to consent, and back again.

The first police forces were created to maintain public order when rulers realized the dangers of using their armies to maintain social control. Repressing riots and demonstrations with armed troops led to a series of bloody massacres in England in the late 1700s and early 1800s. London protests in support of the right of journalists like John Wilkes to criticize King George III without being jailed led to troops being deployed who shot at demonstrators leading to deaths on the streets in the 1760s. British troops had failed to intimidate the American colonists as the popular militias' success led to the 1776 revolution. Back home, the unvanquished spirit of rebellion was the fuel for the fires of London's extensive "Gordon Riots" of 1780, where property and prisons were attacked and hundreds killed.[10] Several more were shot by troops in the Bristol Bridge massacre of 1793.

The French monarchical state had already established a police force from the early 1700s, but it proved incapable of protecting the royal regime from their 1789 revolution. This turn of events so alarmed the British government that they developed a range of legal and policing methods to try and suppress any signs of radicalism in their country.[11] Arguably these in turn stiffened resistance and led to popular democratic organizations of republicans, artisans and Irish nationalists emerging who led three naval mutinies in 1797 and an uprising in the colony of Ireland in 1798.[12] Laws and civil rights were suspended, rebels were hanged by an outraged and terrified government. As society urbanized and modernized into the nineteenth century, Britain's rulers increasingly feared that to continue on this repressive path risked provoking a popular uprising. As Thomas Carlyle wrote in the wake of the slaughter by troops of 19 people and the wounding of hundreds more in Manchester's Peterloo Massacre of 1819: "the number of the slain and maimed is very countable, but the treasury of rage, burning hidden or visible in all hearts ever since...is of unknown extent."[13] The idea behind the formation of London's "new police" in 1829 was that a body of men, selected from among the general population and carrying out the fight against crime in the day to day, would be more likely to gain popular consent than the army, and thus be able to maintain public order when crowds gathered. For this reason, they were unarmed and their uniform was blue, to distinguish them from the troops and convey the message that they were formed to serve the public. Although there have always been "over-criminalized" groups within the general population who bore the brunt of violent and discriminatory policing, majority support for the British police's role evolved to become a reality over the course of the late nineteenth and twentieth centuries, peaking in the decades following World War Two. Nowadays, the proportion of the population questioning police legitimacy is growing far broader, especially among younger people raised in the post-2008 years of austerity and racism. Realist policies aspiring toward "community policing" are being challenged by "idealist" visions of abolition and opposition.

Over time, state institutions have discovered that the best way to maintain control is to combine uniting the ruling classes with dividing the masses beneath them; thus tying the "respectable" sections of the population to their cause by stigmatizing the "other" part. The "dangerous classes" label was therefore functional in uniting feuding rulers against a common foe over whom they must dominate. It is no longer universally acceptable for states and their spokespeople to openly label sections of society as inferior – in theory: But the political value of this labeling process is inestimable for preserving the patterns of social control and, in practice, stigmatization continues despite some governments' claims to be anti-racist and socially inclusive. Popular consent is often the product of the weakness and division that persuades us there is no alternative to complying with those in power and authority.

In their classic study, Stuart Hall and colleagues outlined how moral panics are fermented and the dreaded "folk devil"[14] manufactured; "official society – the state, the political leadership, the opinion leaders, the media, the guardians of order – *glimpse*…the shape of *the enemy*…coercion becomes, as it were, the natural and routine form in which consent is secured."[15] Their *Policing the Crisis* was published in 1978, charting the authoritarian turn in Britain from 1973 onwards, a product of an economic crisis that was international in scope, and marked the end of the post-war settlement as "no longer an appropriate way for the ruling class to exercise its control of society, socially, culturally or economically." In its place was emerging an authoritarian framework aimed at subordinating the whole society ruthlessly to the rule of capital. It focused "a wide range of 'social, moral and ideological dissent' through a lens of racism that, then as now, commands widespread popular support."[16] They concluded with a powerful indictment of their times that certainly resonates with the global crisis and describes the tactics employed by governments and police forces nearly half a century later; "to move swiftly, to stamp fast and hard, to listen in, discreetly survey, saturate and swamp, charge or hold without charge…to keep society on the straight and narrow… The times are exceptional. The crisis is real. We are inside the 'law-and-order' state."[17] Reflecting upon the significance of this "authoritarian turn" helps us to understand our own times and its tendencies toward coercive methods of social control. Hall quite rightly saw the advent of Margaret Thatcher as PM in 1979 as a further turn of the authoritarian screw. As he outlined in a lecture that year called "Drifting into a Law and Order Society": "Make no mistake about it: under this regime the market is to be free, the people are to be disciplined... Its preferred slogan is 'Free Economy: Strong State.'"[18] Indeed it was Stuart Hall who first coined the term "Thatcherism" to describe it.

Thatcher had made no secret of her reliance on police power, organizing significant pay rises for the force in her first year in government, leading to the popular refrain that the police were "Maggie Thatcher's boot boys." This can lead some to imagine that this drift toward coercion started with her 1979 election: Far from it. *Policing the Crisis* demonstrated it began far earlier, evident in Heath's government of 1970 to 1974 when the "mugging" moral panic began in the early 1970s and continued through the era of the 1974 to 1979 Labour government.

In hindsight, the rising establishment fears that allegedly justify authoritarian measures were inevitable in this period, given that a Conservative government had been undermined and unseated by successful strike action in 1974. A series of protests had defeated anti-union laws and won pay rises for millions, "ample demonstration of the simple truth that determined opposition by a sufficiently wide section of the organised working class can render parliament's laws inoperable."[19] Generals, judges and senior civil servants argued for "low intensity operations"[20] which added up to a justification of counterinsurgency; secret services were deployed to liaise between the police and the army in troubled zones such as Northern Ireland, and spying on so-called "extremists."

Similar "strategies of tension" were employed in many European countries in this decade, including West Germany and Greece – above all in Italy.[21] These "secret armies" often used their undercover agents to foment violence and division within far left, anarchist and anti-racist organizations and campaigns. US secret services directed these through NATO while the FBI did the same back home.[22] In 1970s Britain, many concerned commentators pointed out how abuses of human rights allegedly justified in response to the threat of organized terrorism were drifting across from Ulster to the picket lines and to multicultural marginalized communities on the mainland.[23]

A couple of citations from these voices makes clear how things looked from the viewpoint of the capital city of London in 1981, just before riots were to sweep across England. Friend and Metcalf share the belief of Hall and others that the recipe for "policing the crisis" is: "In each historical period there is a particular combination of the two poles of state activity. But in general, during times of relative social peace, the coercive and consent-creating wings of state activity are interdependent and reinforcing – coercive interventions, which tend to be limited, are highly successful precisely because they are underwritten by the majority's broad consent."[24] The result, they conclude is, "the tilt towards the pole of coercion...in response to a loss of consent among various groups...the intensifying struggle of the oppressed Catholic minority in Northern Ireland...the resurgence of militancy...of the industrial working class...the failure of existing mechanisms for disciplining a generation of working class youth...and the intransigent refusal of black people to suffer the consequences of the economic and social crisis."[25]

Riots are evidently an example of the counterpower of the crowd acting against these brutal forms of policing. London was at the center of these developments. The crowd at the 1976 Notting Hill Carnival famously rioted against saturation policing. A total of 18 black youth were then arrested on conspiracy charges.[26] In 1977, more military-style squads of officers were deployed to charge at demonstrators such as the mass of pickets supporting the Asian women Grunwick strikers and the vast crowd of anti-racists opposing a march of the Fascist National Front in Lewisham. This reminds us that "the metropolitan working class has two sexes and a multiplicity of racial origins...and at the same time thrust sexism and racism to the center of the political stage."[27]

Much of this analysis can still be applied to aid our contemporary understanding of protest and policing, social control and institutional racism. The massive surge of anti-racist protest that engulfed the US in 2020, spilling out across many other countries, was a result of police violence targeting black people in a whole series of public killings. These types of actions by forces formally committed to keeping "law and order" have gone on for centuries – especially in countries with a legacy of empire and slavery – but the contemporary scale of global protest, generating violent reaction from the forces of social control, is unprecedented. Even the US civil rights struggles of the 1960s could not match the degree of active involvement by both black and white citizens in coming onto the streets to demonstrate their refusal to tolerate such a racist application of the state's monopoly of the use of violence, with 26 million taking part in May and June 2020.[28]

This points toward the need to revise the traditional understandings of the police that have been generally accepted by broad swathes of the population in previous eras, encapsulated in analyses like "the artisanal... policemen are essentially working class professionals, with authoritarian personalities, engaged in hard and uninspired labour keeping their equals in order."[29] Beliefs in police neutrality are in line with truisms such as "the police are the meat in the sandwich," suggesting that they are arbitrators between opposed sections of the population. In this scenario, like a referee in a football game, their unpopularity stems from having to mediate between groups in conflict – meaning they will never be popular with "both sides." However, as studies of police culture have shown, these are very simplistic and stereotypical characterizations. The police have always been driven by conservative values, mixed with an exaggerated code of "solidarity" that leads them to deny any slights to their reputation and a strict evaluative hierarchy that governs the degree of consideration they are prepared to show to members of the public in the course of their work.[30]

Those groupings who experience the results of this culture, such as the "street corner society"[31] comprising some of those people who live in relatively poorer neighborhoods, non-white minorities and the like, or other groups subject to police stigmatization such as demonstrators or strikers, have generally learned not to trust the police; but their numbers have hitherto not been sufficient to really shake the dominant consensus of pro-police attitudes across society as a whole. To put it more accurately: "What the police have come to define as consent is a passive, grudging acceptance of a police presence."[32] This consensus viewpoint has been periodically threatened, the more powerfully the greater the scale of resistance employed at the time; but the general pattern has been of a return to "normality," where the hegemony of the forces of social control is restored as the challenge has died away. However, hegemony – meaning the successful exercise of social control through our rulers' ability to utilize the combined weapons of physical force and ideological influence – is fragile. Jeff Ferrell describes the dilemma thus: "Both conceptually and historically, it's worth remembering that hegemony is less an accomplishment than a tendency; those who possess inordinate power may be able to deploy that power in 'policing the crisis,' to invoke Hall and colleagues (1978), but they are never quite able to prevent the crisis nor to resolve it. Consequently, across all sorts of systems of domination, meaningful and effective resistance has flourished."[33]

Perhaps this is why we are currently seeing a sea-change

in attitudes toward the police, because of the relatively large numbers of people being propelled into forms of active opposition that bring them into conflict with those forces designated to maintain social control. The police literally become transformed before their eyes from "referees" to militarized servants of an increasingly fragile and belligerent regime. Therefore, a key question being addressed in this book is "why have the police become the new public enemy: And can society keep the peace more effectively with or without them?"

From Sudan to Myanmar, and right across much of the Americas, protest movements are being targeted by governments and their police forces throughout the globe. This concern to stifle protest is shared by a whole range of regimes; from openly authoritarian leaderships in states such as Russia, China, Belarus, Myanmar and Brazil, to so-called democracies including Nigeria, France, the US and UK. A closer examination of the process illustrates some typical features.

Let us begin by considering the social position of the police as a group *vis a vis* other groupings or classes in society. They believe they occupy a defined position in the social hierarchy. Police officers may be less powerful than the richest in society, but their function is to utilize their power to police "the masses" by controlling public spaces, through the exercise of authority and their monopoly of the legitimate use of violence.

In a recent Canadian study, Robyn Maynard spells out what this rather dry description actually means: "Not only is state violence rarely prosecuted as criminal, it is not commonly perceived *as violence*. Because the state is granted the moral and legal authority over those who fall under its jurisdiction, it is granted a monopoly over the use of violence in society, so the use of violence is generally seen as legitimate."[34] Police "have immense discretion in defining, convicting and sentencing. They are central definers, by their actions, priorities and selective interventions, of crime in society...the policies of selective and discriminatory policing...are the embodiment of institutionalized racism."[35] This is why understanding crime is all about the police's discretionary prejudice – their "criminal selectivity."[36]

The coronavirus pandemic allowed the UK police to ban many acts of protest, allegedly to limit the risk of transmitting the virus. However, when thousands gather and march such a ban becomes more impractical to enforce, as we saw when demonstrations peppered the country in summer 2020 in the wake of George Floyd's murder. Smaller actions have been targeted by police, however, such as in March 2021, when a socially distanced gathering of around 50 people in Manchester to protest at the government's 1 percent pay offer for health workers led to a £10,000 fine for its organizer. The protests themselves have generally been exacerbated by the way in which people have been policed, i.e. the police's violent actions have activated and amplified the protesters' reactions: For example, a peaceful vigil to remember Sarah Everard, a woman murdered on Clapham Common in London in March 2021, resulted in several other women being forcibly restrained by police. Their heavy-handed actions led to several nights of further demonstrations where protesters expressed outrage at their treatment, especially given a serving officer of the Met had been charged with her murder.

Up until 2021, the police in both the US and the UK had notoriously managed to avoid being jailed for *any* cases where they have been found responsible for civilian deaths in custody when the victim is black.[37] Arguably, it was the sheer scale of the social movement exploding into life in the wake of George Floyd's murder that led to a sea-change in judicial practice as his murderer, Minneapolis police officer Derek Chauvin, was found guilty and jailed. The echoes of #blm may well have also caused the jailing of a British police officer for the excessive tasering and acts of violence directed toward a black man experiencing a mental health crisis: Dalian Atkinson was tasered until he passed out and then kicked in the head twice while prone by the serving police officer called to the scene.

This breakthrough sentencing breaks the culture of solidarity that had always covered the tracks of police violence up until now. When put together with the wide publicity given to the guilty verdict doled out to the serving Met Officer who had raped and murdered Sarah Everard, this represented something of a crisis in credibility for London's police service in 2021 – especially when it was revealed that the killer had been in uniform – "on duty" – when he abducted his victim. After his conviction the force was put under pressure to respond to the crisis in public trust: Specifically, when asked what women should do when approached by an officer if they felt unsafe, the Met stated "that women in fear of a police officer should flag down a bus or run away." This led to further outrage and calls for the resignation of Met Chief Cressida Dick. The Labour MP Abena Oppong-Asare wrote to Dame Cressida demanding "clarification" of the advice, which she said had been greeted with "ridicule and derision" in her south London constituency, concluding: "The idea that a young black constituent could run away from a police officer attempting to arrest them and not face severe consequences is, frankly, unbelievable."[38]

A fracturing of trust in the police was compounded by the fact that the government at the time was intent on introducing a "Police, Crime, Sentencing and Courts Bill," allowing the police to criminalize protests deemed too "noisy" and/or "a public nuisance." What *Policing the Crisis* explained about the moral panic over "mugging" applies here also: "The paradox is that the selectivity of police reaction to selected crimes [i.e. protests –MC] almost certainly serves to *increase* their number (what is called a "deviancy amplification spiral"). It will tend to produce this increase in the form of a cluster, or "crime wave." When the "crime wave" is then evoked to justify a "control campaign" it has become a 'self-fulfilling prophecy.'"[39] This proposed legislation restricting protest prompted several "Kill the Bill" demonstrations in 2021 across various cities, including several in Bristol.

Another feature employed by all elements of the political police tends to lead to what Ruth Wodak calls "victim–perpetrator reversal,"[40] where the more powerful group claim that they are the victim of the malicious intent of those they are, in fact, marginalizing. For example, the Bristol police maintained that they had come under attack from protesters during the first of the "Kill the Bill" demonstrations in the city in March 2021, telling journalists that two officers had been seriously wounded with a broken arm and a punctured lung. Both claims later turned out to be untrue.

Events in Bristol have a special significance, as in June 2020 around 10,000 Black Lives Matter marchers in the city pulled down a statue of Edward Colston, a prominent slave trader. While protesters and many observers were clearly elated with this powerful demonstration of the links between racist institutions past and present, Home Secretary Priti Patel branded their actions "disgusting" and promised prosecutions. Press statements made it clear that the government put protecting monuments above women's safety, noting "The Police, Crime, Sentencing and Courts bill would increase the minimum term for some serious sexual offenses to 4 years, but increases the maximum sentence for vandalizing a war memorial to ten years."[41] Thankfully, a jury thought differently and acquitted those charged, the "Colston Four," in January 2022.

Another measure the government proposes in the bill is a ban on all "unauthorised encampments" which will enhance police powers to "move on" travelers, Roma and gypsy communities and indeed the homeless. How this will be done was illustrated when a Bristol protest camp was subject to attack by the police, who bragged that they used specialist police dog units, horses, the National Police Air Service and a police drone unit to target protesters. Flowers laid for Sarah Everard, the woman killed at Clapham, were trampled over by officers.

In many ways, the rising tide of protest against the police in the UK since 2020 is a product of the bigger social reaction against police violence in the US. This movement began a long time before the Black Lives Matter campaign became the latest incarnation of popular resistance against institutional racism. In 1961, when the civil rights campaigners known as the Freedom Riders were confronted by racist vigilantes, the Ku Klux Klan, "Mississippi governor Ross Barnett...told [the Klan] to stay home by promising that differently uniformed officers would take care of matters using arrest and imprisonment."

As the Gilmores explain, the association of the police with racist violence endures to this day: "The legitimacy of the badge replaced the discredited Klan hood. Yet the twenty-first century onslaught of police killings suggests that as well as turning the extra-legal units into the legal, more than half a century later, it internalized in police forces certain aspects of non-state organized violence that erupt with regularity in the context of the crisis state."[42] They are arguing that state violence as social control is now official policy, despite the official denials, and this illustrates how vectors of race and class become interdependent: "If, therefore, as Stuart Hall has painstakingly argued, race is 'the *modality* in which class is lived,' then mass criminalization, and the policing it depends on, is class *war*."[43]

Angela Davis is one of the most famous activists from the period of the first US civil rights movement. She endured her schoolfriends' deaths at the hands of Klu Klux Klan bombings in Birmingham Alabama in her childhood, and later spent some time as a member of the Black Panthers as well as many years in the US Communist Party. Davis was herself arrested, accused of involvement in the kidnap of a California judge, writing: "If they come in the morning" from her cell before her acquittal in June 1972, where she was in no doubt about the intersection of protest and police repression, claiming: "As the Black Liberation Movement and other progressive struggles increase in magnitude and intensity, the judicial system and its extension, the penal system, consequently become key weapons in the state's fight to preserve the existing conditions of class domination, therefore racism, poverty and war."[44]

This theme is developed and expanded in Hall *et al*'s pathbreaking climax to "Policing the Crisis":

> Racism is not only a problem for blacks who are obliged to "suffer" it...Nor indeed can it be overcome, as a virus which can be treated by a heavy dose of liberal inoculation. Capital reproduces the class as a whole, structured by race. It dominates the divided class, in part through the internal divisions which have "racism" as one of their effects.[45]

A united class is clearly the solution and, more recently, Davis has explained how these struggles "are already crosshatched, overlaid, intersectional patterns. Class, race, gender, sexuality, ability and other social relations are not simplistically separate. They can never remain uncontaminated by each other."[46]

She remains a champion of abolitionism of all those institutions dividing and ruling states and their peoples

The situation in a typical US city, Baltimore, over the last decade brings out these contradictions clearly. The early 2000s TV series *The Wire* shone a window for millions of viewers on the sociology of a typical US city's key institutions, police, politicians, schools and communities; its racism and rising inequalities, and their human costs. Later, in 2015, the city rioted in reaction to the police killing of another black man, Freddie Gray. Before that, "between 2010 and 2014, 109 people died in police custody in Maryland, and criminal charges were brought against police officers in only two of the cases."[47] After all six officers charged with Gray's killing were acquitted, the president of the local NAACP pronounced: "We have to go back to the drawing board here in Baltimore and Maryland with rules and regulations and laws that affect the police behavior... because it's clear that they can do action that we feel is not correct, but in the courtroom...is not a criminal act."[48]

The Baltimore police had trapped themselves in a double-bind: They still believed only tough coercive tactics would bear down on crime, and therefore continued to replicate the criminogenic conditions where their officers' use of violence and criminal actions were overlooked, thus antagonizing the local population who in turn defended themselves through acts of resistance, civil and criminal. As homicide rates spiraled in the wake of the 2015 riots, the authorities sacked Batts, the police commissioner, who was at least verbally committed to police reform. At a hastily convened meeting officers were told "the Batts era is over. 'It's time to get out there and do what you need to do.'" Eric Kowalczyk, one of Batts' deputies, promptly retired, writing later: "That mentality and operating modality were the exact reasons we had just gone through a riot, the reasons people had protested the department for weeks on end, the reasons nearly 200 officers were injured, millions of dollars in property has been destroyed, and lives were irrevocably changed. No lessons had been learned. Nothing was different."[49]

Two years later, several officers were convicted of multiple cases of serious criminality including violence, robbery and corruption, all bred by the very mentality that Kowalczyk described. Who could tell the difference between police and thieves? As if to prove the point, after their conviction:

The city sought to be excused from having to pay lawsuit judgments resulting from officers' conduct; calling them "criminals who just happened to be officers of the Baltimore Police Department' whose actions were so far 'outside the scope of their employment" that taxpayers should not foot the bill for their crimes. The judges on Maryland's highest court were not swayed.[50]

Presumably they believed it was criminal for the police to employ criminals, just as it would be to have gangsters in the place of judges, deciding on guilt or innocence and administering punishment. Such behavior is associated with the swamp of corruption encompassing the police, the judiciary and the political parties through their association with "organized crime" during the prohibition era of the 1920s. However, it has never gone away, as any number of studies examining the nexus of crime, networks and power reveals.[51] Evidence for the involvement of Britain's largest force in institutional corruption is examined below, by way of a case-study.

The murder of investigative journalist Daniel Morgan took place in London over 3 decades ago, in 1987. At the time, he was investigating evidence of police corruption and collusion with criminals. Despite five subsequent police investigations between 1987 and 2008, no one has been convicted of Morgan's murder, an axe killing in a pub car park. Following several arrests in 2009, the subsequent 2011 trial collapsed when the judge believed the chief prosecution witness, Superintendent Dave Cook, was coaching witnesses. The then Home Secretary, Theresa May, refused to set up a public inquiry in 2013 but did set up an independent panel which reported in June 2021. Its findings are damning; for example, claiming that Cook had been allowed to "operate outside many of the laws, policies and procedures which govern policing." Baroness Nuala O'Loan, the chair of the panel, claimed, "The Metropolitan Police (Met) has placed concern for its reputation above the public interest. This is a betrayal of the Morgan family, and it's also a betrayal of the public." It amounts to behavior which offers "scope for corrupt practices."

The commissioner of the Met from 2017 to 2022, Dame

Cressida Dick, was assistant commissioner when she produced a report jointly with the state's Crown Prosecution Service that outlined where the 2011 trial had failed. This led to her being made the liaison between the Met and the panel. The panel concluded that Dick saw her job as to delay and obscure their search for justice, mentioning the "hurdles" she placed across their path, for example, by refusing to allow panel members to access the police's computer system that held details of how the police investigation into Morgan's death had been carried out. This highlighted the Met's "lack of candour" – a polite way of describing telling lies. As investigative journalist Simon Basketter, who has followed the Morgan case for many years, reports: "The panel inquiry was supposed to take a year. It has taken eight. That's partially because of the successful way that Dick did her job."[52]

In the wake of the panel's publication, Basketter pulls together some of the threads of this web of corruption: "Paul Condon, Head of the Met during most of the 1990s, coined the phrase 'noble cause corruption' – the idea that some police justifiably 'bend the rules' to get a conviction when they 'knew' the accused was guilty, but had no proof. Condon set up a secret anti-corruption squad known as the Untouchables. A number of senior officers – Andy Hayman, John Yates, Paul Stevens and Ian Blair – were in the squad. All are criticized in the Morgan report."[53] Both Stevens and Blair went on to lead the Met, both received peerages when they retired, suggesting that this practice has led to the institutional corruption that the panel describes.

O'Loan has recently pointed out that the police's hostile reaction to the "institutionally corrupt" charge "illustrates exactly the problem that we have been describing…[it] inhibits both personal and individual accountability." Speaking to the inquiry, Daniel Morgan's son, Dan, vehemently expressed his feelings about those responsible for finding his father's killers: "The commissioners of the Metropolitan Police from the past twenty or so years should be stripped of their titles and put in the dock."[54]

This is just one example of the rising degree of criticism directed toward the British police, and the Met in particular. Commissioner Dick has always been a controversial figure. She was the officer in charge of the operation that assassinated John Paul De Menezes, the Brazilian electrician mistaken for an Islamic terrorist suspect in the paranoid climate of fear that followed the 7/7 bombings in London in 2005. In 2011 she was in charge of "Operation Trident" – an anti-drugs trafficking operation which deployed an armed police unit that shot dead Mark Duggan, sparking the widespread riots of that year. While Home Secretary May vowed to reduce the disproportionate stopping and searching of black youth as long ago as 2013, Dick has proudly upheld the right to extend stop and search and refused to address the worsening disproportionality of non-white people targeted by the police. Within one month of the Morgan report coming out the Met faced another barrage of criticism over the failure of the police to prevent hundreds of people breaking through their lines in order to gatecrash the finals of the 2021 European Football championship at Wembley Stadium. Even *The Times* called for her resignation. An open letter from Baroness Lawrence states: "We share a common concern that the leadership of the Metropolitan Police Service will continue to act as though they were above the law."[55]

The government's instinctive reaction was to defend their beleaguered commissioner and Dick's contract was extended for a further 2 years. However, in early 2022 suspicion of high-level collusion between the Met and the prime minister in order to slow the release of information about breaches of Covid regulations at the heart of government looked like another example of institutionalized corruption. Was Dick blocking the disclosure of the "Partygate" charges against Johnson as payback for him keeping her in a job? Finally, the sheer scale of Met police misconduct became apparent when the contents of the Charing Cross Police Station Whatsapp group were revealed by the Independent Office for Police Conduct (IOPC) report.[56] Officers had joked about raping colleagues and suggested they would like to turn African children into dogmeat. Most of those participating had not been dismissed. The Mayor of London informed Dick he was "putting her on notice" and a week later she announced her resignation would take effect in April.

The sexism and racism on display from the Met in a sickening number of cases over the last few years have seen black women's corpses disrespected, rape and murder joked about and women and children strip searched. This poor practice and abuse of power by the police reflects very badly upon not just the officers responsible but the institution of policing as a whole. This is not a new phenomenon, but the power of two protest movements, #metoo and #blacklivesmatter, has made these crimes and brutalities into headline stories and helped shape a broadening consensus that fundamental changes are needed in the policing of Europe's biggest city. The politics of protest movements are anti-sexist, anti-racist and actively challenge the traditional structures and attitudes of those institutions of authority.

However, while it is perfectly legitimate to blame the police for these shortcomings, it is important to remember who they work for. They are the servants of the state and the government of the day. In Britain, as in so many other countries, it is these governments who equip the police with the authoritarian powers and lack of accountability that have led to this situation. Indeed, they rely upon the police to protect them from the justifiable public demands for justice, welfare and opportunity which capitalism systematically denies to so many: Without police protection government laws and policies would be under constant challenge. Causes often only espoused by determined minorities could command much broader active support if they didn't face the repressive power of the police's "thin blue line." The slogan "No Justice, No Peace" articulates this demand for the people's democratic right to a just society. The global protest upsurge that began in 2019 has not been slowed by the pandemic, far from it. Despite the brutality and efficiency of much police repression – which has crushed street protests and nascent popular movements in the likes of Hong Kong, Belarus, Myanmar and Thailand – resistance endures and regroups. In the course of these movements growing, the oppressive nature of the institutions of social control becomes a more pressing issue to call out, challenge and mobilize against. This is why the very nature of policing and the institutions of the criminal justice system are being questioned. The arguments in favor of their abolition for reasons of history, empire, culture and social control have escalated.[57] That's why virtually every politician becomes an "authoritarian" when they are in government, however liberal they appear when in opposition.

This is, of course, a historical phenomenon that goes back to the times when ancient Rome's praetorian guard protected the emperor and beyond. The French novelist Emile Zola created a monstrous fictional version in *His Excellency* – the story of Minister of the Interior Rougon – whose job was to repress the threat of radical republicanism in the 1850s. He declaims to his supporters: "Oh, you know very well what I stand for. I'm an authoritarian. One's born like it. It's not a viewpoint. It's just a need [for those]…serving whoever's recognized to be in power." This contempt for "opinions" in preference to the "needs" of power sounds very like many of today's rulers. Zola explained the psychology: "He had needs more than opinions. He found power too desirable, too essential to his thirst for domination not to grasp it, whatever the conditions under which it came to him. To rule, to plant his heel on the neck of the mob, there you had his immediate ambition."[58]

The mob was a nineteenth-century term, periodically revived in our own times whenever nations face riots and protests that threaten those in power. It represents the masses, the crowd, the counterpower of social movements. The police, then, are state agents for the exercise of social control, which German Jewish sociologist Norbert Elias calls "reinforcement through external restraints, by means of agencies which are specially licensed to threaten or to use physical violence"[59] This was more than merely academic analysis, as Elias himself was forced to flee the Nazi police state when Hitler came to power in 1933, concluding in somewhat of an understatement that "the civilising of these monopolists of physical violence within a state is an unsolved problem."[60]

When the police and protesters confront one another, the nature of their opposition doesn't allow either group to back down: They are trapped in what Elias calls a double-bind: "the mentality of people trapped in a crisis situation can contribute to its inescapable character. A power conflict stands at the center of any double-bind process. The dangers which it brings for the people involved are difficult for them to overcome precisely because their own mentality comes to bear the mark of the threat, and contributes to its recurring reproduction."[61]

To return to the opening question, the institutionalized nature of the police's role of controlling society in the interests of those at its summit is resulting in actions which ever-broader sections of the population of the whole are starting to resent and actively oppose: This is driving the momentum of the debate about the abolition of such oppressive institutions.

Chapter 2

Do Black Lives Really Matter in Britain's Criminal Justice System?
Nicole Nyamwiza

"Civil rights are civil rights. There are no persons who are not entitled to their civil rights. We have to recognize that we have a long way to go, but we have to go that way together."
Dorothy Height

Introduction

Much of the criminological gaze on racial inequality in the criminal justice system and police brutality tends to focus on the African-American experience in the USA (Hetey and Eberhardt, 2018; Donnelly, 2017; Ghandnoosh, 2015; Dunham and Petersen, 2017). This stance is arguably necessary as research has identified that there were only 27 days in the whole of 2019 where the police in the United States did not kill anybody, with Black people accounting for up to three times as many of the 1098 victims than white people in that year (Salisbury, Connelly and Wangari-Jones, 2020). This deeply concerning figure has led scholars to argue that police brutality has become a normalized feature of life for African Americans (Loader, 2020). As a result, the term "Black Lives Matter" was coined to represent a nationwide movement dedicated to eradicating police brutality rooted in discrimination and racism. The unfortunate death of George Floyd in May 2020 shone a light on the "Black Lives Matter" movement as it enabled the cause to capture the attention of policymakers, political activists, mainstream media and major brands and companies (Brunson and Stuart, 2021). However, a further 181 Black people in America have been killed by the police since George Floyd's death. These deaths can lead us to question whether black lives really matter in the justice system, as despite a meteoric rise in the cause, police brutality has continued. While there are heightened tensions between African-American communities and the police, scholars and activists in Britain have argued that the United Kingdom also is not "innocent." As a result, there have been recent discussions around the value of black lives in the UK and how current police practices impact this (Salisbury et al., 2020). Research has demonstrated that policing in Britain can be understood as institutionally racist and, therefore, not designed with Black people in mind. As a result, such institutions are unable to respond to the multiplicity of needs that these individuals present them with. This chapter will focus on how the policing of Black communities can be reformed while also considering how the justice system as a whole contributes to these issues and how these can be addressed. This chapter recognizes that minority groups seek radical changes and have grown exhausted with the light touch approach to change. Therefore, the central argument of this chapter is that institutional racism can only begin to be addressed if we first dissect the collective "BAME" term and recognize the discriminative and oppressive experiences of each ethnic group as their experiences are not the same. Furthermore, this chapter will suggest that the police and justice system must understand and acknowledge the foundations of discriminative bias within their respective practices and develop change from an informed perspective. Such institutions should seek to work in consultation with the communities that are most affected by this practice. Lastly, in supporting the conclusion and to echo the arguments raised by Salisbury et al., (2020), we must all seek to act on the opportunities for learning and change created through the BLM protests.

The impact of the collective term "BAME" on racial inequality in Britain's criminal justice system:

According to Aspinall (2020), all ethnic/racial terminology has often been deemed a form of representation. While it is understandable that collective terms are often used, collective terms when discussing race and ethnicity can become problematic for particular groups. The term BAME (Black, Asian and minority ethnic) first appeared in 1987 and has been widely used ever since. Research has found that the term has been adopted by various organizations in relation to race equality, and in particular in governmental bodies. The use of terms such as BAME provides a convenient shorthand for such organizations; however, the concern is that this term fails to recognize the complexity of the lived experiences of the different individuals in those categories. By assigning a single collective identity for the various ethnic groups in the UK, one may assume that they share broadly similar experiences or challenges within their daily lives. This could be within the justice system, social housing or education. This assertion links closely to findings by Warmington (2014), who notes that education and policing are central to the experiences of struggle for black British communities.

To illustrate this point, the vast majority of literature on this subject identifies that the police are five times more likely to use force on black people than white, and that black people tend to view themselves in the same light that the police see them, as "criminal" (Weitzer and Tuch, 1999; Palmer, 2012).

While this particular experience and viewpoint is mostly unique to black men, the use of the term BAME in official documentation may suggest that this is the lived experience of all people that fall into that category, which unintentionally removes the focus from those that are suffering in that circumstance. Therefore, grouping all minorities together can suggest that they all experience the same types of oppression and racial discrimination in the CJS. Similarly, there is evidence of anti-blackness in the Asian and Arabs communities, and when grouping individuals from all three communities together, we are ignoring that black men and women also suffer discrimination from other people of color. To illustrate this point further, Beaman (2020) highlights that recent COVID-19 pandemic measures and police violence against black individuals has identified how black populations are continuously suspected and marginalized.

Moreover, there are vast differences of experience in the UK black community itself, with Black Caribbean pupils being three times more likely to be excluded from school than other pupils are and twice as likely to be excluded than their black African peers. This example alone should demonstrate that black people are not a homogenous group within themselves, let alone the entire BAME collective (Demie, 2021). Furthermore, statistics found that 47 percent of ethnic minority Britons feel confident using the term "BAME," with 29 percent reporting that they do not recognize the term at all. Moreover, evidence from opinion-based research has found that the word "BAME" has limited acceptability among all ethnic minority communities (Aspinall, 2020). Therefore, it is reasonable to argue that rejecting such a collective label can help progress toward understanding the unique experiences of individual ethnic minority communities. In doing so, institutions such as the police can work toward understanding how to engage with such communities.

Policing of Black communities in the UK

A wide body of research has identified that the earliest studies of policing in both the UK and USA demonstrate that racial prejudice is a consistent feature of street-level policing (Cain, 1973, 2015; Palmer, 2012; Fatsis, 2021; Bowling and Phillips, 2003; Delsol, 2006; Bacchini and Lorusso, 2019). Studies identify that successive generations of Black people in Britain have felt under-protected as victims of crime and over-policed as suspects of crime since the 1950s (Palmer, 2012). An analysis of the language used by news media outlets highlighted that the language used to describe some Black victims of crime was less favorable than that used for their white counterparts. This is particularly true for Black and Black Mixed men, who are often seen as the "ideal offender" instead of as a victim (Christie, 1986). Such theoretical ideals may have influenced the approach to UK policing as findings from a report by The Institute of Race Relations (IRR 2014) identify examples of police malpractice. Historically, some police officers in the UK have proved unwilling to protect Black people against racist attacks and constantly treated Black people as perpetrators rather than victims.

Such ideologies can prove to be problematic as to how Black communities can trust in an institution that has been found to be institutionally racist. This contention is widely supported by previous research, with the Macpherson Report in 1999 labeling the Metropolitan Police as an institutionally racist organization. In doing so, the report defines *institutional racism* as a collective failure of an organization to provide an appropriate professional service to people due to their color, culture or ethnic origin. The report further notes that such practice can be seen in any form of discrimination that disadvantages ethnic minority people (Macpherson, 1999, p.28). However, as Palmer (2012) identifies, the most concerning factor is that such distrust in the police from Black communities has spanned over nearly 5 decades. This leads us to question whether this matter is being strongly addressed within this institution, as the prevalence of innate racist attitudes among police officers has been present since the 1970s and 1980s. Ironically, it does appear that there has been wide recognition of the need for change – despite countless reports and policies being developed, there remains a wider issue.

This argument is based on the statistics between 2019-2020, that highlight that there were only six stop and searches for every

1000 White people, compared with 54 for every 1000 Black people (Home Office, 2020). While crime committed by Black people cannot and should not be ignored, these statistics alone identify that there is still evidence of discriminatory practice within police forces. This practice is further questionable because research has found that police have failed to provide documents to individuals that they have stopped and searched on some occasions. Furthermore, such practice highlights further concerns that some searches in communities are not being recorded, indicating that the statistics may be much higher than we are aware of. It can be argued that a majority of the issues in UK policing, and namely in stop and search practices, are based on stereotypes. Reiner (2010, p. 121) argues that stereotyping is an inevitable tool of suspiciousness endemic to police work. If this is true, then essentially, Black communities are heavily marginalized as they have historically been stereotyped as criminals. Cain (1973) notes how police normalized using force with Black people due to them being "different" and "incomprehensible." Gunter (2003) identified how discussing Black youth in generalized and stereotyped terms could cause one to bypass that they are all unique individuals with their biographies. His arguments lend closely to Cain's comments on stereotyping and magnify that the criminalization of Black people continues to remain as such figures make it difficult not to assume that Black communities are presented as inherently risky due to racialized policing practices (Williams and Clark, 2018).

Therefore, along with the growing body of research on this topic and the vocal message from the recent BLM protests in the UK, we can highlight that many people feel that the "UK is not innocent" in terms of racial disparity within the system of justice. As while literature recognizes that police brutality in the US has amounted to more deaths than police brutality in the UK, only one police officer in the UK has been convicted of a death in police custody since 1969. The conviction rate of police officers does not correlate with the deaths in custody as 509 people from black, ethnic minority and asylum seeker, migrant communities have died in police custody under suspicious circumstances between 1991 and 2014 (Institution of Race Relations, 2015). Unsurprisingly, current research also indicates that black people in the UK are twice as likely to die in police custody as their white counterparts (Office for National Statistics, 2020). This means that while black people account for only 3 percent of the UK population, they account for 8 percent of deaths in custody.

Moreover, current research identifies that black men and young boys continue to be over-represented in all areas of the justice system in England and Wales (Robertson and Wainwright, 2020). This is despite the publication of several recent reports, including the David Lammy Review in 2017, which highlighted the racial disparity within the CJS and offered solutions as to how to address them. However, there still appears to be a limited amount of published research on racial discrimination from other areas within the justice system, for example, the Crown Prosecution Service (CPS) and Her Majesty's Courts & Tribunals Service (HMCTS). This is seemingly concerning as despite there being evidence that the color of your skin has a measurable impact on how an individual is treated at every stage in the justice system, a majority of the literature available on the UK justice system tends to focus on policing and the topics explored above, i.e. stop and searches, but there is still a need for extensive further research on institutionalized racism within the wider CJS. Similarly, much of the literature continues to focus on the experiences of black men, which inadvertently ignores the plight of black women in the justice system. The Corston Report in 2007 reviewed women's experiences in the CJS. It established the need for a radically different and holistic approach to supporting them, noting that black and ethnic minority women were a "minority within a minority" in the system. Therefore, it is clear that institutional racism is embedded at every stage of our justice system and until this is dismantled, there will be no profound changes.

Moving forward

Throughout this chapter, we have explored various areas of issues that can lead one to question whether black lives matter in our justice system and, more specifically, policing. It appears that there is a recognition of the need to address this matter, as there have been several attempts to reform policing in the UK. For example, commissioned reports, interventions and reviews; however, so far, none has appeared to free the black and other ethnic minority communities from discriminatory practice. Therefore, this chapter unfortunately does not bring a new message. Instead, it echoes the arguments raised in previous literature which highlight that it is clear the current policing structure is unable to support and address the needs of such communities. To address the current issues, we must listen to the arguments of abolitionists and consider how we can implement this in practice. We must also step toward identifying the oppression and struggles of communities separately, and shift from using unhelpful collective terms.

Salisbury et al. (2020) identify that abolishing the police does not have to be a negative process of tearing something down. Instead, we can remove some power from the police and shift it into community-led interventions with specialists that are fully equipped to address the emergency at hand. Recent experience has proved that we must not look at the police as a "one-stop shop" to deal with all of the contentious issues in our society, especially in communities where policing has proven to be unhelpful at times. Furthermore, as explored earlier within this chapter in relation to deaths in police custody, the recent conviction of the British police officer who unlawfully killed Dalian Atkinson was the first time in 30 years that an officer has been convicted of manslaughter in the course of their duties, despite there being 10 manslaughter charges against police officers since the 1990s. It brings us to question whether this conviction is a breakthrough in policing equality or a harsh reminder of the constant failings to our communities.

Despite those UK failures and practices highlighted throughout this chapter, the police-funding package for 2021-22 reveals they are to receive a budget of more than 15 billion pounds, with more than 400 million dedicated to recruiting 20,000 extra police officers (Home Office, 2021). Many believe that much of these funds could be more productively redirected to support local communities and expert services. We must take this action to ensure that Black Lives Matter becomes more than a hashtag. Instead, it is recognized as a global activist movement so that black lives can truly matter everywhere, especially within the justice system.

Chapter 3

"Fund the People Not Police!": The Movement to Defund Law Enforcement
Meghan G. McDowell, Luis A. Fernandez, Laura Rethmann and Brooklyn Rincones

Introduction

"You are now entering the free state of George Floyd" read a carefully painted wooden placard that was placed at the entrance of an "autonomous zone" established in Minneapolis, Minnesota during the summer of 2020. The free state of George Floyd, later known as "George Floyd Square," was located at the intersection of 38th Street and Chicago Avenue in south Minneapolis, the site of Floyd's brutal execution at the knee of former police officer, and now convicted murderer, Derek Chauvin. There was a militant, international and sustained response to Floyd's death. Protests, lasting days, and in some cities even weeks, occurred in all 50 US states. In Minneapolis, people burned a police precinct to the ground and people created George Floyd Square.

Faced with these experiments in freedom and (yet another) crisis of legitimacy, the state mobilized quickly to extinguish the uprising through force and via initial concessions such as the arrest of Chauvin. Organizers across the country were also moving swiftly to seize the momentum generated by thousands of people in the streets. Soon, movement spaces were issuing a clarion call to "defund the police" and this soon became the most prominent abolitionist strategy in the United States.

In this chapter, we offer an introduction to the movement to defund the police in the United States. How did we arrive at defunding the police as a mainstream call in the United States? How are cities responding? What are the promises and pitfalls of defund as an abolitionist strategy? Below, we begin by placing these efforts in historical context, both in terms of its antecedents in the Abolitionist Movement to end slavery and by examining the role of police under racial capitalism. Next, we take a closer look at cities where organizers have been fighting to defund local law enforcement. Drawing on these examples, and our own experience as local organizers involved in defunding efforts, we conclude with an analysis and critique of the current strategy.

Context for police abolition in the United States

In 2014, the United States witnessed the first rise of Black Lives Matter (BLM) protests, triggered by the police killings of numerous black, brown and indigenous people. In the streets, people cried out "No justice, no peace, fuck the police!" and "The whole damn system is guilty as hell!" These uncompromising positions were amplified by forceful demands from grassroots collectives aimed at local and state law enforcement agencies. In May of 2020, a Minneapolis police officer named Derek Chauvin placed his left knee on the back of George Floyd's neck, effectively killing him after 8 agonizing minutes. The incident produced a wave of unrest not seen in a generation.

According to some estimates, approximately 15 to 26 million people in the United States demonstrated in the summer of 2020 alone.[1] This is perhaps the largest continuous protest mobilization of people in the history of the United States. And the struggle was rooted in an abolitionist politic. Strong abolitionist movements in the United States are not new. Historically, the idea of abolition was linked to the destruction of an economic system built on the ownership of human beings. What is new is a united, widespread effort to target the police as an institution. Several scholars have noticed this shift,[2] pointing to the grassroots nature of police abolition work. If so, then we can ask why this shift now?

The short answer is that while the intensity is new, the actual focus on policing is not. Calls to abolish police are traceable to at least the late 1960s[3]. And the link between police and racial oppression seems to arise with the emergence of police institutions themselves.[4] As such, institutions have faced periodic calls for reform and elimination. Again, we should ask, why is this so? The answer is because the role of police institutions is to maintain the social order, and thus the *status quo*, regardless of how unjust it is. In a nation where the social order is linked to a racial order, then the function is to maintain the racial divide. Below we describe the rise of police institutions in three areas of the United States, each embedded to a specific type of racial configuration, showing how interlinked the two are.

The early emergence of police-like organizations (or proto-police) in the southern United States is well documented.[5] In the South, proto-police groups emerged as slave patrols, which arose directly from the plantation system in the early part of the 1700s. Slave patrols were organized groups of armed volunteers enforcing corporal discipline on enslaved persons, focusing on "escaped" people or those viewed as defiant. These *patrollers* ensured that enslaved people could not move freely between plantations, were subject to constant surveillance, and brutally punished if found breaking slave codes. These actions were, of course, a basic requirement in maintaining the social order within an economic system requiring free labor. In time, these proto-policing groups were institutionalized as official police departments.

A slightly different proto-police emerged in northern states, from the night watchmen. The night watchmen carried 6-foot poles with a hook to grab individuals and were responsible for maintaining social order in urbanizing cities. In time, cities like Boston, New York and Philadelphia instituted the watchmen into official police departments, intervening in worker strikes, disrupting unions and obstructing labor organizing. Thus, we see police serving social order needs, here around an industrializing economic system.

The Texas Rangers emerged out of a different historical and geographical setting: colonialism. Established in 1835, the Rangers were at first a loose band of irregulars hired to protect the interests of newly arrived white colonialists into the Mexican territory. Once established as a state, Texas instituted the Rangers to consolidate the dispossession of land from indigenous and Mexican citizens alike. D. J. Swanson (2020, p. 10) describes the Texas Rangers as a "violent instrument of repression. They burned down villages and slaughtered innocents, they committed war crimes. Their murders of Mexicans and Mexican Americans made them as feared on the border as the Ku Klux Klan in the Deep South."[6] Here we see, again and again, a proto-police group closely linked to the process of economic accumulation, in this case based entirely on the expropriation and commodification of land.

The three origins of US policing defined above have one thing in common: each exists to help maintain the social order, often described as the maintenance of "peace." However, the so-called peace is embedded in social and economic arrangements that require inequality and human degradation. Thus, we agree with scholar Mark Neocleous and argue that the primary role of the police is one of order maintenance, regardless of the morality of that order[7]. Therefore, it is impossible to distinguish police from an inequitable social order that arises from political-economic arrangements. If the above is correct, then calling for the abolition of police can be read as calling for the abolition of social divisions. And this is what the BLM movement, activists and scholars are advocating. Police defunding, further, should be understood in this broader context.

Approaches to defunding the police

Defund organizers across the United States have taken three

general approaches. First, some have aimed to shrink police budgets and reinvest in community well-being. Second, they have sought to limit the scope of policing, reducing police powers. Third, others have tried to create new (or support existing) institutions, practices and organizations that respond to harm without relying on criminalization, policing or prisons. These approaches are, of course, not mutually exclusive. This section discusses each approach, focusing on seven US cities that made significant efforts in these directions. They include: New York, Seattle, Los Angeles, San Francisco, Portland, Baltimore and Philadelphia.

Shrinking Police Budgets and Investing in Supportive Services

Cities and counties in the United States are generous to their police, allocating between 20–45 percent of local budgets to law enforcement[8]. This does not account for the hundreds of millions of dollars in spending subsidized by the federal government. For example, President Joe Biden, a democrat, has proposed a slate of criminal justice reforms supported by a 300-million-dollar federal investment in local community-oriented policing efforts.[9] Bloated police budgets have become one target of defund campaigns that seek to divest from law enforcement and reinvest in community services to support well-being. In our review of the seven cities noted above, we identified four common areas that organizers successfully (re)funded by shrinking police budgets: (1) mental health; (2) economic development programs for people of color; (3) youth and social services programming; and (4) funding to address homelessness.

For example, organizers in New York City won a 2021-2 budget that reduces police spending and shrunk the footprint of the New York City Police Department (NYPD), one of the largest such departments in the world, by nearly one *billion* dollars. The NYPD budget was cut by $484 million dollars and the council approved an additional $384 million dollars in shifts to outside agencies that are "best positioned" to carry out duties previously assigned to the NYPD, a move that draws on the second approach: reducing the scope of police work. According to a press release by the New York City Council, "The savings will go to critical programs and initiatives, including summer youth programming ($115 million), education ($116 million) and for family and social services ($134 million). In addition, $500 million in capital costs will be moved from the NYPD capital budget which allows investment in other badly needed infrastructure. The capital money will go toward the Parks Department community centers and NYCHA broadband access"[10].

In July of 2020, the Los Angeles City Council voted to cut the Los Angeles Police Department (LAPD) budget by $150 million dollars. Sixty million dollars was used to balance the budget. However, there was a protracted fight over how to spend the remaining $89 million dollars. In May of 2021, the city council successfully voted to allocate $32 million "toward policing alternatives, including community intervention officers, as well as homeless prevention and homeless services."[11] The remaining funds will support education and jobs initiatives, universal basic income pilots, anti-gang initiatives, improvements to parks, youth programming, arts programming, and more. These suggestions came from community activists who had demanded this reform for years.

Addressing the housing crisis and mental health issues with re-appropriated police funds was also a common thread across the seven cities we studied. For example, the city of San Francisco cut $120 million, which represents an 8.7 percent reduction in the police budget. The money is earmarked to address unsheltered people and individuals experiencing mental distress. In Philadelphia, the city council approved a $14 million budget cut from police, with plans to invest in anti-poverty measures and affordable housing. In Austin, Texas, the city council is reallocating police funds to invest in supportive housing strategies for unsheltered people by purchasing local hotels and turning them into affordable housing units.[12] In an effort to address racial and economic inequality, many cities specifically set aside money to support business of color. In Baltimore they are offering black-owned business forgivable loans, alongside plans to build recreation centers, and provide more trauma support services to its residents. In Portland, Oregon, 1 million dollars has been directed toward funding a leadership program for black residents aged 25 and younger. This is reflective of a broader investment in youth services, as nearly every city we studied announced plans to redirect money toward youth programming.

Reducing the Scope of Police Work

A related approach is the reduction of police powers and responsibilities. The main goal is to reduce the opportunities for police-resident contact, hoping thereby to avoid entry into the criminal justice system. The strategy is to divert populations away from law enforcement, while also making it harder for police to engage with vulnerable populations.

This strategy is a response to the expansion of police responsibilities over the past 50 years. In his important book *The End of Policing*, scholar Alex Vitale identifies an array of social problems – homelessness, untreated mental illness, youth conduct in schools, and so on – that local, state and federal leaders have essentially handed off to the police to manage. That violence has resulted from the erroneous attempt to "turn police into social workers" is no surprise, argues Vitale during an interview on National Public Radio's *Code Switch* program. "Police are violence workers. That's what distinguishes them from all other government functions," Vitale explains. "They have the legal capacity to use violence in situations where the average citizen would be arrested."[13]

The defund movement has applied this strategy most successfully to developing police-free alternatives to mental health crisis response and to efforts to eliminate school resource officers from K–12 public school settings. There is historical precedent to draw on here. For example, many jurisdictions are replicating the CAHOOTS Model, a mobile crisis response service that was an outgrowth of efforts in Eugene Oregon in the late 1960s and early 1970s to develop a more holistic, non-punitive and community-driven continuum of care.[14] Today, CAHOOTS is organized around two-person teams, consisting of medically trained individuals and a crisis worker trained in the mental health field. Instead of police officers, this team responds to emergency calls, typically involving youth, unsheltered people, people experiencing a mental health crisis and those struggling with drug addiction. The goal is to provide health care, de-escalation if necessary, and support connecting with social services. According to CNN, at least 13 cities across the United States are working "to minimize or eliminate" law enforcement response to 911 calls involving mental health, substance abuse, or homelessness.[15]

Following the George Floyd uprising in 2020, at least 33 school districts across the US have eliminated school resource officers by ending contracts with local police or sheriff's offices.[16] School districts often pay exorbitant sums to local police agencies to post officers inside schools. There have been numerous harrowing reports detailing racial discrimination, intimidation and violence by SROs across the United States, leading to calls for their elimination. The uprising provided an opening for organizers to renew the call to end SRO contracts. To date, defund campaigns have successfully kicked police officers out of public schools in over 25 cities, freeing up $34 million dollars to be redirected toward student support services.[17] Collectives like the Black Organizing Project are also working to build community-driven solutions to harm in schools, releasing "The People's Plan for Police Free Schools" in 2019.[18]

Reducing the scope of police work eliminates points of contact between residents and law enforcement, thereby reducing the opportunity for harassment, abuse, arrest and premature death that are so often the result of police-resident interactions, particularly for black and indigenous people in the United States.

Building and Supporting Police Free Institutions

The historian and abolitionist Robin D.G. Kelley writes, "Without new visions, we don't know what to build, only what to knock down." The creation of new, life-supporting institutions is central to abolitionist practice. When we stop relying on law enforcement for solutions to violence, the responsibility for community safety and security becomes democratized and collectivized.

The defund movement includes a number of grassroots organizations that are "working to transform the way society views healing and safety [and build] practical models for responding to harm." Common Justice, one such organization in New York, compiled a report titled "Solutions to Violence: Creating Safety Without Prisons or Policing"[19] that details the work of 18 organizations across the United States that are building police-free institutions, practices, and harm reduction models. A sample of the approaches included in this report: the use of restorative justice; the implementation of fellowship programs for young men involved in lethal firearm offenses; reframing violence as a public health issue; using "violence interrupters" instead of police to diffuse conflict; and developing trauma-informed care practices for use by local institutions.

In Durham, North Carolina the local defund movement, led by *Durham Beyond Policing*, successfully fought for the creation of an entirely new city department: The Department of Community

Safety. This department is dedicated to finding ways to address violence without a law enforcement response. Though in the very early stages, the department has already conducted a 911 audit and identified types of calls like minor traffic incidents, quality of life issues and calls for general assistance that do not require an armed officer response. This department will work alongside the Community Safety and Wellness Task Force, comprised of appointed Durham residents, to continue to identify strategies for responding to harm without relying on law enforcement. The staffing of the new department was made possible by freezing and diverting money that would have been spent to fill 15 vacant police officer positions.

What makes these approaches unique is that they are not necessarily tied to state support or state integration. They also are not always scalable – meaning the practices are often place-based and community-driven. This runs counter to the "one size fits all" approach of the criminal justice system. What unites these models is the principle that no human being, even those who have committed grave harm, is disposable.

Assessing the defund movement: Promises and pitfalls

Seasoned organizers know that the state will mobilize quickly to neutralize the most radical demands made in the streets. In this case, the demand to abolish police – full stop – rang out across all 50 states during the George Floyd uprisings. Defunding law enforcement materialized as the dominant approach to police abolition in the months that followed. In this chapter we've mapped three approaches to implementing defund campaigns that are being practiced across the United States. We conclude this analysis by discussing how various governing bodies and state actors have sought to limit the impact of the defund movement. Budgets are fungible, contested and subject to change every fiscal year. This means the fight over how much money police get out of the general fund is always subject to negotiation. To date, the defund movement has made meaningful material gains in the span of just 2 years. According to the *Community Resource Hub* (2021), defund campaigns in cities across the United States have "secured divestment of over $840 million dollars from police departments and secured investments of over $160 million dollars in communities." However, met with a new budgeting cycle in 2021-22, many cities regressed and increased their spending on police. For example, New York City was praised for making a $1.1 billion proposed budget cut to the New York Police Department (NYPD). However, the police budget increased incrementally, and it seems that by 2022 the NYPD could be funded at similar levels prior to budget cuts.[20] Likewise, less than a year after the Los Angeles City Council made significant reductions to their police department budget, the council voted to increase police funding by $36 million for the following cycle.[21]

Divestments from policing do not mitigate against investments in other forms of racialized containment and capture. For example, New York City has invested $10 billion dollars in new jail construction, while other cities move toward e-carceration, a strategy that uses technology to create what some call "digital prisons." City leaders claim to be investing in social services and community safety projects, yet their reinvestment strategies remain opaque. For instance, some cities push the "Memphis Model" of policing, which relies on specialized officers responding to calls of individuals experiencing mental health crises. While these officers may be better prepared to handle a mental health crisis, the scope of power remains within police-centered enforcement. Under this ruse, reinvestment actually keeps funding within police institutions, does not reduce the scope of policing, and permits responders to make arrests and use force.

However, promises made by politicians facing a national

uprising are precarious at best. Case in point, the City of Minneapolis vowed to dismantle the police department in 2020, aiming to replace it with a Community Safety and Violence Prevention Department. To do so meant a change in the city charter, which required a public ballot vote.[22] This process has stalled as politicians fight over disbanding the police in the courts.[23]

Furthermore, while Minneapolis city officials did increase funding for social services, the city council also voted to uphold the current size of the police force, leaving the number of officers intact. In Seattle, protesters called for a 50 percent decrease in the police budget, a number the city initially agreed to during the height of protests. However, the implementation fell well short of the goal, resulting in just an 18 percent reduction in police spending. The Seattle City Council also slowed the process of distributing millions of dollars for alternatives to policing, with the mayor and the council mired in disputes over the process of participatory budgeting.

Another point of caution is the potential to overwhelm social services that are already underfunded. For example, diverting people experiencing mental health crises away from law enforcement may not result in the changes activists hoped for, unless there are meaningful mental health care services available for long-term care. That is, without shoring up mental health services, social workers will be unable to provide meaningful care, since they are already engaged with too many hurting individuals. We need meaningful, consistent investments in community resources alongside divestment from policing. Without long-term alternatives, law enforcement institutions will remain resilient.

Perhaps the biggest challenge facing the defund movement is neutralization through reformist logics that seek to curtail the most radical expressions of police abolition. Reformism uses policing to save policing from policing. As Mariame Kaba argues, any effort that results in more resources for the police is not an abolitionist practice.[24] It is essential that slight cuts in police department budgets are not our end goal. As long as the basic form and function of policing remains unchanged, then police power will continue to be a structuring force, resulting in the premature death, containment and capture of black, indigenous and poor people in the US. "What millions of Americans are looking for right now is real change," explained Alicia Garza, a co-founder of the Movement for Black Lives. "Not tinkering around the edges but going straight and directly to the roots."[25] The movement to defund the police is full of radical potential, can it seize the day?

Chapter 4

Resistant Imagery in Struggles for Justice
Ken Fero

"The media's the most powerful entity on earth. They have the power to make the innocent guilty and to make the guilty innocent, and that's power."
Malcolm X

"Dead is dead it's permanent, it's forever and wanting justice for that death is also forever. It's a forever wanting, I will always want it and will never rest until it's achieved."
Brenda Weinberg.[1]

Migrant Media is a collective of migrant, black and refugee film activists established in 1991.[2] The struggles of race and class are at the core of their resistance-based documentary film-making, and a dominant thread in their work is around campaigns for justice by the families of people killed by the police in the UK. They employ the techniques of *Third Cinema* to incite political change through a provocative strategy of deconstructing established narratives. As Getino and Solanas (1971) state: "Every image that documents, bears witness to, refutes or deepens the truth of a situation is something more than a film image or purely artistic fact; it becomes something which the System finds indigestible."[3]

In this spirit Migrant Media challenges conventional documentary, adopting a position of the filmmakers as the gatherers of resistant imagery. This documentary practice is a radical approach in confronting dominant media and state narratives. Resistance, from a community perspective, is documented over 3 decades, employing a "documentary of force" research method. This is a process where the filmmakers do not just observe but actively participate, and influence the action. It is a praxis summed up by the Dziga Vertov Group in their manifesto attributed to Godard and Gorin (1970): "The problem is not to make political films but to make films politically."[4]

Making films politically, in this instance, has meant that film production ran parallel with the establishment of the United Families and Friends Campaign (UFFC), the coalition of family campaigns of victims of police violence. It was formed in 1996 by Brenda Weinberg, the sister of Brian Douglas, who died in 1995, and Myrna Simpson, the mother of Joy Gardner, who died in 1993. The other founding members were filmmaker and activist Ken Fero from Migrant Media and community activist Minkah Adofo from the African Peoples Liberation Front. Their simple, but militant, idea was to unite the families, strengthen each other and fight the state. As the years went on they were joined by many other families who were campaigning for their own cases. These included Stephanie Lightfoot-Bennett, whose brother Leon Patterson died in 1992, and Janet Alder, the sister of Christopher Alder, who died in the custody of police officers in 1999.

Many individual families already had support from a range of social or political organizations, but their campaigns were tied to whatever the agenda of those organizations happened to be. These groups ranged from the Socialist Workers Party to the Nation of Islam and also a slew of local police monitoring groups. The process of making the film *Injustice* (2001) brought together the families who had previously been isolated from each other into an effective political force, it was led by them, they took control of their own struggles collectively and determined the direction of the campaign. They spoke to the people, without liberal mediation, and appealed directly for help with a set of clear demands, a united voice for a national solution. The approach of UFFC and Migrant Media was to broaden the struggle by expressing the emotional toll of the deaths with a political critique of the failure of the justice system, straight to the public through the use of film. To cite Fanon (1963): "To educate the masses politically does not mean, cannot mean, making a political speech. What it means is to try, relentlessly and passionately, to teach the masses that everything depends on them; that if we stagnate it is their responsibility, and that if we go forward it is due to them too."[5] The spark that created UFFC had occurred a few years earlier, on 28 July 1993 when Joy Gardner died due to police and deportation officers forcibly restraining her with a body belt and ankle straps and gagging her mouth with 4 meters of surgical tape to silence her. She suffocated to death. Migrant Media were commissioned by Channel 4 Television to make *Justice for Joy* (1995)[6], which heard from members of her family about Joy's death, reporting on the reactions to it in the black community. It also examined two other deaths related to immigration control, those of Kwanele Siziba and Joseph Nnalue, and asked what were the political circumstances that allowed these deaths to happen. The film followed the struggle of Joy's family in their fight for justice and for the truth to be exposed.

The public outcry across the country following the horrific killing was met by vilification in the mainstream press. Joy was blamed for her own demise by being an "illegal immigrant." The last outcry following the death of a black mother at the hands of the police had taken place a decade earlier in the case of Cynthia Jarrett which led to the Broadwater Farm uprising in 1985. The political establishment wanted to avoid this reoccurrence and so the manslaughter trial of the police officers that had restrained and killed Joy went ahead. Nevertheless, the officers were later found not guilty. The film explored how the media carried out a character assassination of Joy in order to justify the way in which she was killed. This tactic of blaming the victim is often used as part of the defense of police officers, both in their legal cases but also by mainstream media.

There are critical moments in a crime scene after any homicide termed by police investigators as the "golden hour." It's a time when physical evidence is at its freshest and witnesses have the ability for optimum recollection. These are important elements that need to be secured for a reasonable chance of criminal conviction. The last 5 decades have shown us that, when it comes to police killings of civilians in the UK, there is not just a failure to secure the evidence but the corruption and destruction of evidence.[7] What is clearly crisis management by the state extends to another key area during this 'golden hour' – the manipulation of words and images to attack the integrity of the victim.

This process was outlined by Said when writing about the Palestinian issue where he comments about the "political battle for Palestine in the international world in which ideas, representations, rhetoric, and images were at issue." That political battle, that propaganda victory, was the ultimate triumph over the Palestinians.[8] In considering the lack of justice in the case of fatal police violence in the UK it is clear to see how the political battle to recognize deaths as a result of the violence of state agents has been deflected through character assassination of the victims. There are numerous examples of racialized media coverage of victims of police violence. In the 1990s the press office of the Metropolitan Police made a habit of quickly putting out disinformation and briefing journalists to suggest the victim was to blame for their own death. Without the existence of social media very little could be done to redress that imbalance. In a few cases apologies were made following complaints by the families of the dead but the damage in the public's perception was already done.

The mainstream press was largely sympathetic to the police. Sawyers outlines the blaming process as it pertained to Joy Gardner:

As they normally do in these cases they kind of roll out a propaganda machine, especially the tabloids. The kind of worst elements of the gutter press, and they start making references to the fact that she was a migrant, you see headlines which talk about race row death. There're all these references to how she "snapped" at the police officers. How she was so physically dangerous, and how they had no option but to deal with her in the way that they did. It's really important that we saw this woman as some kind of demon, as a really dangerous person, kind of public enemy number one. The fact that Joy is so violent helps to justify the violence that *they* have committed on her. So, it's really important that they portray her as a violent person, because otherwise they ain't got no justification for what they did, and the fact of the matter is that they haven't got any justification for what they did."[9]

The effect of this strategy in these cases is that everyone is killed twice, once by police violence and once by the words and images that attempt to convince the public that the person they have killed is responsible for their own death just for being in contact with the police. The dominant narrative is the police point of view. It is a story that swathes of the public believe in for their own sense of security. The pervasive impact of this racial profiling and stereotyping is easy to read in the public comments left by viewers and captured on the Channel 4 Duty Log after *Justice for Joy* was broadcast; for example:

"This is giving great offence. I don't think it should ever have been shown"

"Very one-sided – this woman was an illegal immigrant. You are obviously a left-wing station and I hope you get burgled or raped on the way home tonight"

"You have overstepped the mark with this programme. It was so one-sided"[10]

It is perhaps no surprise that the public, primed for a year between the death and the trial by a rabid racialized framing of Joy, was dominated by negative reaction following the national transmission. People only knew the police narrative, and they believed it. Unfortunately, Channel 4 caved in to public and police pressure. They did not appear with the filmmakers on *Right to Reply* – their audience response program at the time – distancing themselves from *Justice for Joy*. The films of Migrant Media critique how the media frame custodial deaths and expose the British state's strategy to prevent the violent deaths becoming national moments of trauma. The film-making approach is critical in understanding mainstream media functioning in maintaining what Zizek (2009) terms fetishist disavowal "I know, but I don't want to know that I know, so I don't know."[11]

One of the most shocking facts exposed in the Migrant Media featured documentary *Injustice* (2001) was the actual numbers of deaths involved. Before the film was produced no media or government organization had actually revealed the figure. It is perhaps telling that even the BBC, with its claimed reputation of objectivity, had failed to take even the most basic journalistic step of collecting data. There was no analysis of the issue beyond individual cases. The filmmakers combined many sources when researching, including the Institute of Race Relations book *A Deadly Silence*[12], the Police Complaints Authority, the organization Inquest and various national and regional newspaper reports. It was a 3-year project which resulted in the figure of over 1000 deaths from 1969-1999.

The film took the approach that this was evidence of systemic violence, that there was a pattern of police crime and also state failure to deal with that crime. The figures alone proved that this issue was worth investigating. Migrant Media approached UK broadcasters to support the making of the film, most notably Channel 4. They declined to become involved on numerous occasions, one senior commissioning editor claimed there was no real story there. Nevertheless, the filmmakers persisted.

The film exposed that the first recorded death at the hands of the police in Britain had occurred in Leeds in 1971 when David Oluwale was found drowned in the river after being chased by the police. In the investigation that followed it was discovered that Oluwale had been harassed by two police officers, Inspector Geoffrey Ellerker and Sergeant Mark Kitching, who had assaulted Oluwale before he died. Oluwale's case went to trial and other police officers testified to the brutality that Ellerker and Kitching had inflicted on David over a number of years. This included beatings and urinating on him as he lay on the floor. The judge did not allow the jury to consider a verdict of manslaughter but the officers were jailed for lessor offenses. (Aspden Kester. (2008). The Hounding of David Oluwale London: Vintage).

Fifty years later with more than 2000 deaths now recorded there have been very few prosecutions of the police. The question is, why? Examining the Oluwale case, the fact that police officers spoke against each other in court caused controversy. The police have built a culture of impunity in the force to ensure officers are more loyal to each other than to the truth. This was easier to achieve in the past, when the police themselves were in charge of deciding whether a case went to trial. From 1986, that role was taken up by the "independent" Crown Prosecution Service. Unfortunately, little has changed since then and the CPS have regularly been accused of preventing cases involving the police going to trial. Instead, the families are forced to go through what is called "the inquest system," a lesser court that cannot make criminal judgments and has no power to sanction or jail offenders. In the face of this inequality of resources UFFC have campaigned for justice for their loved ones. Their efforts have yielded some results in terms of supporting families and impacting policy makers with film as an important tool.

The approach of Migrant Media offers hope around the production of images of resistance, the notion of collective memory is a fundamental part of this. A key example of that is around the screening of *Injustice*. The filmmakers had experienced enormous difficulties in making the film with no support from any broadcaster but defied expectations by completing production and organizing screenings. On 6 July 2001 the premier opening of *Injustice* at the Metro Cinema in London was halted dramatically when two police officers issued last minute legal threats to the cinema owners. News spread about the police action and the ensuing uproar in the cinema. Journalists and diplomats from the UK, Iran and Japan were present. An hour later the filmmakers were condemning the police action on the BBC evening news, with a simple message – they would not let the police kill the film.[13] Five days later, on 11 July, a second attempt to show the film at Conway Hall, a place renowned for supporting freedom speech, was met by more saber rattling from the police. The number of police officers who felt aggrieved by the film had increased to 13. After it became clear that the manager of Conway Hall was going to cancel the screening, a cry from the audience rang out: "Show the film." The audience took control of the venue; barricaded the doors and projected the film themselves.

This action catapulted the story of the attempts to censor the film into the daily newspapers. For some time following this screening, the police continued to harass venues that tried to show the film. The threats of libel to the various cinemas kept coming and a whirlwind of late-night conferences, telephone calls and meetings ended with apologies by cinema managers (the staff were always keen to support the showings) and promises of a screening "once the legal problems had cleared." The public response to the film was incredibly supportive, individuals made sure that there was always a venue near the cinema ready to show the film at short notice that same evening, whether it was a squatted anti-globalization cafe in Manchester, a pub in Hoxton or a community hall in Tottenham. Throughout this period the families of those killed by the police traveled the country showing the film and talking about the struggle for justice.

At every screening there was an outpouring of grief and anger from the audience and also a determination to keep showing the film and supporting the families. Screenings were always full spilling on to the street, Q&A sessions would go on long afterwards. This fight for the truth was helped by many people – workers, students, lecturers, trade unionists, religious leaders, anarchists and even some judges. Screenings were fought for, and won, only because of this support. *Injustice* began to mobilize people to take a stand against police oppression. Screenings cascaded to invitations to show the film, at the Fire Brigades Union conference in Sheffield, at a documentary film Festival in Norway and so on. Commenting on a screening of *Injustice* in Los Angeles, the renowned Oscar-nominated filmmaker David Koff reflected:

> These days films are for mobilizing money and awards rather than for mobilizing people. The fact that a social movement has been generated by the film is evidence of the power of cinema, I would say – a capacity of film-making that is virtually ignored nowadays. I'm very impressed with what they have done with their film and it seems to be taking off.[14]

The threats by the police officers continued. The Police Federation then claimed that the film was not only libelous, but an incitement to riot. Migrant Media decided to push back: In a bizarre move they arranged for a screening of *Injustice* to all the police officers who had been involved in the deaths featured in the film. The filmmakers made it clear that they would go to court to defend the film. If the police went forward with a libel trial they would have to stand in criminal court on account, the very action that had been avoided through the deflection of the inquest system. The police were silenced, no further threats of legal action have been made since.

The police had attacked the film to try to suppress it but the international publicity generated by the film caused them to back down. The public was exposed to the fact that some officers do kill and the government reacted. The ongoing impact of the UFFC campaign combined with the film controversy and screenings contributed significantly to the abolition of the Police Complaints Authority and the establishing of the Independent Police Complaints Commission as part of the Police Reform Act of 2002.

Twenty years later it is clear the deaths continue, earlier reforms have not addressed the lack of justice in the cases of Joy Gardner, Brian Douglas and Shiji Lapite, to name a few. Despite overwhelming evidence against police officers accused of murder or manslaughter, why have they not been convicted? When *Injustice* was released the deaths were framed as human rights abuses. This was ground-breaking at the time as the Human Rights Act had not come into full force in the UK, the very notion that the British state was responsible for such abuses in mainland Britain was clearly a hard pill to swallow and yet what else are they? In fact, the inspiration for the position taken was from Malcom X when he questioned the notion that there could be civil rights for Afro-Americans in the US when even basic human rights, such as the right to life, was clearly not respected due to police killings.[15]

If there is to be any hope of winning the hearts and minds of people in the struggles for justice it is by challenging the very terminology used around this issue; this has been determined by the state for too long. One of the most pervasive concerns on this issue is the very language used. The term "deaths in police custody" is a phrase developed by the state which even lawyers and liberal institutions that support victims of police violence replicate. This is a fundamental mistake because, in reality, it has become an innocuous term that does not fully convey what these deaths really are, killings at the hands of the police. The use of the word "killings" has been rolled back by the state over a number of years and for good reason. During the 1990s a series of highly controversial deaths at the hands of the police, primarily but not exclusively, of black men led to a series of inquest verdicts of "unlawful killing." Oluwashiji Lapite, Ibrahim Sey, Harry Stanley, Roger Sylvester and Christopher Alder were all unlawful killing verdicts.

There was a perceptible build-up of public concern over the period. Now for the general public scanning news media, reading the term "unlawful killing" combined with "police" had a powerful impact. "Unlawful killing" implies a crime has been committed, that something should be done about it. There is a dangerous assumption that action will be taken. Of course, it seldom is and the Crown Prosecution Service invariably decided not to prosecute officers. Nevertheless, the state understood the danger of these verdicts building a consensus for action. In order to suppress the situation, and the growing profile of these deaths, they introduced the option of a narrative verdict. This has been an absolute failure for the families of victims as it dilutes the impact of the "unlawful killing" verdict which it has largely replaced. While inquests allow families and legal representatives to gather facts, in reality they function to ensure that criminal trials do not go forward. They act as a release valve for the state. There have been numerous government reviews, most notably the Angiolini Review, which act as smoke screens. Played out endlessly they are ineffectual as they are never acted on and come from within the system.[16] This deflects from what the families want, the reopening of their cases.

Developing long-term relationships is central to Migrant

Media's film-making approach.[17] As an example, one of the participants, Myrna Simpson, the mother of Joy Gardner who died during police restraint in 1993, appears in the documentaries *Justice Denied* (1995), *Injustice* (2001) and *Burn* (2014). There is a process at play in which the participants have a vested interest in the research and its dissemination, becoming central players in the debate and dialogue of the outputs. Gramsci (1971) writes of the organic intellectual being "in active participation in practical life, a constructor, organizer, 'permanent persuader' and not just a simple orator."[18] Myrna Simpson played that role within the community following her daughter's death and, at several points in the films, her words clearly reflect the longevity of this position. Cooper (2001) notes this in relation to *Injustice* and the context of the attempts to suppress the film: The voices silenced in the present broadcasting landscape aren't so much those of the filmmakers as of people like Myrna Simpson. "You don't know the pain, you don't know the suffering, you don't know how I've cried. My tears will catch them. My tears will catch them."[19]

Ultraviolence (2020) has been released 19 years after *Injustice*, and demands to know what has changed since then? One of the clearest pieces of evidence in the new film is the escalation of violence, culpability, neglect and collusion within the state. The research for *Injustice* revealed that over 1000 people had died after coming into contact with the police during the 30-year period we investigated. In the 20 years since then there have been another 1000 deaths. The kill rate is rising. Anyone that claims, as many have in the light of the George Floyd killing, that the UK is somehow different, that those things "do not happen here," is mistaken. They had better look at the cold hard facts and stop feeding themselves the lie that the police in this country are less brutal. They should also hear, as is presented in *Ultraviolence*, the words of Frank Ogboru, the killing of whom predates Floyd with the cries of "I can't breathe" as he died on the streets of southeast

London, physically restrained by the Metropolitan Police. Those in denial may also want to make themselves aware of the last words of Paul Coker, who screamed: "They are killing me," when a gang of more than 12 officers restrained him in his girlfriend's flat in Plumstead. (Statewatch UK: Black deaths in Custody — No Justice, 1 July 1996: https://www.statewatch.org/statewatch-database/uk-black-deaths-in-custody-no-justice/).

A society that refuses to even acknowledge the last words of the dead is a chronic monstrosity. Is the collective amnesia and desperation to trust the police so overwhelming that society will continue to allow police officers to kill with impunity? *Ultraviolence* asks these questions and many more. The film presents new evidence in the cases followed in *Injustice* such as that of Brian Douglas, who was killed by PC Tuffey in south London. Brian was struck with a police truncheon, a blow so severe it fractured his skull. This stop and search escalated when the officer decided that a man with his arms raised was fair game as he cracked his skull from behind. What happened in that case? Nothing. Essentially Douglas was blamed for his own death and the officer was free to pursue more racist violence which is presented in *Ultraviolence*.

The process of the production of *Injustice* helped promote a review of the Crown Prosecution Service by Lord Justice Butler, in which he deals with Douglas and the CPS decision-making process:

Having considered the papers, Senior Treasury Counsel advised that he was satisfied that it would not be right to bring proceedings either for manslaughter, or for attempting to pervert the course of justice, against these officers. There were, however, two contrary opinions obtained on behalf of the relatives of the deceased each by a Queen's Counsel with experience in the criminal law. Senior Treasury Counsel maintained his position even after he had read these opinions. The decision was taken not to prosecute. I have expressed my concern at this decision to the DPP and to the CCP at Central Casework. I have been given an undertaking that this case will receive full and careful re-consideration.[20]

The CPS did review it and came to the same conclusion: Insufficient evidence.

Ultraviolence also investigates a spate of killings in the early 2000s, including that of Jean Charles De Menezes. He was shot with seven bullets in his head by police in Stockwell in a train full of commuters. In this, as in other cases in the film, we follow the resilience and campaigning of the families for truth, accountability and justice. In this case the commanding officer that gave the order to shoot Jean Charles dead was Cressida Dick, the Metropolitan Police Commissioner shamed into her resignation after a string of scandals in 2022. What's the message in this illustrious promotion? The film deals with the whole state apparatus that ensures there can be no justice in these cases. Senior figures, including Sir Ian Blair, the Metropolitan Police Commissioner, are implicated. Nick Hardwick, chair of the now discredited Independent Police Complaints Commission, only offers excuses for the actions of the officers. The Crown Prosecution Service also fails and we see, in exclusive access to both institutions, film of the families confronting the individuals that preside over a system which investigates itself. Corruption, collusion, containment are all forensically exposed. Another case that is retraced is that of Christopher Alder and, presented for the first time, is a comprehensive analysis of his death which is seen on camera. There is disturbing footage in *Ultraviolence* but now is the time for people to be disturbed. Now is the time for these cases to be reopened. The editing of *Ultraviolence* took place over the same decade that the Black Lives Matter movement has emerged in the UK. Despite the outcry over the Floyd killing, and other US citizens, there is a growing complacency in the UK that issues of inequality around Black Lives Matter are being dealt with by institutions. To a certain extent they are but only out of an embarrassed realignment which does not concede power. Are those same organizations actively responsive to the fact that police violence against black people in the UK is fatally disproportionate? We need these organizations to follow through with long-term depth, power and commitment to confront fatal police crimes here in England. Why are the names of those killed by US law enforcement so well-known and yet few in the UK can name even one of the 2000 people that have died in in England? (Hattenstone, Simon. (2020). "Ultraviolence: The shocking brutal film about deaths in police custody." The Guardian, 12 October 2020: https://www.theguardian.com/film/2020/oct/12/ultraviolence-ken-fero-documentary-injustice-deaths-police). The methodology of killing is just as horrific, just as brutal, just as racist. Unless the cases in the films, and others, are acknowledged, reopened and dealt with in a robust way then racist police violence, or police violence in general, will continue to run unabated. It needs to be challenged.

Ultraviolence presents, for the first time, evidence of the first successful prosecution of a police officer for manslaughter. On 12 February 1985, Henry Foley, a 67-year-old retired bus driver from Merseyside, died from injuries inflicted on him by a police officer while in custody. Sergeant Alvin Sawyer went into the cell where Foley was handcuffed, he brutally assaulted him, stamping on him and rupturing his spleen, his bowel and detaching his left kidney. Sawyer was convicted of manslaughter and sentenced to 7 years in prison. Why has that story been suppressed? How were that jury able to come to that conclusion and what has the CPS and the other organizations that are concerned with custodial deaths done to acknowledge that prosecution and build on it?

We have also recently seen another guilty verdict for the manslaughter of Dalian Atkinson. That's two successful prosecutions out of 2000, a shameful figure. After half a century of killings this country has got nothing credible to say for itself on this issue. Governments, media, judiciary and all the liberal apparatus continue with their inquiries and recommendations that lead to excuses. This has not gone unnoticed by the families, as Brenda Weinberg comments in *Ultraviolence* (2020) "I was one of the ones that had a certain faith in the British judicial system and to have it continually turn around and let us down, time after time after time. So, for every meeting we have you come away thinking oh right, okay, yes, they're on our side. They're on their side. They're on the side of the job that it entails and that is to contain and we are being contained." In comparison to the UK, larger numbers of law enforcement officers have been charged and convicted of murder and manslaughter in many European countries, and internationally as well. There is a tidal wave of hypocrisy as UK institutions, desperate to be woke, respond to the cry for George Floyd yet refuse to even accept that Joy Gardner, Ibrahim Sey, Shiji Lapite, Roger Sylvester, Sean Rigg, Leon Patterson, Mikey Powell, Edson da Costa, Rashan Charles, Jason McPherson – and many others – need lamenting. More than that, though, their families need visible support in their struggles for justice.

Despite the trauma in the film, especially in the form of the powerful testimonies of the pain of the families, *Ultraviolence* is full of resistance and, dare it be said, hope. The film reflects on periods when people have stood up against war, historic periods where imperial and colonial oppressors have been defeated. The film makes a direct parallel between deaths at the hands of the police and the deaths of Iraqis during the US- and UK-led invasion that was happening while the film was being made. Many people will find the parallel imagery in the film shocking and the film reflects on this imagery of violence and how society denies its cause.

The images of Vietnamese children running down a road after the US bombing of their village with napalm in 1972, shocked the world. Crying with skin and flesh hanging off them, they are naked, shocked, traumatized. They run toward the camera and toward the US soldiers who pour water on the children's flesh as the chemicals burn into them. Shock and awe, the torturer is also the savior. Those images of the chemical assault on children in Vietnam did not prevent the US army using white phosphorus in Falluja in 2004 and burning Iraqi children. Once we see these images we cannot forget them – much as we may try – these images are part of our psyche yet we seem unable to act when shown this evidence. The weakness of film as reality is, ironically, the deniability of film as evidence of truth. We consume these images but we do not process them. With the increased speed with which we see each atrocity we become desensitized, we give no time to have a "long take." A process which may lead to a deeper analysis and perhaps some action, or even resistance.[21]

Ultraviolence follows the struggles for justice of the families in the context of a country at war with itself and abroad. In many respects, the resilience of the families in their relentless pursuit for the truth and accountability has been called engaging and admirable. It's a role they never wanted but they undertake it with a passion and .commitment that should inspire anyone watching. This reflective film work of Migrant Media offers lessons in *how* to fight state violence, because many people already know *why* they must fight it if we consider the current state of the world. The film is also full of bittersweet hope, written to the filmmaker's son, it laments the failure of the generation currently in power but outlines a history of resistance that today's youth are already taking up. Our children are marching for racial justice, they march for gender equality, they march against environmental catastrophe, they march against war. Will you march with them?

Chapter 5

Riots as the Language of the Unheard
Jonathan Havercroft

In the late 1960s and early 1970s prominent political theorists such as Hannah Arendt, John Rawls and Michael Walzer began to reflect on the implications of the tumultuous 1960s. They quickly reached a consensus that the non-violent direct political action of Martin Luther King was a legitimate form of political protest and that the black urban riots of the same era were illegitimate. Curiously King himself refused to condemn urban US riots of the late 1960s, instead describing riots as the "language of the unheard" (1968). Following Martin Luther King Jr's assassination, many white liberal American's developed a romantic myth of King and the civil rights movement, that equated "non-violence" with passive acquiescence by black citizens in order to bring about racial equality (Hooker, 2016). One by-product of this myth of non-violence as passive acquiescence was the delegitimization of other modes of political resistance, including rioting.

This chapter exams how mainstream political theorists appropriated King's political strategy to delegitimize rioting. I review Arendt's, Walzer's and Rawls's arguments against the legitimacy of political rioting. I then examine how the leading figure of non-violent direct action came to see the riot as a cry for help from the urban poor. This survey will demonstrate how the distinction between civil and uncivil disobedience has become so central to liberal-democratic theory. This chapter argues that mainstream political theorists appropriated King's strategy of strategic non-violence to delegitimize the black uprisings of the 1960s while ignoring what King actually said about those events. White liberal academics have framed the debate about civil disobedience on a narrow set of protest tactics that have delegitimized non-lethal militant protest.[1] By tracing how riots have been delegitimized in liberal political theory over the last 50 years, we can better understand recent responses to riots. This chapter demonstrates two things. First, political theory's delegitimization of the riot is comparatively recent. It is a response by white political theorists to militant black protest. Second, political theorists misunderstood the urban uprisings of the late 1960s, and used a false narrative about these protests to shape subsequent discussion about civil disobedience and militant protests.

Arendt on the distinction between violence and power

Arendt's reflections on political violence first appeared in a New York Review of Books essay published in February 1969. The essay is part theoretical reflection on the tumultuous events of the previous year and part phenomenological analysis of the concepts of violence and power. The essay is most influential in political theory circles for the distinction Arendt draws between these two concepts. While many political theorists and social scientists see violence as an extreme form of power, Arendt's main claim in the essay is that they are conceptually distinct.

In Arendt's schema power comes from acting in concert. It is an inherently pluralistic form of action, and it forms the basis of democratic politics. Power emerges when a group of people come together and through speech and deed decide to act together for a common purpose. Her paradigmatic examples of this form of action include revolutions, her proposal for a federated council system, activist groups such as the French resisters during World War II, and the ancient Greek and Roman practices of direct democracy. Her concern was that modern mass democracies lacked the spaces of freedom that could foster political action. So this form of political power was being lost to the tyranny of administrative bureaucracy, and the threat of totalitarianism.

Arendt's primary concern in the essay was to counter the common place assumption that violence was an extreme form of power. We can see examples of this assumption in expressions such as Clausewitz's claim that "war is politics by other means" or Mao's statement that "power grows out of the barrel of a gun." The idea behind these sayings is that politics is about a command obedience relationship, where the ruler has political power and uses it to issue orders that the ruled must obey. Arendt argues that this understanding of political power actually confuses power with two other phenomena – authority and violence. Authority, on Arendt's account, refers to the ability of one in a particular position to issue orders that others will follow simply because of the status of that office. For example, a police officer can issue an order to a member of the public, and in most instances the person will obey simply because of the authority of the police. Violence, on the other hand, is purely instrumental coercion. One uses the direct threat of violence to compel someone to do something. For example, a robber pointing a gun at a person and demanding their money is expecting compliance not because of the office they occupy, but because of the threat of violence that goes with their demand.

Arendt saw these concepts as ideal types, that often overlapped in practice. In the modern world it is easy to confuse authority, power and violence because individuals often combine the three in specific actions. For instance, a head of state issuing a declaration of war relies upon the authority of their office, the instruments of violence amassed in the state's military, and the power that comes from the support of the public. Yet crucial for Arendt was the idea that power could only be exercised collectively, and hence democratically. In dictatorships, the head of state often had to use more violence against the public precisely because the regime did not have the *power* that came from being supported by the people. The crucial moment in a revolution comes when the state agents of violence simply stop following the commands of the old regime because the rulers no longer have the power that comes from being supported by the people.

With these conceptual distinctions in mind, we can now make sense of how Arendt responded to the riots of the 1960s. The essay "On Violence" does not contain a sustained analysis of a particular riot, but does reference several kinds of riots throughout, and singles out for critique Frantz Fanon and the Black Power movement. In particular Arendt critiques the black inner-city riots of the 1960s, student riots including the People's Park riot at Berkeley, and occupations of administrative buildings by students at Cornell, Columbia, and City University of New York, the student uprisings in France in May of 1968 and student protests at German universities.

Her objection to the riots was two-fold. First, she felt that the violence of the riots could not be transformed into political power. The danger with violent protest rested in its instrumental nature. It used violence to compel political adversaries to yield to the group's demands. Yet this always ran the risk of the means—violence—overpowering the ends—racial inequality or student demands for reform (Arendt, 1972, p. 177). In the case of the inner-city riots of the 1960s, Arendt argued that because the black community lacked political power, the risk was that the riots would provoke a white backlash, in which whites would endorse a police state in the name of protecting their material interests against demands for economic equality from blacks. Second, she objected to the specific demands of the rioters.

The essay is dismissive of black protesters' demands for housing reform, school integration, affirmative action in university admissions and the creation of African studies programs in universities. Her opposition to these demands was not merely that she opposed them on policy grounds, but that she believed that "since the tactics of violence and disruption make sense only for short term goals, it is even more likely...that the established power will yield to nonsensical and damaging demands" (Arendt, 1972, p. 177). For Arendt, because the riot was an expression of collective violence rather than collective power, it would always be more "the weapon of reform than revolution" (Arendt, 1972, p. 176).

In Arendt's mind the violence of the riots meant that they were futile. Implicit in her critique was a call for non-violent collective political action. By arguing that violence and power were two distinct and incompatible phenomena of action, Arendt implied that modes of civil disobedience were effective, whereas riots were ineffective. She argued that the rise of riots was in response to the rise of bureaucratic politics. The unique feature of bureaucracy was that it was the "rule of nobody" (Arendt, 1972, p. 178). This new mode of rule meant that there was no obvious person or group against which an oppressed group could effectively air its grievances. She concluded by speculating that because the rise of bureaucracy meant the decline of political power, the rise of riots might either be the beginning of a new mode of politics, or "the death pangs of a faculty that mankind is about to lose" (Arendt, 1972, p. 181). In either case, the riot would be the sign of the loss of political power. Far from being a mere political tactic with which Arendt disagreed, riots represented a mode of political action that undermined human freedom.

Walzer on the obligations of oppressed minorities

Walzer's consideration of rioting appears briefly in an essay first published in *Commentary* in 1970. The main topic of the essay is the obligations of oppressed minorities within democratic societies. Resistance theory, stretching back to the writings of John Locke, has long recognized the right of oppressed groups within a society to rebel if the regime infringes upon their basic liberties. Yet, it is unclear, Walzer argues, how such a right can be exercised within a democratic state, when a majority uses its power at the voting booth to systematically frustrate the will of a minority. Walzer makes clear early in the essay that what he has in mind is a situation akin to that faced by black people in the United States (1982, p. 48). This situation presents a unique challenge for democratic theory because the majority dominates the minority precisely because it has a permanent electoral majority in a free and open democratic system. The system as a whole may meet the formal criteria of being a just democratic system, but the tyranny of the majority ensures that the minority will be oppressed, and leaves few options to them for legitimate resistance within society.

Walzer argues that non-violent forms of resistance are always acceptable in these conditions. He cites consciousness raising activity and political work as two examples of such forms of resistance (Walzer, 1982, p. 54). The bigger question for Walzer is whether oppressed minorities within a democratic society have a right to use violence in order to resist their oppressors. Walzer considers three possible modes of resistance: conspiracy, armed revolution and terrorism.

By conspiracy, Walzer means any attempt by an armed militant group to replace a ruling elite with themselves. The danger here is that the militant group acts on behalf of the oppressed group without their approval, and it overthrows a democratically elected government. Armed revolution occurs when an insurgency wages guerilla war against the government in the hope of overthrowing it, and establishing a new regime that works on behalf of the oppressed minority. The danger in this case is three-fold. First, the equal rights of an oppressed group cannot be secured by destroying the social structure within which equal rights are being sought. Second, an armed revolution is not likely to improve the situation of those on behalf of whom the insurgency is being waged. Third, the results of a revolutionary war are likely to lead to more oppression by the victors over the vanquished. As such, Walzer rejects armed revolution as a possible means for liberating oppressed minorities, although he does concede that such tactics may be justified in cases of an ethnic minority seceding from a larger state (Walzer, 1982, pp. 61–2). The third mode of resistance Walzer considers is terrorism, which involves targeted acts of violence against members of the oppressor group in order to intimidate them into meeting the demands of the oppressed. Walzer rejects this approach because it does not empower the oppressed.

Walzer then turns his attention to acts that he describes as defensive violence, such as armed resistance by blacks to white lynch-mobs, and acts of violence against "marauders, vigilantes, sadistic policeman, and so on" (1982, p. 63). According to Walzer the aggression of the oppressors means that the oppressed are justified in using violence in self-defense. Furthermore, if the state fails in its obligation to protect the oppressed minority, then collective self-defense against the majority is justified. Yet, Walzer is clear that such acts of defensive violence are limited to "the immediate context of violence" (1982, p. 63), and do not justify acts of pre-emptive or retaliatory violence.

After examining these four instances of violent resistance (conspiracy, revolution, terrorism and self-defense), Walzer then considers the riot. He classifies the riot as "a kind of spontaneous terror, generally concealed in the crime statistics, occasionally exploding in riot and *jacquerie*, which expresses only the inchoate rage of oppressed men" (Walzer, 1982, p. 65). Walzer argues that "it is wrong to attach any honor to such violence or to attempt to justify it (it is not wrong, obviously, to try and justify it)" (Walzer, 1982, p. 65). Part of Walzer's reason for dismissing rioting as unjustifiable is that he deems the participants as apolitical (Walzer, 1982, p. 65). Yet he also twice expresses concern that the violence of the black rioters would be directed against "us" (Walzer, 1982, pp. 65, 66) – presumably the white American readers whom Walzer addresses.

While the rage that the black underclass in the US feels against the white majority is justified according to Walzer, he places the obligation to address those injustices on the white majority. It is unclear, however, from Walzer's brief critique of black rioting what the black minority is supposed to do. The three activities Walzer says in the essay are permissible are consciousness raising, defensive violence and leveraging the hypocrisy to the oppressive majority in order to compel them to live up to the democratic ideals they claim to support. In a brief footnote Walzer states that he has in mind the "recent riots" as an example of the unjustifiable political violence he is talking about. Presumably Walzer had in mind events such as the Holy Week uprising in 1968, in which there were a large number of black riots in the US in response to the murder of Martin Luther King Jr. Yet Walzer leaves unsaid both the specific cause of this rioting (the assassination of the civil rights leader), and any possible solution to both the violence against civil rights activists protesting non-violently, and their concrete demands. There is a double de-politicization at play in Walzer's dismissal of the riot. First, he claims the rioters are apolitical, when the clear political cause of the riots—the murder of a political leader—was clear for all to see. Second, he offers no political solution for an oppressed minority to resist its oppression apart from vague platitudes about consciousness raising and pointing out the hypocrisy of the oppressors.

Rawls and the justification of civil disobedience

John Rawls does not directly address riots in his political philosophy, but his account of civil disobedience shaped the way the political practice has been understood by philosophers for the last 50 years. Rawls, drawing on the ideas of Henry David Thoreau, Hugo Bedeau and Martin Luther King Jr, developed a justification for civil disobedience in *A Theory of Justice*. The puzzle that Rawls's grapples with is how can civil disobedience be justified within a democratic society as the action breaks the law, and acts against the will of the majority. At first glance, there can be no justification for such actions so long as the society itself is "well ordered for the most part but in which some serious violations of justice nevertheless do occur" (Rawls, 1999, p. 319). Democracy requires that its citizens comply with laws passed by a legislative majority. So, breaking that law, even in the case of an injustice, poses a problem for democratic theory. If citizens are free to disobey the law whenever they disagree with it, then there seems to be no obligation to obey the will of the majority ever. Yet, if one must always obey the law, then how is one to respond when the law infringes upon liberty and the "duty to oppose injustice" (Walzer, 1982, p. 319)?

To resolve this dilemma Rawls develops a theory of civil disobedience to differentiate between dissent and other forms of opposition to political authority, establish the criteria by which civil disobedience is justified, and to explain what the function of civil disobedience is within society. Rawls defines civil disobedience as "a public, nonviolent, conscientious yet political act contrary to law usually done with the aim of bringing about a change in the law or policies of the government" (Rawls, 1999, p. 320). While he acknowledges crucial differences between his ideal model of civil disobedience and its historical practice, he cites Thoreau and MLK as two inspirations for his theory. In order for civil disobedience to work, it is not enough that it breaks the law; it must break the law in such a way as to provoke the majority to reconsider an unjust political policy that it supports. Crucially for Rawls, civil disobedience is a non-violent action.[2] Rawls opposes the use of violence in the instance of political disobedience for two reasons. First to engage in acts of violence violates the civil liberties of the victims. As civil disobedience hinges its appeals to justice on claims of the rights of the protesters, it is a contradiction to violate other's rights when fighting for your own. Second, Rawls opposes the use of violence in civil disobedience because in order for it to be *civil* it must disobey the law "within the limits of fidelity to the law" (Rawls, 1999, p. 323). That is, while civil disobedience breaks specific laws, it does so by remaining supportive of the rule of law in general.

Rawls's point is that civil disobedience's prohibition on violence rests on the protesters breaking the law in order to demonstrate the hypocrisy of the majority's claims of justice. For example, in the paradigmatic example of the anti-segregation lunch counter sit-in, protesters explicitly broke laws that prohibited blacks from eating in diners in order to demonstrate that it was the segregation laws that were themselves unjust, whereas the actions of the protesters, while law breaking, were appealing to a broader principle of justice. For Rawls, a turn to violent protest would undermine the normative leverage that protesters would receive from non-violently breaking the law.

Rawls uses the non-violence feature of civil disobedience to distinguish it from a different category of political dissent that he labels "militant action and obstruction" (Rawls, 1999, p. 323). While Rawls does not explicitly say that a riot would fall under this category of dissent, it is reasonable to place it here. Rawls argues that the militant, unlike the civil disobedient, does not accept the justice of the existing system, and is not seeking to "appeal to the sense of justice of the majority (or those having effective political power)" (1999, p. 323). Instead the militant is trying to evade legal sanction, whereas the civil disobedient invites legal punishment. The militant does this because they believe the basic structure of society is itself so unjust that the system requires radical change. In these instances the militant is "trying to arouse the public to an awareness of the fundamental reforms that need to be made" (Rawls, 1999, p. 323). While Rawls concedes that this type of militant action could be justified in certain circumstances, he declines in the text to examine those cases. The reason the riot falls under Rawls's category of militant action is that it is violent, the participants do not invite legal punishment, and it aims to arouse awareness about fundamental reforms in society rather than pointing out a contradiction between a principle of justice the majority professes to hold and how they fail to enact that principle with respect to a minority within society. While Rawls does not explicitly spell out the circumstances in which militant actions, such as riots, might be justified, he does do so with respect to civil disobedience. By considering those circumstances we can infer the circumstances in which militant protest might be justified. In the case of civil disobedience, Rawls lists three criteria which would justify it. First there must be a "clear and substantial injustice" (Rawls, 1999, p. 326). For Rawls this means violations of his principle of equal liberty. Examples he provides include being denied the right to vote, the right to hold public office, the right to own property, freedom of movement, freedom of religion, and freedom of opportunity.

All of these rights are what are called civil and political rights, and are classified as negative rights—rights that protect citizens from violation of their basic liberties by the state. Rawls does not believe that social rights, or questions of economic justice, are appropriate justifications for civil disobedience because they involve clashes of competing interests (Rawls, 1999, p. 327). The second criterion is that the practitioners of civil disobedience must only use this tactic as a last resort after exhausting other legal avenues such as petitioning their legislators for change. And third, acts of civil disobedience cannot lead to a "breakdown in respect for law and the constitution" (Rawls, 1999, p. 328). Civil disobedience on Rawls's account is always reformist and never revolutionary. It seeks to correct an injustice in a democratic society, while leaving most of that society as it is. Conversely, more militant actions, such as riots, do seek a breakdown in law and order, even if only temporarily, to protest the injustice of the system as a whole.

We can infer why this may be from Rawls's first criterion for justifying civil disobedience: that it addressed violations of civil and political liberties, not economic injustice. The riot, however, has a long history of protesting social issues. In the seventeenth through nineteenth century most riots contested issues such as the price of grain, unjust enclosure of common land by elites, and the displacement of workers by new technologies. The grievance expressed was not a violation of negative liberty, but a defensive act by a marginalized people fighting to protect their means of subsistence. The US riots of the 1960s were triggered by issues of police brutality, lack of affordable housing, and chronic unemployment among inner-city blacks. These are precisely the kinds of issues that Rawls says are off the table for civil disobedience, because they are largely a matter of economic redistribution rather than basic liberties.[3] Yet it is unclear from Rawls's comments whether he would justify riots in these circumstances, because he declines to consider militant protest in his theory of justice. Regardless of what Rawls might have thought about rioting, the consequence of his theory of civil disobedience is that political philosophy has largely ignored the question of what might justify a riot until very recently.[4]

King on riots as the language of the unheard

We can observe two connected moves in early 1970s political theory. First, Arendt, Walzer, and Rawls all either implicitly or explicitly cite the example of Martin Luther King Jr's non-violent civil disobedience as the one justifiable model for an oppressed minority to challenge the rule of the majority within democratic society. Second, Arendt and Walzer explicitly argue that the riot is not a justifiable form of resistance for oppressed minorities, and Rawls argues that militant action (such as riots) is only justifiable in the context of unjust democratic regimes. The effect of all three prominent political theorists denouncing the riot as an unjustified political activity was to keep it off the agenda of political theory until very recently. Political theorists did not develop sophisticated arguments about why riots were unjustified, they simply did not talk about riots. At the same time, the model of non-violent civil disobedience associated with King and Gandhi has generated significant scholarly research. What is curious about this silence is that since at least 2015 King's own description of the riot as "the language of the unheard" has been widely circulated by political defenders of anti-police violence riots in the US. So on the one hand we have white liberal political theorists invoking King to demarcate the riot as an illegitimate mode of political resistance, and on the other hand we have activists invoking King's description of riots in defense of Black Lives Matter protests in 2020.[5]

What are we to make of the conflicting invocation of King? King used the phrase "language of the unheard" to describe riots several times after 1965. According to his autobiography the crucial event for his rethinking of riots was his visit to Watts, Los Angeles after the riots in August 1965. The riots broke out just 5 days after the passage of the Voting Rights Act by Congress, the event that is normally celebrated as the culmination of King's non-violent campaign against segregation in the US. King himself was shocked by the event, noting that, "As soon as we began to see our way clear in the South, the shock and horror of Northern riots exploded before our eyes and we saw that the problems of the Negro go far beyond mere racial segregation" (King, 2002, p. 290). King deplored rioting, but crucially he did not condemn the rioters. Instead, his repeated invocation of the riot as the language of the unheard was meant to point out to his audience that a riot was a crisis that called out for a response rather than condemnation.

King himself went to Watts in the days after the riot, and met with rioters and community leaders. For King, the root cause of the riots was "the depth of despair which afflict a people who see no way out of their economic dilemma" (King, 2002, p. 291). Whereas Arendt, Rawls and Walzer all set aside economic considerations in their analysis of civil disobedience, King recognized that the political grievances he addressed through his campaign against segregation did not address the broader economic inequalities that drove the riots in the US north in the late 1960s. King noted that there was a significant class divide between the middle-class leadership in his anti-segregation campaign, and the underemployed and unemployed in US inner cities that participated in the riots (King, 2002, p. 292). In the South, both the working-class whites and the black population were poor. So the issue that divided them was primarily race. But as he turned his attention to campaigns in LA and Chicago, King quickly realized that the interplay of race and class, combined with deep-seated economic inequality, drove much of the conflict.

It is for this reason that during the last 3 years of his life, King shifted the focus of his activism from de-segregation to addressing economic inequality. It was precisely this economic inequality that he diagnosed as causing the riots. King noted that the key demands of rioters in Watts were work and dignity. He argued that looting, largely condemned by the white mainstream media, "was a form of social protest very common through the ages as a dramatic and destructive gesture of the poor toward symbols of their needs" (King, 2002, p. 293). King noted that humans are "consumers first" (2002, p. 295), as they need to consume in order to first survive, and then to enjoy life. The US of the 1960s was excluding black people from the consumer circle, by denying them the means of earning a wage. King felt this was the primary driver of unrest, and of resentment of the urban black population toward the affluent white community. Looting and rioting was an expression of dissatisfaction with an economic system that was blocking black people from participating within the economy.

It is worth noting here that King's diagnosis of riots accords with a longstanding academic tradition that has interpreted rioting not as spontaneous mob violence, but as a form of moral economy by the least well-off members of society.[6] According to the research of Rudé (2005) and Thompson (Thompson, 1971), the primary cause of rioting in the eighteenth and nineteenth centuries was economic. Peasants used riots as a form of collective bargaining to enforce fair prices on grain, and to protest about practices that infringed on their wages and employment. The inner-city riots in the 1960s can be read in that same way. As the US experienced its long, post-World War II economic expansion, black people were increasingly left behind. And despite the expansion of political rights through the civil rights movement, black social and economic rights were not addressed at all.

In addition to the direct economic causes of the riots, King also identified two other social drivers of the conflict. The first was the repeal in 1964 of California's housing discrimination law, which King noted made California "the first major state to take away gains Negroes had won at a time when progress was visible and substantial elsewhere" (King, 2002, p. 295). It is worth noting here that Arendt, in her dismissal of riots, specifically cited housing, and housing discrimination laws, as a problem that could not be solved by protest as it was a matter of clashing interests between landowner and renter. For Arendt, questions of housing were not political. Yet for King, the message of the riots was that economic segregation was as politically damaging as political segregation.

The second driver of the riots was police brutality. King noted that "the Negro of the ghetto was convinced that his dealings with the police denied him the dignity and respect to which he was entitled" (King, 2002, p. 292). Most major riots over the last 60 years, from Watts, to LA in 1992, to the suburban Paris riots of 2005, through the Tottenham riots of 2011, to the

George Floyd riots of 2020 have been triggered by instances of police violence against black people. None of the white liberal theorists considered here have an analysis of the appropriate form of resistance for a minority group that experiences systematic violence and death at the hands of state authorities. King's own non-violent civil disobedience has struggled with how to confront this problem. It is worth noting that within the liberal tradition dating back to Locke there has been a generally recognized right of resistance when the state threatens the life and liberty of its citizens. If the riot is conceived as an act of resistance against police violence, then it is wholly legitimate within the liberal tradition to riot in defiance of police brutality.[7]

King, himself, did not advocate rioting. He made clear that he opposed riots on two grounds. First, on principle he was committed to non-violence as the morally correct way of resisting oppression. Second, on pragmatic grounds he worried that riots, and any form of political violence by blacks, would alleviate white liberal guilt about systematic racism in the US (King, 2002, p. 294). He felt that the moral suasion of non-violent activism was the most effective means for bringing about political change in the US.

But, unlike the white political theorists, King refused to condemn the rioters. He wrote "a mere condemnation of violence is empty without understanding the daily violence that our own society inflicts upon many of its members" (King, 2002, p. 295). He argued that all Americans were responsible for the violence (King, 2002, p. 291), and he warned President Johnson that if the demands of the rioters were not met, that his non-violent civil rights movement might be overtaken by a wave of violent urban uprisings. Part of what King confronted in Watts, and later in Chicago and Detroit, was a possible limit to non-violent civil disobedience. King's tactics were effective when confronting the denial of civil and political rights, because protesters leveraged the hypocrisy of a political establishment that claimed to be democratic by manifesting how it denied basic political rights to some of its citizens. Yet there is nothing hypocritical about economic inequality in a capitalist system. Capitalism, after all, professes to sort society into winners and losers. While King himself turned his attention to poverty after 1965, that campaign was far less successful than his civil rights campaign.

The unanswered question from King's engagement with the riots is: if non-violent civil disobedience is not effective at confronting economic inequality, and the riot is taboo because it breaches the norm against violent political action, then what options do the urban poor have to confront an economic system that leaves them behind? The fact that the root causes of the Minneapolis riot in 2020 were so similar to the root causes of the Watts riot in 1965 means that we have not yet found an answer to that question.

Chapter 6

Policing the Crisis – the Criminalization of Racial Minorities

Ken Olende

Introduction

The British government was unsettled by the international growth of the Black Lives Matter (BLM) movement following the murder of George Floyd in the US. In July 2020 it set up an inquiry on racial disparity which resulted in the Sewell Report, a document that denied the existence of institutional racism, with the dismissive comment: "The linguistic inflation on racism is confusing, with prefixes like institutional, structural and systemic adding to the problem" (Commission on Race and Ethnic Disparities, 2021, p. 34). This is not an insignificant issue as it points to an argument about whether racism is a series of outdated prejudices held by individuals or is systemic and linked to the central organs of the state. Almost simultaneously, the government advanced a new law to extend police powers, notably regarding protest and travelers (UK Government, Police, Crime, Sentencing and Courts Bill, 2021), and another to criminalize certain refugees depending on how they arrive (UK Government, The Nationality and Borders Bill, 2021). These issues are about more than simple law and order and raise questions about how government and the wider establishment maintain influence and furthermore how the understanding of crime can be racialized.

Before Sewell the position on institutionalized racism had been established by the 1997 Macpherson Report into the police's botched investigation into the murder of black teenager Stephen Lawrence. This report branded London's Metropolitan Police Service (MPS), Britain's largest police force, institutionally racist, something it defined as:

> The collective failure...to provide an appropriate and professional service to people because of their color, culture, or ethnic origin. It can be seen or detected in processes, attitudes and behavior which amount to discrimination through unwitting prejudice, ignorance, thoughtlessness, and racist stereotyping. (Macpherson, 1999, p. 49)

The term institutional racism first emerged in the US Black Power movement in 1967 (Ture, 1967, p. 4). In Britain, long-term director of the Institute of Race Relations (IRR), A Sivanandan, further defined it, saying that, once the government introduced discriminatory immigration controls in the 1960s, it "made racism respectable and clinical by institutionalizing it" (Sivanandan, 1976, p. 73). In this chapter I will argue that institutional racism, particularly as it relates to so-called common-sense racism, is key to understanding why race is central to discussions of crime and policing in Britain. In so doing I will make use of arguments put forward by Stuart Hall and his colleagues at the Centre for Contemporary Cultural Studies (CCCS) in the 1970s, particularly in their 1978 book *Policing the Crisis: Mugging, the State and Law & Order* (PTC). I will draw parallels between the racially charged crisis of the 1970s and the current racially charged crisis. The book became influential in several fields, including sociology and criminology, but its method of detailed conjunctural examination of the social and political make up of a time is difficult to replicate.

'Iron times' and the criminalization of ethnic minorities

Though the post-war establishment favored large-scale immigration, this did not stop racially discriminatory views from the top. Weeks after *Empire Windrush* brought the first 500 immigrants from the Caribbean in 1948 Labour prime minister Clement Attlee replied to a group of Labour MPs who opposed non-white immigration, saying that "British subjects...of whatever race or colour...should be freely admissible to the United Kingdom." But he qualified this by adding an unwarranted suspicion of criminality; "If our policy were to result in a great influx of undesirables, we might... consider modifying it" (Gupta and Bhattacharya, 2002, p. 204). Nevertheless, through the 1950s governments actively encouraged immigration from the Caribbean and elsewhere in the empire.

West Indians faced unfounded prejudice that they were likely to be criminal, as is evidenced by the following memorandum sent by the Home Secretary to chief constables in 1957:

1. What is the number of colored people in your area?
   a. West Indians
   b. Non-West Indians
2. Is there any definite evidence of large-scale crime?
3. Do they mix well with white people?
4. What are the facts of illegitimacy relating to West Indians?
5. What is the evidence concerning brothel management and colored people? (Cited in Howe, 1988, p. 25)

While black people may have been prejudicially associated with crime, the police and the establishment did not see them as a destabilizing force. Academic Paul Gilroy has noted that though racist, the 1958 Notting Hill Riots in London "may have marked a turning point in the history of modern racism, press coverage... is notable for the degree to which the crime theme, though present, is again subordinate." (Gilroy, 1987, p. 81)

PTC sets out to explain how the ending of the post-war political consensus brought race to the center of British politics through the 1970s. It is long and complicated, bringing together arguments from a range of disciplines to understand a key shift in the mindset of a significant part of the British population. It starts by looking at the development of the "moral panic" over mugging around 1972. It then examines how "primary definers" such as the press attempted to fix the panic in a cultural space of ordinary people as white and respectable in opposition to black criminality. The book then presents this use of ideas in a wider context of ideological hegemony and discusses why there was a "crisis of authority" (Hall et al, 1978a, p. 175) for Britain's rulers. It examines how "blacks became the 'bearers' of those contradictory outcomes; and black crime becomes the signifier of the crisis in the urban colonies" (Hall et al, 1978a, p. 333).

There was nothing new about the crime of mugging or street robbery, "except the label itself" (Hall et al, 1978a, p. 10). The MPS commissioner's annual report for 1964 had noted a significant increase in "robberies or assaults with intent to rob" but commented that such robberies had been common since "further back than the days of highwaymen and footpads" (Hall et all, 1978a, p. 9). No new crime of mugging was ever legally defined, though in his 1972 report the commissioner was able "to reconstruct statistics for its incidence back to 1968" (Hall et all, 1978a, p. 9).

What had changed was the suggestion that this was a crime particularly carried out by young black men. The term "mugging" had emerged in the US, where it had been used as part of a law-and-order offensive, which tried to draw groups previously hostile to the government in with a defense of the "national interest" (Hall et al, 1978a, p. 24). *PTC* argues that the creation of mugging "transforms the deprivation of the class, out of which crime arises, into the all too intelligible syntax of race, and fixes a false enemy: the black mugger" (Hall et al, 1978a, p. 388). Mugging is not presented in isolation, but as part of an ideological process, which will be detailed below.

The idea of "crime" is part of a hegemonic set of ideas about how society is run and who is likely to be a victim or a criminal. Such beliefs affect how the population at large understands or identifies with violence or surveillance carried out by the police (Hall et al, 1978a, p. 168). The ruling order will often argue that such "iron times" require the state to move "away from consent towards the pole of coercion" (Hall et al, 1978a, p. 214). Often support for such a move can be won by "othering" certain groups such as non-white immigrants. In this context race can operate both as a marker of similarity and otherness (Hall et al, 1978a, p. 325). To explain these developments, the authors draw on arguments put forward by the Italian Marxist Antonio Gramsci in the 1920s and 30s. He suggested that in relatively advanced capitalist states social norms are maintained from day to day not by direct coercion, but through ideas which are accepted by the majority, becoming "hegemonic" or simply seen as "common sense." These tend to be the ideas of the ruling group, but especially in times of social crisis they will be contested. (Hall et al, 1978a, p. 153). At other times their rule is "founded on the conjunctural mastery of class struggle. But this mastery is displaced, through the mediating form of 'the consensus,' and reappears as the disappearance or pacification of all conflict" (Hall et al, 1978a, p. 213). So specific forms of oppressive and exploitative rule become hidden in an apparent societal agreement.

The book spends some time linking this to how political legitimacy developed in the British state before discussing the breakdown of the post-war consensus and the development of a more authoritarian "law-and-order" state, that would culminate in Margaret Thatcher's government and racial confrontations through the 1980s. *PTC* talks of "the spontaneous and successful" hegemony in the post-war period, in contrast to the crisis that followed. Cultural theorist Martin Barker is right to point out that it can be "dangerous" to suggest that even in confident periods, "no hard work had to be done" by a country's rulers to assert hegemony (Barker, 1992, p. 88). The authors wrote it as an intervention in the fight against racism, so it finishes with a discussion on how such a resistance can develop.

A key issue in *PTC* is the interaction between social class and race. It states:

> Blacks are ascribed to a position within the class relations of contemporary capitalism which is, at one and the same time, roughly coterminous with the position of the white working class (of which black labor is a fraction), and yet segmentally differentiated from it. In these terms, ethnic relations are continually overdetermined by class relations, but the two cannot be collapsed into a single structure. (Hall et al, 1978a, p. 382)

The authors were challenging a tendency among many left theorists at the time to reduce the ideological complexities to "economism," that is challenging oppression entirely through the struggles of the organized working class in workplaces. This was one of the issues that Gramsci had also challenged. However, while agreeing with the broad argument, Sivanandan rightly pointed out that there is a danger of dividing off oppressed groups from the wider working class, leaving it "stripped of its richest political seams – black, feminist, gay, green etc – and left, in the name of anti-economism, a prey to economism" (Sivanandan, 1985, p. 77).

Hall himself could take a somewhat reductionist view as to how the various kinds of resistance developed through the 1970s. He saw a split between cultural and trade unionist responses, "the massive displacement of political class struggle into new forms of social, moral and cultural protest and dissent, as well as in terms of the revival, after 1970, of a peculiarly intense kind of 'economism' – a defensive working-class syndicalism" (Hall et al, 1978b, p. 33).

For me, this analysis does not square with the way much of the trade union movement in Britain shifted its activity to challenge sexism and racism as part of the militancy in the 1970s – for instance in disputes at Ford Dagenham and Grunwick. As Satnam Virdee has put it, "From being attached to a narrow understanding of class that nested neatly within dominant conceptions of race and nation, key groups of workers had moved towards a more inclusive language of class that could now also include racialized minority workers" (Virdee, 2014, p. 135). The shift by the 1980s to seeing trade unions as a central part in such community struggles was not an inversion of an earlier economism.

Gramsci made a further, related point, that people involved in such ideological tussles have a "contradictory consciousness," part of which comes from personal experience and another, the "common-sense" part, that is "inherited from the past and uncritically absorbed." To counter this, "the concept of hegemony represents a great philosophical advance as well as a politico-practical one" (Gramsci, 1971, p. 333). Gramsci was talking about working-class militants, who can challenge the hegemonic "common-sense" ideas of their rulers, through political organization and struggling to make their own ideas hegemonic, but the same argument can be applied to people suffering from racism who challenge prejudicial arguments about the necessity for authoritarian rule in iron times.

How race became central to British politics in the 1970s
The post-war hegemony began to crack in the 1960s. While living standards and expectations continued to rise, the end of empire and the Cold War nagged at rulers and ruled alike. Debacles including the invasion of Suez in 1956 and the Profumo scandal in 1963 undermined respect for and deference to the establishment. At the same time and also central to undermining the existing hegemonic common sense were demands for social

change around increased rights for women, workers, LGBT and ethnic minorities. The transformation in political attitudes to race can be seen most clearly in the rapidly shifting rhetoric of Conservative front bencher Enoch Powell. In 1964, he stated that he would "set my face like flint against making any difference between one citizen of this country and another on grounds of his origin" (Foot, 1969, p. 66). Just 4 years later he made his infamous racist "Rivers of Blood" speech. This included the words, "While, to the immigrant, entry to this country was admission to privileges and opportunities eagerly sought, the impact upon the existing population was very different... they found themselves made strangers in their own country" (Powell, 1968). Powell had moved from an imperial view that saw subjects of empire as "citizens of this country," who should be supported, to an attempt to "other" migrants. Thus, complex social changes, which unsettled sections of his constituents, could be blamed on a small minority of the population (See Foot, 1969, p. 10). Gilroy noted that from this point on, "The idea that blacks are a high crime group and the related notion that their criminality is an expression of their distinctive culture have become integral to British racism" (Gilroy, 1987, p. 109). While many people were disgusted by Powell's speech and it lost him his place in the shadow cabinet, some groups of workers came out on strike in support, and he became a figure idolized by the far right through the next decade. Powell made the speech during a bid for the leadership of the Conservative Party. Though this was unsuccessful, many of the assumptions in his arguments would be taken up by politicians through the 1970s. In the run up to the election where she became prime minister Margaret Thatcher said, "The British character has done so much for democracy, for law and done so much throughout the world that if there is any fear that it might be swamped people are going to react and be rather hostile to those coming in" (Thatcher, 1978).

PTC argues that Powell's speech spoke "to fears, anxieties, frustrations, to the national collective unconscious, to its hopes and fears" (Hall et al, 1978a, p. 242). But this is to go too far. It was not just a shift in an unconscious, untheorized "common sense," but a thought out and ideological response among conservative theoreticians, as Martin Barker demonstrated in his book, *The New Racism: Conservatives and the Ideology of the Tribe* (1981), which goes through the philosophical development of this "instinctive" response. The change in policing that *PTC* focuses on occurred between Powell's calculated racist outburst and Thatcher's assertion of a cultural difference between the supposedly law-abiding natives and questionable immigrants. This was the time of the oil crisis, that dramatically ended the post-war boom, and unprecedented levels of social unrest and industrial militancy.

Hall was right to assert later that:

The fact of the matter is that it is no longer possible to fight racism as if it had its own, autonomous social dynamic, located between white people or the police on one side, and black on the other. The problem of racism arises from every single political development which has taken place in Britain since the new right emerged. (Hall, 1985, p. 79)

Sivanandan talked of how new identities in Britain were built as communities of resistance: "Cultural expression came not from government edict, but from the joint fight against racial discrimination – on the factory floor and in the community – by Asians, Afro-Caribbeans and whites, thereby creating unity in diversity" (Sivanandan, 2006). In this the self-images of different sections of the population develop in a dynamic relationship with each other and change over time. So "black" was seen by activists as a unified term for people who had been "colonized" by the British Empire, rather than defining people from an African-Caribbean background as is more common in the twenty-first century. It is also worth examining changing public attitudes to and the self-image of the police – in these examples the MPS. It is no coincidence that the Mangrove Nine judgement, Scarman Report, the Macpherson Report and indeed the Sewell Report are all responses to different kinds of resistance – acts that call the role of the government into question.

The Mangrove Nine case resulted in an official assertion that racism exists within the police, showing as it did elements of the MPS actively criminalizing the West Indian community. In 1970 local activists organized a protest after 12 drug raids on the black-owned Mangrove Restaurant in Notting Hill, west London – none of which had found any drugs (Bunce and Field, 2010). The restaurant was also a community center, which provided legal representation for black people, who were picked up by the police and, activists maintained, randomly charged with criminal offenses (Howe, 1988, p. 50). The protest ended in a violent confrontation between police and protesters. Nine of the organizers were arrested in dawn raids and charged with inciting a riot. They fought the case through a 55-day trial and were acquitted of all the main charges (Details in Howe, 1988, pp. 50-59).

The judge said in his summing up that the trial had "regrettably shown evidence of racial hatred on both sides" (Bunce and Field, 2010). The MPS complained about this statement and tried unsuccessfully to get it withdrawn. The result did not see a significant change in police tactics. Raids on the Mangrove continued, until in 1992 the owner was awarded £50,000 compensation for the harassment (Mills, 1992). From the mid-1970s the Notting Hill Carnival in the same area was treated to increasingly heavy policing and became an early flashpoint in the kind of confrontations with young black men that would become increasingly common in the 1980s.

Police increasingly demonized black people as the key cause of unrest, at a time of ever-greater instability. *PTC* argues that, "Policing the blacks threatened to mesh with the problem of policing the poor and policing the unemployed: all three were concentrated in precisely the same urban areas...The on-going problem of policing the blacks had become for all practical purposes synonymous with policing the crisis" (Hall et al, 1978a, p. 325). MPS commissioner Sir David McNee said in 1979 that: "Policing a multi-racial society is putting the fabric of our policing philosophy under greater stress than at any time since the years immediately after the Metropolitan Police was established in 1829" (cited in Gilroy, 1982, p. 146). In the early nineteenth century it was the emergent working class that had to be trained to accept the then novel idea of being "policed." McNee is contrasting a class that he saw as being acclimatized to alien immigrants who – for whatever reason – could not be.

Gilroy notes that, "The black mob...opened a new chapter in the lexicon of racialized crime imagery...The shift towards a plural collective image rather than the lone and isolated figure of the 'mugger' reflected the partial de-racialization of the mugging concept which had followed once white muggers had begun to be caught." (Gilroy, 1987, p. 99) Rioting was and has continued to be seen as a black activity, even when a significant number of those arrested are not black, as was the case in the 1981 Brixton riot. As with all the riots from St Paul's in 1980 onwards it was multiracial, even if young black men dominated (for more on how this was replicated in the BLM protests see Monti in this volume). This has remained true in more recent disturbances; for instance, 40 percent of those arrested in the 2011 riots across England were white (Home Office, 2011, p. 4). Brixton was at the time seen as unprecedented in its scale and was followed by a summer of rioting across the country.

Unconventionally, the Scarman Report into the riots "broke the prevailing law-and-order consensus by firmly locating the sources of unrest in 'insecure social and economic conditions and in an impoverished physical environment'" (Hall, 1999, pp. 189). However, Scarman also categorically stated that, "'Institutional racism' does not exist in Britain: but racial disadvantage and its nasty associate racial discrimination have not yet been eliminated" (Scarman, 1981, p. 209). Though they went against the instincts of the Thatcher government, the report's recommendations were far from radical, saying little more than that more must be done to challenge racial disadvantage. Scarman argued elliptically that, "If we eliminate racial prejudice from our society, it will not be difficult to achieve good policing" (Scarman, 1981, p. 210). Jenny Bourne of IRR wrote, "Scarman had effectively reduced (objective) institutional racism to (individual) black perception, on the one hand, and personal (white) prejudice, on the other, and so shifted the object of anti-racist struggle from the state to the individual... from improving the lot of whole black communities, mired in poverty and racism, to improving the lot of black individuals" (Bourne, 2001, p. 12).

An idea of the world Scarman's understanding of policing envisaged can be seen in John Brown's *Policing by Multi-Racial Consent* (1982), for which Scarman wrote the introduction. The book looked at policing in the multi-racial inner-city area of Handsworth in Birmingham, one of the areas which had rioted in the summer of 1981. Brown presents the problem as finding a way to deal with black youth who, "drift into lives of idleness and crime, justifying themselves with half-digested gobbets of Rastafarian philosophy. Many of the couple of hundred 'hard-core' Dreadlocks who now form a criminalized subculture in the area live in squats...they constantly threaten the peace of individual citizens, black, brown and white" (Brown, 1982, p. 9). This maintains the idea of a criminal infection, even if it reduces it to a small part of the whole immigrant-background community. And it sees cultures of resistance – such as Rasta –

as part of the problem. While the police are seen as a first aid point rather than a part of the problem. Brown blames this on wider society and a loss of communality, that means "losses in society's capability to protect life and property, to control crime and to keep the peace" (Brown, 1982, p. 153). Once more this assumes that the problem is created by an external disruption, and at this level is not divorced from the ideas put forward by Powell, Thatcher and others.

In practice there was no major change in policing after Scarman and further riots followed. A far more serious attempt to change the way Britain is policed came with the Macpherson Report into the botched investigation into the 1993 murder of black London teenager Stephen Lawrence. Stephen's friend Duwayne Brooks, who survived the attack, recalled being treated as a suspect rather than a victim (Cathcart, 1999, p. 356). Let down and spied on by the police, Lawrence's parents led a high-profile campaign to get justice for their son, supported by protests and building support among trade unions (Evans, 2019). This was the watershed investigation that condemned the MPS as "institutionally racist" in 1997.

Though the MPS reluctantly came to accept the report, it showed enormous hostility. Hall argued that, "The idea of 'institutional racism' strikes at the heart of one very English kind of racism, which thrives, not against, but cozily inserted within, liberalism" (Hall, 1999, p. 194-5).

However, the government and police did attempt in the early years of the twenty-first century to get rid of racist attitudes and practices. Cressida Dick, who was to become MPS commissioner from 2017-2022, retrospectively stated that the Met "can be proud of how it has been transformed in attitudes, practice, training and professionalism" (Dick, 2012, p. 92).

Unfortunately this tendency was blunted by responses to the subsequent crisis.

The current crisis

The centrality of racial politics that Hall refers to ended in the late 1990s, which is not to suggest that racism was not a major issue afterwards. However, the situation changed dramatically once the current crisis began with the financial crash in 2007. But the shift is complex. The drivers are not crudely economic. The rise in racism in the 1960s preceded the economic collapse of the 1970s, as I argued with the case of Powell above. Some similarities can be seen in the period before the shift around the recession, with Britain's continued relative economic decline and its rulers once more attempting to redefine their role. This was reflected in the crisis of confidence in the West after the 911 attack on New York in 2001 and the subsequent "War on terror," which saw a marked increase in the view of Muslims as a particularly violent and lawless group. As with the view that black people tended to be lawless, violent and immoral, this did not appear out of the blue. It can be dated back at least to the Iranian revolution in 1979, and in a British context the controversy over whether Salman Rushdie's *Satanic Verses* was blasphemous in 1989. Looking back on the period, Jon Burnett of the IRR complained that, "instead of analyzing the local racial fallout from, say, asylum policy or the wars in Afghanistan and Iraq, politicians and opinion-formers turn the tables and define problems in terms of mistrust and antagonism between individuals in communities that do not cohere because of self-segregation" (Burnett, 2012, p. 95). A recent Home Office report raises the same issues that Gramsci and Hall discuss in different language, as it talks of "crises in the legitimacy of policing or trust in the state generally" (Home Office, 2020a, p. 61).

Enoch Powell was used above to exemplify an ideological shift in the 1960s. Former prime minister David Cameron can be cast in a similar light 50 years later. He won the leadership of the Conservative Party in 2005 as a modernizer, who complained that too many party MPs were "white men" and promised "no more grumbling about modern Britain" (Cameron, 2005). However, as his government's austerity measures cut into most of the population's standard of living, Cameron shifted to a much more critical stance on multiculturalism. He protested that immigrant communities, and particularly Muslims, were not law abiding and did not accept Western values, stating: "Frankly, we need a lot less of the passive tolerance of recent years and a much more active, muscular liberalism" (Cameron, 2011).

As in the 1970s, once the authoritarian trend had been set it accelerated as the crisis intensified through subsequent leaders Theresa May and Boris Johnson. And it was not an inevitable, impersonal process, but was enacted ideologically through specific policies that were intended to change people's attitudes. The return to a racialized nation reached fever pitch during the 2016 "Brexit" campaign over whether to leave the European Union (EU). The shift is not peculiar to Britain, and in many ways has been more extreme in EU countries such as France, with its criminalization of various Muslim practices, and the presidency of Donald Trump in the US. However, the authoritarian right has not become hegemonic and, despite the Covid pandemic, Britain has seen both the revival of BLM and a campaign against the controversial police bill, generating the nationwide "Kill the Bill" protests that followed in its wake.

The revived racialization of crime

The ideological offensive to convince people that crime is a particular problem and to continue the racialization of crime can most clearly be seen in several policies, notably the treatment of "black-on-black" crime, the Prevent Duty and the arguments around the "hostile environment." The first makes immigrant-background communities, and particularly African-Caribbeans, appear exceptionally criminal, the second does something similar to people who look Muslim, by tending to associate whole communities with terrorism.

Meanwhile, the hostile environment makes ordinary people into border guards. And as the victims of the Windrush scandal discovered, people who are black can be assumed to be illegal immigrants. The ideological intervention from the top is pushing people to see black people, immigrants and refugees as a central problem in crime. As Liz Fekete of IRR has stated:

> Because the state has been so effective in cordoning groups off as 'special cases', by manipulating fear of 'Islamic terrorists', 'black gangsters', 'Gypsy thieves', and 'criminal chavs', it is securing the transition from policing by consent to policing by enforcement, while maintaining the fiction of policing by consent (ie we all consent to the use of force as long as it is not against us). (Fekete, 2013, p 73)

The racial division is most clearly seen in stop and search figures. Since there is "only marginal association between stop and search and, in particular, violent and indeed 'volume' crime," criminologists Ben Bradford and Matteo Tiratelli query whether it "is not really 'about' crime, but rather relates to wider processes of social control directed particularly at deprived and marginal populations" (Bradford and Tiratelli, 2019, p. 9). The statistics appear to speak for themselves. The proportion of stop and searches conducted on white suspects decreased from 75 percent in 2014/15 to 59 percent in 2018/19 and increased for all minority ethnic groups, but the largest increases were from 13 percent to 22 percent for black suspects and from 8 percent to 13 percent for Asian suspects. From 2014-19 in London, the proportion of stop and searches involving black suspects increased from 30 percent to 37 percent, now equal to the number of white suspects searched.

But is such a distortion justified by the fact that black people are almost wholly responsible for knife crime? This is not the conclusion drawn by the Office for National Statistics, which reports, "Around one in five (21 percent) suspects were identified as black, seven times higher than the general population (3 percent). Differences in these figures are likely to be related to the ethnicity of the population differing by age, region and socioeconomic factors which have not been taken into account" (ONS, 2020). Indeed, as another study notes:

> In England and Wales, the recording of "knife enabled" offenses did not start until April 2007 (with the exception of London, where such records started to be collated in 2003), which makes it impossible to make any comparison with preceding periods...The fact that offenses of illegal knife and gun possession are not routinely collected for the Home Office makes it difficult to establish the impact of strategies aimed at deterring young people from carrying weapons. (Silvestri et al, 2009, p. 10)

The issue of stabbings among young people is a serious one, but it is not simply a black issue as it is often presented. A similar response can be made to the issue of so-called "black-on-black" crime. This has concerned the MPS, which has set up a series of task forces, including Operation Trident, and more recently the Gangs Matrix to confront gang violence. As Amnesty's report on the MPS Gangs Matrix in 2016 notes, the ethnic bias in people included, "87% were from black, Asian and minority ethnic (BAME) backgrounds (78% were black). Eighty percent were between the ages of 12 and 24, and 15% were minors (the youngest was 12 years old). Ninety-nine percent were male" (Amnesty International, 2018, p. 2). The vast majority of these are not people who have been involved in organizations recognizable as gangs. Clare Alexander has detected a cultural bias in examining Asian gangs, "a media-infused strategy to represent the Asian gang as a new problem. The accompanying discourse marks a shift away from a 'dualistic racist/anti-racist' dialogue toward a more nuanced 'new racist' discussion of nation and belonging'" (C. Alexander, 2000, quoted in Williams, 2015, p. 22). Think of the stereotype beloved of the far right of the Pakistani "grooming gang." A recent government report has stated that to the extent that such a category is useful, "Research has found that group-based CSE offenders are most commonly White" (Home Office, 2020b, p. 8).

The government's anti-terrorism strategy, Contest, was first launched in 2003 and has since been expanded. It focused on "four Ps" – Pursue; Prevent; Protect: Prepare (HM Government, 2011, p.6). The Prevent strand is of interest here because it criminalizes people who are not involved in any kind of terrorist activity. The 2015 Counter Terrorism and Security Act moved it from being a policy to the statutory Prevent Duty, which specifies that an array of people in universities, colleges, schools, local authorities need to have "due regard to the need to prevent people from being drawn into terrorism" (Home Office, 2015, p. 3).

It assumes that certain groups of people are vulnerable to being drawn into terrorist activity. Campaigner Robert Ferguson argued that: "Prevent is a disguised but systemic form of institutionalized Islamophobia," and that the core message of the training "is a 'statutory duty' to report 'concerns'... A typical resource notes that cause for concern in child behavior may include: 'trying to make sense of world events'" (Ferguson, 2020, p. 234).

Though there have been attempts to rectify the imbalance early Prevent guidance focused on Islamic extremism at the expense of the far right.

An example of how this shading of legitimate issues into apparent matters for concern can be seen in a now withdrawn counter-terrorism policing guide for the southeast of England aimed at "managers, senior officers and safeguarding leads at all levels of local authorities" (Counter Terrorism Policing,

2020, p. 2). Included among signs to help spot extremists, "You may hear someone...voice concern for 'oppressed' Muslims in other countries" (Counter Terrorism Policing, 2020, p. 7). Another example of the racialized double standards is the treatment of Shamima Begum, who was born in Britain, but left in 2015 to join Isis in Syria aged 15. Rather than treating her as an underage victim of grooming, the British government subsequently stripped her of her citizenship, seeing her as a criminal rather than a victim. The human rights organization Liberty complained that the government used discriminatory punishment, "stripping people who have non-British heritage of their citizenship" (Liberty, 2021).

The hostile environment policy, launched in 2012, which came out of an attempt to demonize refugees, probably affects the greatest number of people, as I argued in "The Hostile Environment for Immigrants" (Olende, 2020). Home Secretary Theresa May stated that, "the aim is to create here in Britain a really hostile environment for illegal migration" (Kirkup and Winnett, 2012). The policy also aimed to increase pressure on legal immigrants, as evidenced by May's comment that the legislation would "ensure that legal immigrants make a proper contribution to our key public services" (Home Office, 2013, p. 2). It was part of an attempt to turn round public sympathy for refugees. In part this has been a longer-term process of trying to make people legitimately seeking refuge under international law appear as criminals – economic migrants or failed asylum seekers, with attempts to deport them before they can appeal (as a large proportion of appeals are granted). As criminologist James Banks has argued, "the 'securitization of asylum' has provided for the successful integration of criminal justice and migration systems of control" (Banks, 2011, p. 191). Similarly, the deportation of people who were jailed for more than 12 months, introduced in 2008 (Banks, 2011, p. 193) is punitive punishment, for people who have already served their sentences, but doubly so for people who may have been Windrush generation with a right to stay but no papers. A 2021 investigation found that a disproportionate number of people from the Caribbean were deported (Walker, 2021). A plane that left in August 2021, initially scheduled to take 90 former prisoners to Jamaica, flew with seven once people had been able to get legal representation (Taylor, 2021).

The policy was more formally implemented via the Immigration Acts of 2014 and 2016. These new legal frameworks were intended to draw a far wider section of society into the role of de facto border guards, with "measures seeking to restrict illegal immigrants from renting property in the UK, driving, having bank accounts and accessing benefits and free healthcare" (House of Lords, 2018, p. 1). In practice this criminalized large sections of the immigrant population – not just people who were doing something illegal, but people who "everyday" border guards might suspect. The Windrush scandal emerged as a direct result of these policies. It emerged that thousands of British residents, mainly of Caribbean origin, who had legally come to the UK before the 1971 Act's restrictions were enacted in 1973, were being treated as illegal immigrants and losing their jobs or being deemed ineligible for pensions, benefits or health care.

The process of criminalization included the decision to restrict the use of Home Office records to establish the legal status of those affected. It had "not been using central tax and pension records, which could prove someone has been working, to support people's applications" (BBC, 2018). Other Windrush generation people have continued to be treated as criminals, unable to get compensation. Although the Home Office has admitted its mistake in classifying Windrush generation arrivals as illegal immigrants 2 years later, by July 2021, only 412 of the 2367 compensation claims submitted had received their final payment. The scheme expected to have to pay out on up to 15,000 claims in total (Syal, 2021).

The concentration on areas such as the NHS bolstered the idea that a crisis developing in emergency provision could be blamed on "health tourism," that is people traveling to Britain to illegally use NHS services. This is reminiscent of Powell's equally specious argument that his constituents "found their wives unable to obtain hospital beds in childbirth, their children unable to obtain school places" (Powell, 1968). In 2015 the King's Fund noted that the estimated cost of "health tourism" was "between £60 million and £80 million per year. This compares to the annual NHS budget of £113 billion" (King's Fund, 2015). That is less than a tenth of one percent. This does not take into account migrants who are resident in Britain and work, not infrequently, in the Health Service.

Conclusion

Prime minister Boris Johnson announced at the launch of the Sewell Report that he intended to "change the narrative so we stop the sense of victimization and discrimination" around race (Honeycombe-Foster, 2020). This attitude is part of a process of moving away from talking about race in terms of systems and institutions and going back to the softer language of "unconscious bias" and individual ideas. This is not new. The anti-racism solution that followed Scarman was Racism Awareness Training, where individual white people were supposed to confront their individual racism, rather than seeing it as part of a systemic problem (Sivanandan, 1990, p. 114).

Racism is never primarily about individuals and their prejudices. Dealing with racism is not a matter of "race relations," which suggests that it is a matter of dealing with prejudice in different communities. For these reasons Gramsci's hegemony model is useful – it shows that the problem is wider than limited mindset issues. The police cannot be understood without looking at their role in capitalist society. The social crisis cannot be reduced to an increase in criminality. Gramsci's view was closely linked to an analysis of who benefits from making people see crime as the main thing to fear. The debates during the summer of 2021 highlighted the fact that an unprecedented number of law makers were themselves descendants of non-white immigrants, including Home Secretary Priti Patel, Chancellor of the Exchequer Rishi Sunak and Equalities Minister Kemi Badenoch.

The ideas of mugging and the need for a more authoritarian state in the 1970s and 80s were not givens and were fiercely contested. They met a great deal of resistance, both from the black community and the wider working class. The same is true of the current attempt at scapegoating. It goes far beyond simple arguments about policing and the solutions to it belong in an area of wider social change.

My argument is not that there are not specific reasons for the racialization of individual crimes or the invention of new crimes, but that the whole can only be understood by seeing that this is not primarily an issue of criminality or policing, but of policy and an adjustment of common sense in the interests of one group rather than another, and that ways to respond to it must be developed in that light. This is not about refusing to take crime seriously, but to say that focusing on individual crimes loses the bigger picture of why shifts in attitudes and behavior happen at particular times.

Chapter 7

"A Momentary Brotherhood of Uncomfortable White Men, Trying to Figure Stuff Out" Cultural Unity, Political Divisiveness, and the Black Lives Matter Protests

Daniel J. Monti

With the support of: Contributing Authors
Carla Brown
Iordyem Ma
Shreya Nagendra
Nicole Nelson
Rachel Rimmerman
Students in the graduate program in Public and Social Policy Studies
Saint Louis University

And Lauren Billeh, Kaitlynn Borik, Cassidy Eckert, Shelby Highlander, Caitlin Mussey, Larisa Nesimovic, Alonna Robertson and Tayla Slay
Undergraduate Students at Saint Louis University

Delhi, New York would seem an unlikely place to have a protest, much less one of the Black Lives Matter protests that swept over the United States in 2020. Three hours and 150 miles north of New York City, Delhi is in a lovely rural setting. It is unnewsworthy, except perhaps for the presence of a campus of the state university system whose students had already left town for the summer.

Not counting the students, over 90 percent of the 5100 people who live in Delhi are white. That was consistent with the makeup of the protesters who were in the protest or watched it along Main Street (O'Hehir, 2020).

More than 700 people, the vast majority of them white and most under age 40, lined Main Street for several blocks in both directions – maintaining appropriate social distancing, and wearing masks – outside the tractor supply store and the speedway mini-mart and the Delaware National Bank and Dubben Brothers Hardware. They did call-and-response chants and held up the now-familiar array of signs protesting police violence or white silence and honoring the equally familiar litany of black people's names: George Floyd, Breonna Taylor, Eric Garner, Sandra Bland, Tamir Rice, Mike Brown – as you know, we could go on.

The Delhi police chief posted a cheerful Facebook message in support of the protest, while making clear that whatever bad things involving cops may have happened elsewhere had nothing to do with him.

After 2 hours of largely upbeat protest on a beautiful Saturday in Delhi, nearly everyone up and down Main Street "took a knee" in commemoration of George Floyd and other victims of police violence.

To the reporter looking at both the protesters and counter protesters, "it felt like a momentary brotherhood of uncomfortable white men, trying to figure stuff out."

Which is precisely what people in places as small as Delhi or as big as New York City are doing when they meet in public to register their concern about something that bothers them as much as George Floyd's murder obviously did. What else they can do may not be clear right then and maybe not for a long time. But coming together in public and "making a statement" is an integral piece of the figuring out process.

Such gatherings are an invitation to a cultural reckoning of sorts about the event and its meaning to the community. The airing need not be of the community's dirty laundry, though that often is the purpose served by such public displays. Dramatic public outings can be used just as readily to celebrate or acknowledge something good about a community that is not commemorated often enough in the estimation of the people who are rallying, marching or demonstrating.

Of course, the protest over the murder of George Floyd was anything but a celebration. The Delhi event dealt with the unwarranted and shocking public execution of a black person by a white person who had the power but not the right to do what he did as far as they were concerned.

When community sentiment is clear, as it was in Delhi, a public demonstration looks more like a big exclamation point than a question mark about what to do. People in all the places where protests happened made a loud and life-affirming "Not in My Back Yard" statement for everyone to see. An important gesture, to be sure, but nothing that would necessarily lead town leaders to take a formal action to address the killing, which happened in Minneapolis more than a thousand miles away.

It is different in cities and not only because such killings are more likely to happen in urban areas that have large minority populations. City people deal with all manner of crowds every day and sometimes use crowds to register their sentiment on matters they believe need commemorating or a public reckoning. Finding a collection of fellow residents upset and engaged enough to take to the streets is not necessarily easier in cities, but city people are more accustomed to using crowds for just such a purpose.

Crowds (or protests, marches, or demonstrations) are not something people in Delhi see all that often. The same probably could be said for most of the 2000 towns and perhaps even some of the cities that had a Black Lives Matter protest (Wikipedia, 2020). It turns out there were no precedents in US history for the number of protests that occurred after George Floyd was murdered. Just as surprising, perhaps, are the self-reports people gave of their participation in the protests. In the United States alone, the number who said they were involved fell somewhere between 15 million and 26 million.

These numbers greatly outshined the 3 to 5 million who participated in the women's march of 2017 (Buchanan, Bui, and Patel, 2020). Even more surprising, the number of Black Lives Matter protesters might well have dwarfed the total number of participants in demonstrations that took place during the civil rights movement more than a half-century ago. Adding further significance to the protests that occurred after George Floyd was murdered was the fact that most of them were homegrown affairs. Organizations such as Black Lives Matter provided "materials, guidance and a framework for new activists." But the protests were inspired by what local people saw in the media and posted online.

White people across the country were inspired just as they were in Delhi. As *The New York Times* reporters put it:

More than 40 percent of counties in the United States – at least 1360 – (had) a protest. Unlike previous Black Lives Matter protests, nearly 95 percent of counties that had a protest recently are majority white, and nearly three-quarters of the counties are more than 75 percent white.

Quoting Doug McAdam, who has long studied social movements, the reporters added,

(w)ithout gainsaying the reality and significance of generalized white support for the movement in the early 1960s, the number of whites who were active in a sustained way in the struggle were comparatively few, and certainly nothing like the percentages we have seen taking part in recent weeks.

Noteworthy, too, is the way some governments responded: quickly, surprisingly so. Public officials in many communities were taken aback by the killing and/or sobered by the countrywide protests just as millions of other Americans were. In Minneapolis, the city council pledged to dismantle its police department. In New York, lawmakers repealed a law that kept police disciplinary records secret. Cities and towns across the country passed new laws banning chokeholds. Mississippi lawmakers voted to retire their state flag, which prominently includes a Confederate battle emblem. The federal government, at the time this chapter was being written, was working through proposals to deal with police misbehavior.

The George Floyd protests were exceptional in all these ways. In other important ways, however, the protests were anything but exceptional. The reasons why tell us a great deal about the social and cultural significance of popular unrest and what, if anything, as a practical matter it accomplishes.

First, unconventional acts such as protests, no matter how peaceful or violent, carry the cultural blueprint of public celebrations, commemorations and grievance-sharing customs long practiced in Western societies such as the United States (Davis, 1986; D'Arcy, 2013; Tilly and Tarrow, 2015; Delgado, 2016). They have been around for a long time.

Their staying power does not make them any less unconventional, disruptive or threatening, of course. It just means events very much like the Black Lives Matter protests have a storied history in Western societies. They are one way people have traditionally made themselves heard when they had something important to say about their community or their place in it.

Second, people willingly break commonly accepted standards for decorous behavior to make clear they are upset. No matter what specific grievances may have inspired their public display, every demonstration provides clues to who is (or is not) a community member in good standing and who is accountable for keeping the whole community in good working order.

Third, and just as important, no matter how dramatic demonstrations are, including the more violent ones, larger questions about why the community is organized the way it is and who benefits (rightly or wrongly) from the arrangement are not raised publicly. This is no less true of the aggrieved parties than it is for persons who might become less privileged, powerful, and well-off if the community were organized much differently.

The questions raised around protests, demonstrations, boycotts and even riots are not trivial and can be quite sensitive, which is why they are often presented publicly as parodies of real-world practices so they invite laughter and head shaking as much as they do serious reflection. But people's concerns and grievances usually deal with problems whose solution is well within the reach of all the parties implicated in a public kerfuffle.

Typically left untouched are the underlying social arrangements that help to produce problems and misunderstandings and the foundational values upon which these arrangements are built. These could be invoked but are not often called into question or openly challenged, by anyone. They are the elephant in the room people do not want to talk about but cannot stop themselves from poking or at least dancing around.

The protests following George Floyd's murder satisfied all three of these criteria and, as such, were successful pieces of street theater. They brought together as good a mix of exceptional and unexceptional cultural features as one would hope to find in a good stage play. The performers were dramatic enough to capture our attention but not so over-the-top that we focused on them and forgot to talk about the larger moral of the story they were trying to tell.

However angry people may be, burning down the theater is not an option. The building next door, perhaps, depending on how outraged they are. The one around the corner from the theater, a safer and more likely target. But not the whole theater.

A closer look at some Black Lives Matter protests

People involved in protests or simply observing them provide good hints about the message trying to be conveyed. But it is not just what they say and do that matters. Just as important and sometimes trickier to discern is what they do not say or do in public. Their unwillingness to use deadly force, for instance, is, if you will, a dead giveaway in this regard. So, too, is the mismatch between the overheated rhetoric people might use compared to the less aggressive way they act when confronting their real or imagined opponents in public.

Our task is to not to figure out people's motives for becoming involved in different kinds of unrest but the moral of the story they are trying to tell with their provocative behavior. The fact is people are not particularly self-aware and may have only a vague idea, if they have any notion at all, of what they hope to accomplish. People's lack of clarity is itself a clue to the cultural significance of popular unrest and why people use it as often as they do.

People are not supposed to know how unrest will turn out. If they did there would be no point to raising an alarm. Popular unrest works only because it is a surprise and shocks people who have become too comfortable and certain about the way their community works and their place in it.

Figuring out and perhaps controlling the ingredients that make unrest a surprise in the hope we might avoid the confusion it sows and the mess it sometimes leaves for us to clean up may not be a fool's errand (Collins, 2008; Nassauer, 2019). But that is not where the cultural secrets to understanding unrest and putting it to some good use lie. Unrest helps us clarify the uncertainty we have built into our world and gives us the time and push we often need to figure stuff out, especially the big stuff.

The motivations of participants and observers – interesting, ill-defined and irrelevant as they usually are – tell us little of what we want or need to understand about unrest. Here I will try to identify and unpack what was (and was not) being communicated in the Black Lives Matter protests and what important community matters become clarified when people go public with their concerns in a big and sometimes even violent way.

The information presented here came from news accounts about Black Lives Matter protests across the country. Stories were scoured for word and behavioral clues attributed to the people who were there. Most of the protests in these news stories were in bigger cities such as Minneapolis, Louisville, Atlanta, New York, and Portland, Oregon.

But a crucial feature of the Black Lives Matter protests was all the smaller and much whiter towns that had one demonstration or a series of protest events. What happened in those places might be different from what was done and said about protests in bigger cities. There were news accounts about these demonstrations, but not a lot of firsthand and after-the-fact assessments of what had happened there.

I had students choose pairs of smaller communities in states whose towns had protests but had not been mentioned in national news stories. (A list of places we surveyed appears at the end of this chapter.) Students collected media accounts of the protests in those towns and then interviewed local officials and anyone they could find who had been mentioned in the newspaper stories about their protest.

The principal question asked of the people students managed to track down was about what happened in the town *after* the protests ended. My guess was that life would have returned pretty much to what it was before the protests, but I could not be certain, which is why we asked.

Students certainly uncovered more about what had happened from the perspective of the reporters and citizens who were there. But people had much less to say about changes they saw. Students got a lot of "not much" or "not really" answers when they asked whether much change had happened. Some towns reportedly were planning to change how they policed their communities. In other towns, local people hoped to keep conversations about racism and race relations going at least in the near-term and established groups or committees to carry on such discussions.

As a practical matter, that might be all the protests accomplished. But that is not all the protests told us, albeit indirectly or unintentionally, about the community or why they were important. Much more telling, from my perspective, are the answers people provided to the three questions I posed earlier about community membership, rule breaking and accountability.

What follows is a bare-bones summary of what we learned.

Protests in smaller towns

Black Lives Matter protests in places as geographically dispersed as Nome, Alaska; Millersport, Ohio; Chambersburg and Wilkes-Barre, Pennsylvania; and Moscow, Idaho had several features in common (Abdalla, 2020; Dennis, 2020; Gajanan, 2020; Robertson, 2020; Shuler, 2020). They were relatively small, with one or two hundred people at most, but were still big stand-out affairs for towns with a few thousand residents.

The protests were often led by white and minority teenagers and twenty-something year-olds. Older adults known to them, including parents and grandparents, and others they did not know well or at all came out to support them. Sometimes a town official was reported to have joined the protesting crowd. There were occasional comments about the protests being "family affairs."

There principally to speak out against the killing of George Floyd, protesters added issues of local concern to them and their community. On a few occasions these included calls for a public official or chief of police to resign.

Lined up against the protesters in some communities were smaller numbers of white people who jeered at the protesters or just stood in place and tried to look menacing. It did not appear to bother the protesters, who seemed satisfied calling out police misbehavior and decrying racism.

For their part, black protesters and observers were surprised at how many white people showed up to protest and give voice to complaints they have had for a long time. They were even less certain how they could use it. Apart from calls for greater police accountability, it was hard to know what issues local black residents might raise in the future or which initiatives white people would support or take a pass on.

The protests were much more revealing of people's sentiment on broader social or cultural questions such as how welcomed black persons would be in the community, whether whites and blacks would be held to the same standards for how to behave in public, and how accountable different groups were for keeping the town in good working order (Monti, 1999).

The sense we made of their words and actions goes something like this. Most people wanted their town to be open to black people. Police officers were expected to behave professionally and most certainly not single out black people for abuse. And people who mistreated black citizens and townsmen should be held accountable for their misdeeds.

Local people who disliked the protests and the ostensible reason for staging them made their sentiments clear mostly by what they *didn't* do during the protests. White people did not act out as much as they did decades ago when black people first showed up in predominantly white neighborhoods and townships. There was no widespread fighting this time. Most counter-protesters exercised self-restraint in front of their neighbors. Protesters, whose numbers included even more whites than the counter-protesters, drew a new metaphorical line in the sand that counter-protesters understood, might have groused about, but did not cross.

The story conveyed in the words and deeds of the people at the protests contained an important moral about the kind of community they had made and how it measured up to the one they wanted to make in the future.

The question of community membership

However much or little white people may have welcomed black people in the past, protesters made a strong bid for black people to be considered credible members of the community where they were demonstrating. George Floyd was a stand-in for all black persons in this regard. But the bid was just as important for the younger black and white persons who led so many of these protests. Counter-protesters made smaller, less demonstrative, but still noteworthy challenges to these claims. Who could or should be considered full-fledged members of the community was still open for debate, but community sentiment leaned more toward recognizing the protesters and the people on whose behalf they were demonstrating.

Misplaying by the rules

To make their bid more credible, protesters frequently paired their obvious "coming out" with equally obvious attempts to play by rules people already vetted and certified as members of the community were expected to follow when they wanted to make a public show. Demonstrating fidelity to community rules, even as people purposely turned them upside down for a moment or two, is an important way people use to identify each other as credible members of the community.

The single most important way protesters made this clear was by working with local police departments to keep their protest peaceful. In many towns, both protest leaders and town officials commented on how well their planning and collaboration had gone. Counter-protesters, whose status as members of the community was not in dispute, made no public attempt to work with local officials to keep their obvious displeasure with the protests in check. They did this on their own by not acting out in most instances. But when they did act out the police were there to keep the two sides separated.

Playing by the rules and sometimes ignoring, bending or breaking them matters to everyone, even if they do not recognize it or are unwilling to acknowledge the importance of unrest as a cultural practice. When people are concerned, upset or shocked by events they do not understand, how they respond is limited only by their imagination and experience.

There are good reasons why experience takes precedence over people's imaginations under such circumstances, and they all have to do with history and the power of customs. As a matter of history, people are likely to ignore, bend or break some previously agreed upon understanding about how to deal with their problems when they face something new or unprecedented. Unclear or unsettled situations challenge those understandings. On those occasions where the misunderstanding is substantial, people struggle to find something they can do that will work. To that end they often find themselves splitting the difference between using past solutions, which probably will not work as well as people hope, and their imaginations, which are less constrained but whose proposals for action are not well tested.

Nothing people have invented splits that difference better than popular unrest, which is all about ignoring, bending or breaking rules until such time as they figure out something else, presumably better and longer lasting, to do. Peaceful disruptions to everyday routines are closer to one end of the ignoring, bending and rule-breaking continuum. Violent disruptions are closer to the other end of that continuum. But in unsettled situations rules are always the first things thrown out the window.

The reason this is not as off-the-wall as it sounds has to do with where our ideas about unrest come from and how practiced we are in using it: history. Unrest works because its form and timing are guided by customs that are well-traveled, tried out and flexible. In popular unrest we have a customary way to ignore, bend and break rules so we can deal with unexpected events and troublesome conditions. And, to repeat, nothing works better to alert the wider community there is a problem in search of a solution than a good display of public outrage or concern.

Making people accountable

The other way protesters made their claim for membership in the community more credible was by asserting or reaffirming that everyone needs to be held accountable for what they do and say in public. Given the multi-racial and multi-generational makeup of the protesters, the demand for accountability would have applied not just to powerful, well-to-do and more well-regarded persons in the community but also to persons who were not. This would have included all the young people who took prominent roles in the protests and people like George Floyd.

The calling out of Derek Chauvin as a stand-in for all errant police officers and public officials who abuse their authority was the single most powerful message about accountability conveyed in the Black Lives Matter protests. No one missed it. Not the public officials who would soon be rushing to pass new rules about police conduct. And not the counter-protesters whose inaction spoke louder than the individual jeers and catcalls a few made from the sidewalk as much larger numbers of children and adults, many of whom looked like them, walked down the middle of the street.

Another way public accountability was an important value and part of the story protesters wanted to tell was in bringing more local issues and problems to the attention of their neighbors. Included on this list were proposed changes to their schools' curriculum, voting rights, black persons' mental health, gentrification, black-on-black violence, the removal of Confederate statues and other symbols, drug abuse, black men's respect for black women, the treatment of immigrants, white fragility and the importance of an ongoing community dialogue on matters involving race. Here were items they wanted put on the community's public bulletin board for future consideration and further action.

Protests in bigger cities

In small towns, younger white and black people had a noticeable and perhaps unexpectedly large presence in Black Lives Matter protests. Both the protesters and counter-protesters behaved better than people may have expected. Confrontations with "counter-protesters" were rarely more than shouting matches.

In cities, protesting crowds were larger, noisier and more likely to be challenged by police officers than civilian counter-protesters. Young white persons and adults were more involved in racial unrest in some communities until the early-1970s (Hinton, 2021). White people grudgingly ceded cities and neighborhoods where they had once been dominant but could no longer exclude black people scare them away. Large numbers of them "escaped" to suburban safehouses for a while and have been all but missing in confrontations with fellow black citizens since then.

This left police departments (and sometimes a state's National Guardsmen) to keep restive black populations in check. The principal mission of police always has been to maintain public order, especially against the real or imagined threat presented by newcomers and cultural outsiders. Since the 1960s, the police have proven overzealous and ineffective in carrying out the mission in cities where the people being targeted had become too numerous and assertive to control that way. This is the reason there were more fights with police, looting and arson associated with Black Lives Matter protests in cities.

The question of community membership

The question of community membership was unsettled in the small towns that had Black Lives Matter protests. The number of black residents was too small to threaten white persons' social and political dominance. This had not been the case in many cities for more than a half-century. By 2020, black people's presence in cities was not open to question much less being challenged. But exactly where and when during the day they could assume all the rights and duties that come from being fully vetted members of their own community was still up for grabs.

In bigger cities, such questions were raised in the Black Lives Matter protests in ways they had not been raised in a half-century: how far the limits of unconventional behavior could be pushed; where protesters could assert such control (if only for a little while); and why protesters should be held any more accountable for their unruly behavior than the police had been for theirs were put to a momentary test after George Floyd was murdered.

Misplaying by the rules

Big-city protesters ignored, bent and broke rules for acceptable public behavior that small-town protesters never approached, much less crossed. But then, so too did city police who were sent to keep protesters moving someplace else or, barring that, to contain, tear gas, "kettle" and arrest them back into compliance for their disorderly and sometimes destructive behavior.

The longest and most challenging acts of civilian-inspired resistance to public authority and police intervention during the Black Lives Matter protests occurred in Seattle, Washington and Portland, Oregon. There mostly white protesters declared certain parts of the city off limits to any authority except their own and kept it that way for months.

Annoying, provocative and at times violent as these takeovers were, they stood as a counterpoint to what happened in the other cities where the question of who "controlled" public spaces often arose only for a matter of hours or a few days, or was revisited on a predictable weekday or weekend schedule. For however long city protests lasted or were repeated, though, the people who were involved made a much bigger point of playing almost exclusively by their own rules than small-town protesters did. Again, so too did the police (Barker, Baker, and Watkins, 2021).

Making people accountable

Unlike small-town protests where local concerns having little or nothing to do with the police were added to demands for police accountability, big-city protesters appeared laser-focused on efforts to limit police discretion and greatly diminish the presence of police by cutting their funding. A large part of the reason why, as I already noted, probably had to do with the indiscriminate use of police power going back many decades for blacks and even longer for earlier collections of outsiders and newcomers to the city.

Memorializing the struggle to enforce new levels of police accountability and new standards for police conduct, protesters in some cities made the places where police offenses or their standoff with the police had occurred into shrines. The most notable and perhaps permanent of these was the corner where George Floyd was murdered.

Absent a physical spot to memorialize, the unrest itself and the clashes with police that were such an integral part of big-city protests could be invoked long into the future as a memorializing event and a warning. Clashes with police and open defiance to the authority of public officials would become the closest thing to a shrine that protesters left behind. The memory of how the community (or part of it at least) had been mobilized on behalf of "the greater good" could be recounted and rallied around the next time the question of who was accountable to whom was asked and community members demanded a different answer from the one they might otherwise have expected.

Conclusion

There were several instances when people described their Black Lives Matter protest as "doing community." They were right. Protesters and counter-protesters made moral claims about what being a credible community member looked like, the values they should embrace and how their behavior should reflect those values when they were out in public. Black Lives Matter protests were an occasion for teasing out which standards would be embraced in the future and for affirming why changing their standards might be a good and necessary thing to do. It is how people figured stuff out.

Americans have had more than a few disquieting and unsettling racial moments to deal with in the past decade that required us "to figure stuff out." The main point made here is that however well or poorly Americans have worked our way through such moments in the past, we seem to have come to a clearer understanding about how we want that part of our world to look in the future. We are ready to write a different story, and that includes how we will police ourselves.

The moral arc of our new story was apparent in the Black Lives Matter protesters and, by way of a comparison, in how different they were from the Capitol Hill insurrection on January 6, 2021.

The crucial moral of the Black Lives Matter protests is that we have more in common culturally than we recognize and acknowledge. Black people more like George Floyd than Martin Luther King have earned the privilege and duties that go along with being full-fledged members of the community where they live. They deserve the same public regard and treatment white people have long taken for granted. (Here is where the protests come in. They affirm a new community standard for the fair treatment of black persons by people granted public authority and power.)

By comparison, the moral of the story embedded in the Capitol insurrection is that our politics today is all about keeping us divided and not being held accountable to anyone except your kind of people. The ire of the insurrectionists was directed at legislators who do not appreciate how marginal and culturally irrelevant white people supposedly have become in their own country.

White people made their displeasure clear in their attempts to reinstate Donald Trump as president by disregarding votes made by persons who lived in urban areas with lots of black people. It also was made clear by their rejection of every decision made by courts that disagreed with what they wanted. (The insurrectionists staged their 4-hour rebellion after every attempt to redress their grievances had been publicly and legally rejected. The unrest they fomented was supposed to reaffirm an older community standard and storyline that had kept their fellow black citizens legally marginalized until the mid-1960s. That older community standard also was rejected.)

The popular unrest reflected in the Black Lives Matter protests and Capitol Hill insurrection raised important cultural questions about the people we are and the kind of community we want to make in the future. It also gave us a clear cultural answer: all kinds of Americans, including more white ones than at any time in the past, have publicly declared they no longer buy trumped-up claims of racial superiority and inferiority and will not tolerate the use of force to reimpose them.

Smaller communities sampled for this work

Florence and Anniston, Alabama

Russelville and El Dorado, Arkansas
Safford and Nogales, Arizona
Aspen and Alamosa, Colorado
Carrolton, Dacula and Lawrenceville Georgia
Decorah and Ottumwa, Iowa
Emporia and Liberal, Kansas
Belfast and Lewiston, Maine
Aberdeen and Pierre, South Dakota
Covington and Winchester, Tennessee
Issaquah and Shoreline, Washington
Morgantown and Clarksburg, West Virginia

Chapter 8

Searching for Justice in the Twenty-first Century
Karen Evans

The twenty-first century has seen explosions of protest and resistance around the globe. It was born with the slogan "Another World is Possible"[1] and has witnessed the birth of numerous and significant social movements which have galvanized large numbers in protest against the status quo. These are movements which have spread out beyond their local, regional or national beginnings and have touched raw nerves in many places across the planet. They have expanded and multiplied to become truly transnational in their scope, offering the possibility of activism without borders – proposing a global solution to problems which are keenly felt at every level from individual, family, community and wider society.

These movements emerge, demand, create and seemingly fade away, but their legacy continues and the voices which they raise are sustained and amplified by others protesting further arenas of inequality and sites of injustice. There is a clear, red thread which runs through the anti-globalization movement, World Social Forums, Make Poverty History, Occupy, the Arab Spring, Extinction Rebellion and Black Lives Matter, for example, which can be traced back to the indigenous and urban workers movements which swept through Latin America in the late twentieth century (Chodor 2015). They are reactions to the unfettering of global trade in the 1980s and the release of a rampant neoliberal form of capitalism which has succeeded in viciously overturning many of the reforms and concessions made to labor and the poor following the ending of the 1939-45 World War.

The shock and after-effects of the attacks made by a revitalized capitalist class have reverberated across the globe and culminated in wave upon wave of social unrest. The injustices heaped upon the global majority – the "ninety-nine percent" – by this class have generated renewed calls for justice which have gone beyond those which were envisioned in the past, including aspects which are environmental, social, economic, political and cultural. They are informed by the knowledge that reforms, hard-gained, can be snatched away and that a more permanent alternative must be built instead. The environmental movement has succeeded in adding a further layer of urgency to the struggle for change as it has raised issues of grave concern for the entire planet.

Such is the scope of global emergencies faced – social, political and environmental – that the demands made by these movements continued even in times of global pandemic. In 2020 Black Lives Matter protests exploded around the globe in the most difficult and circumscribed conditions. State after state employed the carceral language of "lockdown" in their attempts to curb a virus that has been spawned from the economic and environmental destruction wreaked on the world by the scramble for profits within advanced globalized capitalism[2] – but still we rose.

Justice envisioned and re-visioned

The concept of "justice" has been raised time and again by activists searching for alternative social arrangements which would allow society a sustainable future, but what "justice" might look like in such a future has not been articulated – and perhaps cannot be before those future societies come to fruition. Our current concept of justice is far from "natural" and each society fashions its own forms of justice to suit its own purposes.

Much of what we now consider "justice" is the product of occidental intellectual and conceptual development based in a very particular place and period and is consequentially extremely limited. The eighteenth-century philosophers such as Rousseau, Smith and Kant were concerned with achieving a smooth transition to market-based capitalism and perceived justice as that which ensured the protection of private property. They were therefore concerned to grant the state the legitimate use of force in order to maintain social order and to enforce a new set of social relations which were fundamentally based on financial and social inequality. For these thinkers, the "state of nature" was "uncivilized" and government authority was necessary to enforce and sustain their idea of just relations in society.

These philosophers' particular take on justice paved the way for "modern", "enlightenment," notions of punishment and criminal justice which we still largely rely on today (Hanley 2018). In so doing they underpinned and legitimized the employment of state violence, the militarization of society and the carceral politics which define so many governing principles. The idea that justice acts as the defender of private property, to protect the haves from the uncivilized "have-nots," has been used to justify the spread of rampant capitalism, the market, empire and slavery. Clearly these are not the visions of justice which energize and inspire significant social movements of today. This is not the justice of which we speak in the streets when we rally under the cry of "No Justice, No Peace!'

Rawl's (1971) theory of justice, imagined for a liberal society and developed in the second half of the twentieth century, may at first sight appear closer to the ideals to which many progressives in society now aspire (Sarangi 1991). Developed during a period in which welfare capitalism seemed to offer some hope to society, Rawls' thesis is based on the concept of a fair and equitable society, in which each individual should be given an equal opportunity to thrive. A just society, for Rawls, is one that does not favor any individual as a consequence of an accident of their birth, but is one in which merit alone should contribute to each individual's outcome. However, Rawls still allows for social difference to be maintained, and he is accepting of inequalities in wealth and status, as long as these are fairly come by and that those who benefit from such outcomes utilize them for the common good – the goal of any just economic order being to continue to strive to maximize opportunities for those who are the least well-off.

The post-war period also seemed to offer a resurgence of democratic over totalitarian values and therefore, not unsurprisingly, Rawls envisaged a just society as inclusive of some kind of representative democratic and political structure in which those elected would maintain the conditions within which reciprocity, egalitarianism and fair distribution of resources would be assured. Citizens would abide by laws and regulations made by others because they would understand that it is in their best interests ultimately so to do.

Those who violate these regulations he considered to be of bad moral character or as exhibiting flawed reasoning. It is a hierarchical view of society in which the nation-state is placed at center-stage of penal policy, endowing it with the moral authority to punish transgressors – in his eyes this is done for the collective good and continued maintenance of the just society (Honig 1993). Looking back from our current vantage point, Rawls' ideas surrounding the beneficent state seem at best naïve and at worst as giving state violence a cover of moral authority.

As this paper's opening remarks reveal it has become increasingly clear that the political and economic systems upon which all these past formations of "just" society have based their visions of the common good have not served the planet nor its peoples well. Systems of private property have entrenched inequality and division and sustained harmful systems of class and privilege. The pursuit of profit above all social and environmental good has wreaked havoc on human and eco-systems alike which it may be difficult, if not impossible, to heal. Those forms of democracy which have dominated have afforded only a modicum of power to a narrowly-defined electorate and have proved both fragile and fractious. National government and state authority have more often been used to stake territorial, economic and political gain over others than to protect citizens. The state has been prepared to use significant and sustained violence against its own citizens to ensure the maintenance of the status quo. However, rather than achieve stability and security, we have stumbled from crisis to crisis.

A politically significant number of voices raised through the social movements of the twenty- first century are arguing that the time for reforms of the current system has long gone, that extant economic, political and social organizations should be set aside and new ones created. Our views of what a just society might look like must also be reconsidered. Recent social movements have created new sets of demands and many have attempted to build alternative forms of social organization which contain within them the seeds of how a newly emerged post-capitalist society might be organized (Webb 2019); as Ferrell and Greer (2009:5) note, "a shuddering social order can shake loose new hopes and possibilities." The following sections of this chapter look at a sample of the protest and resistance movements which have made significant contributions to building alternative visions over the last 2 decades and asks whether they might indeed be able to offer a set of ideas and possibilities which could take us to an alternative conceptualization of what the "justice" of tomorrow might become.

A justice without borders

A striking feature of many of the significant social movements which have emerged over the last 2 decades is the manner in which they have very quickly, and spontaneously, transcended national borders. Some of these movements have been explicitly global in their reach while others have grown internationally from more regional beginnings, as their cause speaks to those living within other nations.

The World and Regional Social Forums, for example, took an explicitly transnational perspective from their inception. They were organized in many different countries from 2001 to 2018 and at their height brought tens of thousands of people together to discuss alternatives to international capitalism and its domination of regional and national economies and cultures.[3] These forums were made up of disparate groups, from landless farm-workers and indigenous activists from the global south to a wide range of non-governmental organizations and trade unions from across the globe, each with their particular focus but coming together to fight for a common goal and in order to create and sustain a "global justice movement" (Hammond 2003).

Other movements, however, have arisen as a consequence of local events and circumstances but the injustices which they sought to reveal and overturn have been no respecters of national boundaries themselves. Black Lives Matter protests, for example, initially protesting manifestations of racism in the US, exploded across the globe precisely because racism is a structural and systemic failure of capitalism – a world system. As the violence of racism and white supremacy have been embedded in the practices of international and national economy-building, the protesters who came together in city after city under the banner of Black Lives Matter recognized that the conditions which they face locally were embedded historically in global practices. Imperialism and slavery were, and remain, global endeavors and Black Lives Matter have specifically stated that their movement must move beyond "narrow nationalism" if it is to succeed in its goals of "freedom, liberation and justice" (Black Lives Matter 2020). Less spectacularly but no less important, the call for a justice which is global in scope can also be seen in the many organizations which have rallied to the defense and protection of vast numbers of people seeking refuge and asylum from intolerable national conditions. These organizations have often manifested as small-scale, locally-based groups which form to welcome and provide for those who arrive after hazardous journeys over land and sea or who find themselves corralled into camps and unable to travel further to their preferred destinations (Theodorou 2018). Nevertheless, in their determination to assist those who have been displaced from their homelands and cut adrift into statelessness, the care that these activists show, often in the face of threats from national policies and border-enforcement agencies, is also intensely political and reflective of the need for a justice which is without borders. Far from being anchored in ideas of nation and self-interest they bring to the discussion the need to formulate a concept of global citizenship, mirroring the idea of global justice which has been central to so many social movements of our time.

A trauma-informed justice

Existing notions of justice, and the systems built to represent them, have developed little understanding of the profound effects of centuries of violence and discrimination on the shaping of the dominant institutions of today. Neither have they anything like an adequate comprehension of ways in which the legacy of a violent past weigh heavily on individuals, who may not have personally experienced violations such as war, slavery or state violence, but who are part of a social group within which there resides a "collective memory" of such injustices (Corredor et al 2018). As the recent discovery of the unmarked graves of First Nation children across Canada reveals, the suppression of such memories can take horrific, and sometimes physical, form (Lee 2021).

Those inhabiting the social spaces where such collective

memories are real and still raw feel the pain of living is at odds with their personal reality and therefore cannot fine peace or security. Campisi (2014) suggests that justice can only be attained where personal, collective and expert (or "historical") memories co-exist and are given equal value and attention. Only at this point can necessary healing occur and can there be any attempt at reparation for past wrongs. Only then may perpetrators of injustices be held accountable for their crimes, victims released from blame and there be a possibility that a public discourse can be created to restore the personal and psychological well-being of those negatively affected. Only in these circumstances can we begin to imagine a world where future harms might be prevented. Current conceptions of justice have been largely blind to this notion of collective memory and trauma. Legislative fixes against discrimination have been predicated on individual rather than collective recourse to what is deemed justice. Legislation has focused on outlawing individual acts of discrimination against named persons but has been slow to understand institutionalized forms of abuse, let alone begin to comprehend or deal with the historical legacies of violence which are collectively felt. Indeed, current systems of justice are likely to perceive the collective sharing of histories of violence as conspiracy and statutes of limitation severely restrict the time period in which an accusation of injustice can be considered. Movements such as Black Lives Matter, however, have shown us that it is only through an understanding of collective memory that demands for the removal of offending statues or the renaming of spaces to remove the constant triggers of damaging collective memories can be understood. Rather than erase memory and history, these actions declare that history should be publicly acknowledged and its legacy recognized, that collective memory should be more widely shared beyond the affected group and injustice challenged as a society. It is a call for a justice which can attempt to heal trauma and ensure that harmful practices are not repeated.

A public justice

The public occupation of private space has been a central feature of a number of social movements and demonstrates a rejection of models of private ownership. The refrain "Whose Streets? Our Streets!" is often adopted by activists to symbolize the taking control of physical spaces but also to signal that these spaces have been, albeit temporarily, freed from the control of the state and its agencies.

From event-based protests such as Critical Mass bike rides which take control of the streets as they momentarily pass through (Ferrell 2001) to the more open-ended occupations of the temporary autonomous zones inspired by the Indignados movement in Spain and later adopted to such effect by Occupy (Pejcha 2020), both public and privatized spaces are taken into a common ownership and declared open and available to a wider public to use as an arena or forum of protest. These are declared as communal sites without formal membership or residence where anyone can drop in and stay for as long as they desire. Bystanders are invited in and given a voice.

These spaces challenge the concept of private property and ownership in general and, in addition, are organized on an egalitarian basis wherein no one individual or group possesses power over others. The rules and regulations which are adopted in these zones in order to allow disparate individuals to live together harmoniously are based on the values of mutual respect and the adoption of an inclusive perspective. These are, therefore, "public" spaces in more than their physical presence and herald a future in which control is taken away from the few and where the many search for ways to forge a different notion of "the public" which exists outside of the narrow definitions supplied by the idea of citizenship bounded by the nation-state (Pejcha 2020).

The temporary autonomous zone embraces a much wider view of what is "public" than current paradigms allow. Alongside physical occupation of land and the declaration of autonomous living is the adoption of horizontal connections instead of hierarchical representation. An attempt is made to create spaces for public expression which may take many different forms. Art, music, culture, intellectual curiosity and utopian dreaming are all afforded a significant arena within which to develop a new and public form. Temporary autonomous zones allow a real taste of alternatives to extant structures and thereby offer a physical embodiment of new forms of public life which inspire new ways of thinking about the future.

The occupation of space for a wider political and social agenda has been considered a form of prefigurative politics in which attempts are made "to create a desired future world in the present" (Naegler 2018:507). Klein calls for "collective spaces in which to confront the raw terror of ecocide" as the only means to disturb prevailing paradigms and to articulate alternative worldviews (Klein 2015: 461). Nevertheless Pejcha (2020) contends that the temporary autonomous zone does not fashion itself as an experiment in utopia or as an attempt to offer a blueprint for a new way of living, merely that it reminds us that other ways of organizing society are both possible and desirable.

A participatory justice

That Black Lives Matter demonstrations rebounded across the globe in the midst of pandemic and lockdowns during the summer of 2020 took many by surprise. However, the social movements of recent decades have been characterized by methods of mass participation and direct action which have often erupted spontaneously and in rapid succession. The organizing principles of these movements demonstrate a commitment to mass action which is inspired by a non-violent civil disobedience organized from below (Extinction Rebellion 2021). As a consequence they do not follow top-down leadership models in which bureaucratic maneuvers can easily stifle action and dissipate anger.

Similar grassroots organizing can be seen in the Climate Emergency school strikes inspired by Greta Thunberg's Friday sit-downs. School students across many different countries heard the call for action and left school in their hundreds to emulate Thunberg, but there was no central organizational model for them to follow. Instead each strike acted as its own, leaderless, act of disobedience and an emancipatory moment of empowerment for the many who took part – what Piketty (2020) has termed "collective deliberation." These were actions which demanded that the climate crisis be recognized and acted upon, but were also forms of organizing that rejected existing forms of authority which had proved unwilling and unable to take action, despite their own experience and knowledge of global emergency (Fridays for Future 2021).

This form of activism displays more than the adoption of non-hierarchical organizational models, creating what Black Lives Matter activists have termed "a collective of liberators" where each individual plays an active and engaged part in the greater movement, street protest or moment of resistance (Black Lives Matter 2021). Extinction Rebellion too builds autonomous "chapters" which may act independently so long as they subscribe to and respect the commonly-held values "of radical ecological action and non-violence" (Burgess and Read 2020: 173).

These alternative democratic spaces are far from the models of democratic engagement which have hitherto been formulated to encourage and ensure civic engagement and the provision of justice. The forms of direct democracy which are adopted within these movements reach further than any previous forms of representative democracy, requiring in their place a deep level of engagement with both strategy and action. Decision-making is considered a collective process, with active engagement encouraged and where participants are given both the right and the means by which to engage in decision-making. Extinction Rebellion has employed Citizen Assemblies as its democratic model, highlighting the importance of the need to listen to disparate voices before decisions can be made (Extinction Rebellion 2021). These alternative democratic structures embed decision-making and power within the collective, rejecting internal hierarchies of power and denying the right of external authorities to limit actions which have been arrived at through direct and democratic decision-making (Patriquin 2019). They therefore offer new and powerful methods through which justice might be attained and sustained throughout society.

A justice sustained by mutuality

While contemporary mechanisms of justice foreground the rights of the individual there is in the significant social movements of today a clearly expressed element of mutuality and engagement with society outside of the narrow needs of the self. Over the last 2 decades there has been a growth of activism based on people "stepping in" as neo-liberalism dismantles what is left of the welfare state and the creation of what Robins and Newman (2021) have termed an "advice ecosystem" within which those who have access to skills and resources share these with others who have need of them. Robins and Newman point to the growth of refugee and migrant solidarity networks, debt crisis centers and food banks as well as the resurgence, in the UK, of the Law Centre movement to illustrate this move.

Many of these movements have likewise demonstrated an orientation toward mutuality and the provision of ongoing social support. The temporary autonomous zones created by movements such as Occupy and Indignados have been built around "egalitarian social relationships based on mutual aid" (Naegler 2018:509) within which both visitors and those resident have banded together to provide food, shelter and support networks to sustain the activists involved. Some have expanded beyond the immediate needs of the activist group to include the provision of advice and material benefits to all in need in their immediate environs. Indeed, when the Occupy spaces were cleared it was this provision which was carried on in their name (Pejcha 2020).

The mutual aid demonstrated within these sites was based on more than a charitable replacement for the care of the state but as a manifestation of the activists' rejection of both private interest and the profit motive. This mutual aid should therefore be read as a rejection of the marketization and commodification of care and its replacement by the provision of mutual support extended as an act of love and respect for others, without thought for self-interest. These are acts then, not of charity, but of solidarity and self-organization. They specifically reject the neoliberal idea of the "flawed citizen" (Bauman 1998) and replace this with one of the failed society.

These acts of self-organization, love and respect for those in need were also made apparent in the many small acts of kindness and support, neighbor to neighbor, which blossomed in pandemic lockdowns. At a time of medical and social crisis, with many states and economies paralyzed and unable to find functioning solutions, community self-help and organization filled a widening hole (Lashua et al 2021). There is much to be written about the resetting of lives forced by the global pandemic (Monbiot 2020) but that which is beginning to emerge reveals that life outside the normalized routines of the labor market can be inventive, supportive, reflective and characterized by care for others' well-being and can even embrace more regenerative and sustainable models of living (Lashua et al 2021). These values are a fundamental requirement of a decentralized, inclusive and mutualized approach to social relationships (ER 2021). All these examples suggest that just human relations will be sustained through mutuality rather than the constant threat of state-legitimized violence and force meted out by the police, prisons and military today (Graeber 2011).

A transformative justice

Calls for a world without borders (Social Forums), fair and equitable distribution of the world's resources (Make Poverty History, Drop the Debt), the common ownership of land (Indignados, Occupy), the adoption of sustainable consumption (Extinction Rebellion) and the defunding of the carceral state (Defund the Police, Black Lives Matter, Kill the Bill) have been a few of the most prominent demands which have been central to recent protests. Each of these, and more, represent fundamental challenges to the current system.

Beyond this demand for whole-scale system change for the future, however, a number of these movements have developed bold and radical demands which they are making in the here and now. These insist that the institutions which have entrenched power in the hands of the minority over the centuries cannot be corrected through piecemeal reforms. Therefore, transformative demands are made which go beyond the idea that these institutions can be rehabilitated or improved in any way – instead they must be replaced. Calls to defund the police, to abolish carceral systems, to overthrow patriarchy, to end the devastation of the planet should be read as radical abolitionist perspectives (Fleetwood and Lea 2021) wherever they are linked to the dismantling of structures of power.[4]

Many social movements which have emerged over the last 2 decades have offered a total critique of the dominant institutions and their values which have come to prominence in liberal democracies. The criminal justice system has already been exposed as one which is based on negative discrimination and stereotypes and which holds certain groups as suspect populations, surveilling, arresting and incarcerating young black men in particular in disproportionate numbers (Alexander 2010).

Movements such as Black Lives Matter were formed as a consequence of the state violence meted out to the black population of the US but in demanding justice for all have revealed that current political and legislative arrangements have continually favored certain groups and entrenched the rights of these groups while remaining oblivious to, or disregarding of, the grievances of others. They have revealed that such imbalances of power and interest are not exceptional but that liberal accounts of (in)justice have been unable to see the depth of institutionalized power or understand the persistence or magnitude of the problems which have been created (Delgado and Stefancic 2007).

Many now understand that the law, and social institutions more widely, do not speak for, or protect, them and that human rights mean nothing without access to justice and the means to enforce rights and have grievances heard. Liberal-democratic structures have proved inadequate in bringing about the real changes that are necessary and the institutions which they have spawned must be replaced, however 'natural' they may currently appear to be.

Concluding thoughts

This brief look at the values and alternative perspectives which might generate new understandings of how justice is defined and deployed in future societies is limited and partial but designed to open up a dialog for others to take further. According to Naegler (2018:507), "The post-crisis movements of the early 2010s have been widely perceived as a revival of anarchist politics," but they cannot be so easily categorized. While many of the prefigurative actions have indeed been claimed as inspired by anarchist philosophies this overview suggests that there is more complexity and diversity in the responses to the many crises engendered by the violence of neoliberalism. Solidarity and community are actually quite old concepts which are at the heart of other political and organizational responses to the toxicity of class-based societies, and have been seen as essential to humanity by people with a range of political perspectives and organizational forms, from trade unionism to mutual societies, co-operatives and experiments in utopian living.

This discussion should not be read either as an evaluation of the effectiveness or the "rightness" of the politics and organizational choices of the movements featured, nor an assessment of their authenticity or value. There are certainly criticisms to be made of the functioning on the ground of all of these moments and movements. Indeed, ideals of perfection cannot be attained in an imperfect world.

Rather, it should be read as an attempt through description to begin to explore and analyse the myriad ways in which significant reactions to the violence of the state and the economy might allow us to see a range of alternative possibilities. These examples allow a glimpse into what social beings can create when they attempt to throw off the shackles of past and present and imagine another world is possible for our future.

Chapter 9

A History and Analysis of Police in the United States: The Need for Community Control of Budget and Public Safety
Virginia Rodino

Racist beginnings of policing in the United States

Socialists understand that the police are the first line of defense for the ruling class. The first police force in the United States that employed full-time officers paid with public funding was created in Boston in 1838. It is no surprise that at the time, Boston was a large shipping commercial center and business owners felt compelled to protect their property from non-property owners, such as the Irish immigrants who lived in deprivation in the port city. During the same period in the South, police forces were created not for the protection of shipping interests, but for the preservation of the slave system. Slave patrols — organized groups of armed white men — enforced discipline on slaves in the antebellum South, chasing down runaways and quashing slave revolts. The first formal slave patrol was created in North and South Carolina in 1704. After the abolition of slavery, during Reconstruction, the slave patrols were transformed into sheriffs' departments, enforcing segregation and disenfranchizing freed slaves.[1] Describing this period, police studies expert at Eastern Kentucky University Victor E. Kappeler writes:

...New England settlers appointed Indian Constables to police Native Americans...the St Louis police were founded to protect residents from Native Americans...and many southern police departments began as slave patrols. In 1704, the colony of Carolina developed the nation's first slave patrol. Slave patrols helped to maintain the economic order and to assist the wealthy landowners in recovering and punishing slaves who...were considered property...The similarities between the slave patrols and modern American policing are too salient to dismiss or ignore. Hence, the slave patrol should be considered a forerunner of modern American law enforcement.[2]

Controlling unions, strikes and elections.

When workers began forming unions to fight for improved working conditions and fair wages, the police served the interests of the factory owners. By the late 1880s, all major US cities had police forces, borne out of fears of the unionizing of large waves of Catholic, Irish, Italian, German and Eastern European immigrants. At the same time, the police were used as a tool to wield political power. Olivia B. Waxman notes in a 2017 *Time Magazine* article that "the late 19th century was the era of political machines, so police captains and sergeants for each precinct were often picked by the local political party ward leader, who often owned taverns or ran street gangs that intimidated voters. They then were able to use police to harass opponents of that particular political party, or provide payoffs for officers to turn a blind eye to allow illegal drinking, gambling, and prostitution."[3] Police departments have a 400-year-old history of racism that is built upon the capitalists' need to control large, defiant crowds in order to protect their wealth, property and position in society.[4] Those in defiance have often been people of color, have often been immigrants and have always been members of the working class.

Why not reform?

The police have become increasingly militarized and have been trained to escalate rather than deescalate explosive situations. Because of the militarization of the police, how the police are trained, and who the individuals are who join the police,[5] ordinary people need to start to make the decisions about what safety looks like for their communities—we have to end this racist institution. We are seeing a revolutionary turn in the present movement to defund the police. BLM has moved from trying to make the police "nicer" to taking control of the capitalists' tool of disciplining us.

In his book *The End of Policing*, Vitale (2018) observed that:

> by conceptualizing the problem of policing as one of inadequate training and professionalization, reformers fail to directly address how the very nature of policing and the legal system serve to maintain and exacerbate racial inequality... At root, they fail to appreciate that the basic nature of the law and the police, since its earliest origins, is to be a tool for managing inequality and maintaining the status quo. Police reforms that fail to directly address this reality are doomed to reproduce it.[6]

As Brett Grant, director of research and policy for Voices for Racial Justice, a Minneapolis nonprofit, explained in a June 2020 *CS Monitor* interview, the campaign to defund the police represents nothing less than a chance to redefine the social contract. "We can't just focus on the police if we're talking about addressing systemic oppression and historical racism," he says. "We have to talk about inequities across society. We need to connect the dots."[7]

Victories by the Movement for Black Lives

The Brennan Center for Justice released a report in May 2021[8] detailing the reforms of state policing since the murder of George Floyd and the enormous uprisings that his killing sparked across the globe. The center first described the racial disparities among the targets of law enforcement and mass incarceration. Comprising only 13 percent of the US population,[9] black people face 21 percent of police contact,[10] make up 33 percent of people behind bars,[11] and are more than three times more likely to be killed by the police than their white counterparts.[12] The center also looked at how cities and counties have begun restructuring their budgets and how police are deployed in service of public safety. For example, Austin, Los Angeles, and at least 12 other cities, pledged to cut police budgets with plans to reinvest in community programs[13] such as supportive housing,[14] violence prevention[15] and other services.[16] Some local governments made commitments but then rescinded some of these promises: Minneapolis never disbanded its police department,[17] instead spending $6.4 million to recruit more officers.[18] San Francisco[19] launched crisis response teams to respond to behavioral health calls in lieu of police, and Berkeley[20] voted to limit law enforcement involvement in low-level traffic stops. Minneapolis[21] and other cities[22] made commitments to end or reduce police presence in schools. New York City,[23] home to the nation's largest police force, just became the first municipality to end qualified immunity for officers (joining Colorado[24] in doing so).

Importantly, community activists in Chicago won a seven-member Community Commission for Public Safety and Accountability which will be among the strongest community commissions in the country.[25] The commission creates direct community input and power, including being able to issue a vote of no confidence in the superintendent and to set policy, which could only be reversed by a mayoral veto. The mayoral veto could be overcome by a two-thirds council vote, enacting the policy anyway. The Brennan Center also listed the changes that occurred through ballot initiatives, with at least 18 of them strengthening law enforcement oversight nationwide, including in towns and cities like Kyle, Texas and Columbus, Ohio.[26]

Throughout the past year, at least 30 states and Washington, DC enacted one or more statewide legislative policing reforms,[27] ensuring greater policy uniformity within each jurisdiction. In

25 states and DC, at least one of three areas directly related to the circumstances of Floyd's killing were addressed in these pieces of legislation:

- use of force
- duty for officers to intervene, report or render medical aid in instances of police misconduct
- policies relating to law enforcement misconduct reporting and decertification (i.e., the revocation of a person's authorization to serve as a police officer)

Many states restricted or clarified the types of force that officers are permitted to use and in what circumstances, often spelling out that deadly force is justified only as a last resort after exhausting all nonviolent options. These states now require law enforcement agencies to report specified use of force incidents to the state or federal government. According to research by the Brennan Center, although the FBI maintains a national use of force database,[28] compliance is voluntary and only 5030 of the nation's 18,514 law enforcement agencies submitted[29] data in 2020.

The state of Colorado now bans[30] the use of deadly force to apprehend or arrest a person suspected only of minor or nonviolent offenses. Also, though many states permit the use of deadly force to prevent "escape," five states enacted restrictions or prohibitions on shooting at fleeing vehicles or suspects. Additionally, nine states and DC enacted complete bans on chokeholds and other neck restraints while eight states enacted legislation restricting their use to instances in which officers are legally justified to use deadly force.[31]

Some states, reported the Brennan Center, also focused on the standard by which use of force is reviewed, removing subjective knowledge from the equation to focus on whether the officer's actions were objectively reasonable or to lay out what alternatives the officer should have considered or circumstances that should affect the decision-making process. Meanwhile, states also passed laws to restrict law enforcement's use of less-lethal weapons such as rubber bullets, pepper spray and tear gas during demonstrations. At least seven states passed laws in 2020 and early 2021 restricting the rights of protesters, joining 23 states that made similar moves between 2015 and 2019.[32] In Florida and Oklahoma the backlash against protests went so far that legislators passed bills protecting drivers who deliberately hit protesters with their vehicles from liability.[33] From late May to early July 2020, at least 72 such incidents occurred, some involving police in law enforcement vehicles.[34]

Duty to intervene, report and render medical aid

Despite pleas from onlookers for the brutality to stop,[35] three officers watched or aided Derek Chauvin as he took George Floyd's life.[36] In reaction, 12 states and DC created a duty for law enforcement officers to intervene in cases of excessive or illegal force or misconduct,[37] with penalties for officers who fail to do so ranging from discretionary decertification to criminal liability. All but one state also included a requirement for officers to report excessive force or misconduct to supervisors. And eight states now have a duty to render medical aid for anyone under an officer's custody or care.

Even without state action, many localities are taking the matter into their own hands: Twenty-one of the nation's 100 largest police agencies have adopted duty to intervene policies since June 5, 2020, bringing the total to 72 agencies.[38] Although the details of each law vary, some states now require officers to intervene, report or render medical aid when witnessing the use of chokeholds. Others apply this duty to a broader set of misconduct behaviors, including any use of excessive force, assault, bribery, theft or tampering with evidence.

Decertification processes and centralized misconduct reporting

Prior to killing George Floyd, Derek Chauvin had been the subject of 22 misconduct complaints or internal investigations.[39] Other officers involved in other high-profile killings, like those of Eric Garner[40] and Tamir Rice,[41] also have histories of past misconduct. Timothy Loehmann, the Cleveland officer who shot and killed Rice, had been found "unfit" to carry out his duties by a police department he previously worked for.[42] Without statewide certification and decertification processes, or an easy way to look up prior misconduct, "wandering officers" like Loehmann can travel from department to department unnoticed.[43] To remove officers who are deemed unfit to serve and more closely monitor the prevalence and types of police misconduct, at least 14 states enacted laws in 2020-2021 that established or strengthened law enforcement decertification processes, and 13 states added laws requiring law enforcement agencies to report misconduct data to the state.[44] Massachusetts and Hawaii created their first centralized bodies tasked with decertifying law enforcement officers, leaving only California, New Jersey, Rhode Island and DC lacking this authority.[45] Twelve states created additional statutory grounds for the suspension or revocation of law enforcement officers' certifications.[46] Massachusetts, for example, will now automatically revoke officer certifications for making false arrests, creating or using falsified evidence, destroying evidence, perpetrating a hate crime, using excessive force that results in death or serious bodily injury, and more.

New laws also mandate that law enforcement agencies report specified data to the state, such as the names of officers who resign while under investigation, are terminated for cause or receive misconduct allegations. And ten states have created databases or now require state-level maintenance of data regarding officer decertifications, disciplinary actions or misconduct, with some mandating public access. With these additions, 11 states now maintain public databases containing officer misconduct records,[47] although more states—such as Colorado—have mandated that these records be available to the public upon request.[48] Only in Indiana, Massachusetts and Washington do new laws require reporting to the National Decertification Index,[49] the voluntary national database that houses information on decertified officers.[50]

National Public Radio also took a look at what has changed or not at the one-year anniversary of Floyd's murder. It interviewed Bowling State University criminologist Philip Stinson, who for the past 15 years has been painstakingly maintaining one of the country's most thorough databases of information on police officers charged with on-duty killings.[51] Stinson described The Henry A. Wallace Police Crime Database, a collection of more than 18,000 cases since 2005 of officers across the country who have been arrested. About 1100 new cases are added each and every year. In that exhaustive database of nearly 20,000 officers arrested, fewer than 150 have been charged with murder or manslaughter. Only seven or eight of those officers to date have actually been convicted of murder.

Defunding and abolition is the revolutionary turn we need

Divesting from the police and investing in other social programs that communities want and need is a serious revolutionary step forward, showing ordinary people that they can control the budgets for their states and municipalities and take over state apparatuses. Students on college campuses, parents and teachers in schools, and working families in communities across the country are eliminating one of the most powerful and reactionary institutions on the planet—the militarized US police force. They are proving to themselves and others that it is possible to take complete control over significant parts of society and that the existence of police is not an innate, unchangeable factor. By empowering ordinary people with the ability to dismantle this racist and corrupt institution, the cracks are forced even wider to reveal how unnatural the entire system is. We are seeing how we can control the wealth we produce.

In March 2021 *The Guardian* reported that more than 20 major cities[52] have reduced their police budgets in some form,[53] an unprecedented trend. In 2020 budget votes, advocacy groups won more than $840 million in direct cuts from US police departments and at least $160 million investments in community services, according to an analysis by Interrupting Criminalization, an initiative at the Barnard Center for Research on Women.[54]

In 25 cities, such as Denver[55] and Oakland,[56] officials moved to remove police from schools, saving an additional $34m. Portland, Oregon cut $15 million from its budget and disbanded a gun violence reduction unit and transit team that had both long been accused of over-policing black communities.[57] San Francisco officials pledged to divest $120 million from police over 2 years with plans to invest in health programs and workforce training.[58] Minneapolis is using police cuts to launch a mental health team to respond to certain 911 calls.[59] Austin, Texas directly cut about $20 million from the police department, and moved $80 million from the agency by shifting certain services out of law enforcement. The city has gone from spending 40 percent of its $1.1 billion general fund on police to now allocating about 26 percent to law enforcement.[60]

New York, Los Angeles, Chicago, Seattle,[61] Milwaukee, Philadelphia, Baltimore and a dozen other cities have all also reduced police spending. More than 100 community groups and unions in Chicago helped craft and push the passage of a historic civilian policing oversight commission in July 2021, among the strongest community commissions in the country. The ordinance gives direct community input and power, including being able to issue a vote of no confidence in the superintendent and to set policy, which could only be reversed by a mayoral veto. Then, the commission could overcome that veto and enact the policy anyway with a two-thirds council vote.[62]

Challenges to Reimagining Real Public Safety

However, this campaign for change faces major roadblocks: In May 2021, President Joe Biden announced a 5-point strategy to fund more police, and urged cities and states to use $350 billion of funding from a Covid-19 relief bill on public safety efforts, including adding more police officers, even beyond pre-pandemic levels. Echoing sentiments he has expressed his entire political career, Biden exclaimed, "This is not a time to turn our backs on law enforcement or our communities." As a senator, Biden had written a 1994 crime bill that allowed for the mass incarceration of black people.[63]

Another of the greatest obstacles to defunding law enforcement agencies are powerful police unions, which have long opposed reforms and negotiated strong protections in their contracts that typically make it impossible for cities to terminate or lay off officers. Unions have launched aggressive PR campaigns to counter the movement. In Austin, the Texas Municipal Police Association (TMPA) created highway billboards saying "Warning! Austin Police Defunded, Enter at Your Own Risk" and "Limited Support Next 20 Miles" – and put up the signs in September, before the new budget had gone into effect.[64] The Republican governor of Texas, Greg Abbott, has also repeatedly threatened to try to force Austin to restore its police budget through legislation,[65] and other state Republicans have spread misinformation about crime rates in the city.[66]

In July of 2020, as Black Lives Matter protests against police violence were sweeping America, the AFL-CIO, a coalition of unions representing nearly 15 million people, formed a "Racial Justice Task Force" to formulate the plan for "taking concrete action to address America's long history of racism and police violence against Black people."[67] In early May 2021, *In These Times* obtained and published excerpts of an unreleased draft version of the report. The substance of the final report's recommendations have not changed since then: it calls for the creation of a new training and enforcement program administered by police unions to weed out bad officers, effectively aiming to make police unions themselves the primary mechanism for reforming police practices. It amounts to a definitive embrace of the importance of police unions to the labor movement, and a rejection of calls from progressive union members for the AFL-CIO to separate itself from police unions.[68] The report also rejects the idea of defunding the police, and calls instead for additional funding. Unsurprising, since the subcommittee itself was made up solely of unions that represent police members.

During the insurrection at the US Capitol on January 6, 2021, and its aftermath, the racist roots of the nation's police force and its interconnectedness with the white supremacist movement was broadcast to the world. Numerous media outlets reported on how at least 13 off-duty police officers[69]— with some saying as high as 31[70]—participated in the attack on the Capitol which killed five people. While many of the police participants were not charged after internal investigations, it is not difficult to surmise that many more were missed altogether in the investigations.

Conclusion

Despite this pushback and back-sliding, communities across the country have made great strides in 2020 and 2021 in dismantling the racist police institution. Police forces are not a natural part of human nature or human society, but were created to protect the interests of the ruling classes in the capitalist economic system in which we live. The police arose from the formation of the state, which itself is a manifestation of antagonisms among classes, between workers and those who own the workplaces and dictate the conditions of these workplaces—and the struggle by the workers to change those conditions. The struggle to defund and to abolish police forces is a key component of class struggle, a result of the oppressed in our society struggling to create something new that is "capable of serving the exploited instead of the exploiters."[71] The fight by ordinary people in communities across the globe who are resisting the oppression and misery caused by the police is inseparable from the struggle to build a better world.

Chapter 10

Why Defund the Police?
Brian Richardson

2020 was an extraordinary year. At its outset very few people had heard of coronavirus, let alone the variant of it that had emerged the previous year. By the end of January it was still regarded as a dim and distant contagion, confined to an obscure city in China. Within 2 months, however, much of the world was in lockdown as Covid–19 developed into a global pandemic. Normally bustling and vibrant city centers were transformed into ghost towns as we were forced to limit contact with the outside world and live in isolated units. It was all the more remarkable then that within another couple of months a movement erupted whose size compared favorably with the civil rights and Black Power struggles that had been such a powerful feature of the United States in the 1950s and 60s.

Black Lives Matter (BLM) was not an entirely new movement. It had been initiated in 2013 by Alicia Garza, Patrice Cullers and Opal Tomato in the aftermath of the acquittal of vigilante George Zimmerman for the 2012 killing of 17-year-old Trayvon Martin in Sanford, Florida. In the years that followed it developed into a decentralized and international network as the killings of people like Michael Brown, Tamir Rice, Walter Scott and Sandra Bland highlighted the issue of racism and police brutality. As with any movement, BLM has ebbed and flowed in the years since its inception. It has been suggested that 2016 was both the year "Black Lives Matter protesters returned to the streets" and "the year (BLM) went global." The deaths of Alton Sterling and Philando Castile in Louisiana and Minnesota were among those that caused this uproar, and Britain, France, Australia and Brazil were just a few of the countries where protests erupted and chapters were formed. Impressive though all of these were, they are now completely overshadowed by the events of 2020.

The murder of George Floyd

The fact of George Floyd's death on 25 May 2020 was entirely predictable. As initiatives like *The Guardian* newspaper's "The Counted" have illustrated, 1000 plus deaths at the hands of the police per annum is routine.[1] Despite the promise that "change had come to America" that accompanied Barack Obama's election in 2008, his 8 years in the White House did little to shift the disproportionate number of black men among that grim total. It was no surprise that such brutality continued during Donald Trump's divisive presidency. Nor in this particular context was there even anything surprising or novel about the fact that Floyd's death was recorded and broadcast or about the dying man's final words. Back in 2014 Eric Garner had gasped "I can't breathe" as he was wrestled to the ground and choked to death by New York City police officers for the alleged crime of selling loose, untaxed cigarettes. Every sudden, violent death is shocking for those who witness or become aware of it. The fatal shooting of 26-year-old Breonna Taylor at her partner's home by two white plain-clothed policemen on March 13, 2020 was no less of an atrocity than Floyd's. It has rightly been cited by a number of campaigners to highlight the fact that black women are victimized too. Clearly, however, for millions of people there was something particularly harrowing about the sight of a forty something man begging for his mother as the life was crushed out of him over the course of 9 painstaking minutes.

So it was that in the days, weeks and months that followed, millions of people erupted onto and occupied the streets. In the United States alone, an estimated 26 million people participated in protests in the first few weeks after Floyd's killing.[2] By early autumn, over 2000 demonstrations had been held with every US state affected. Moreover, seasoned veterans such as the professors August Nimtz and Angela Davis have opined that the 2020 uprisings were more diverse than those that they participated in during the heady days of the 1960s. Davis is a particularly iconic figure. In the early 1970s she was charged with, among other things, conspiracy to murder for her alleged role in a shootout at a court in Marin County California. Following this she was declared a public enemy after going on the run. She was eventually acquitted of all charges and as such is well placed to comment on the inconsistencies of the criminal justice system. In a characteristically astute intervention, Davis spoke at a rally organized by the International Longshore and Warehouse Union on 19 June 2020. This was significant for a number of reasons. The union had called strike action in support of George Floyd, and Davis's presence reflected her long-term commitment to workers self-activity. Moreover, the date is known as Juneteenth and was a national holiday in many states to commemorate the emancipation of slaves in 1865.[3] Davis celebrated the BLM struggle declaring that she was "just so happy to have lived long enough to witness this moment." But she also recognized that this was only a start and that the hard work of transforming an "extraordinary moment"[4] into a movement for lasting change still lay ahead:

The protests offered people an opportunity to join in this collective demand to bring about deep change, radical change. Defund the police, abolish policing as we know it now. These are the same arguments that we've been making for such a long time about the prison system and the whole criminal justice system. It was as if all of these decades of work by so many people, who received no credit at all, came to fruition.[5]

Davis was careful to avoid lecturing the new generation. She recognized that they must find their own way of organizing and articulate their own demands. At the same time, however, she noted that there is a continuity with the struggles of the past and lessons that can be learned by standing on the shoulders of the giants that have gone before. Indeed she used this very phrase to suggest that in so doing, Generation Z activists will be able to see further and more clearly than their twentieth-century counterparts. As Davis's comment suggests, a very specific focus on the oppressive role of the police has long been a central feature of the activities of political campaigners. She herself was very briefly a member of the Black Panther Party for Self Defense (BPP) and remained sympathetic after her departure. Founded in Oakland, California by law students Huey P Newton and Bobby Seale, the BPP was established "in the spirit" of Malcolm X and a central feature of their activity involved confronting the police and driving them out of black communities.[6]

Britain

As had been the case in 2016, the 2020 BLM protests were not confined to the United States. They broke out across the globe taking in 60 countries in all continents apart from Antarctica[7] and their impact ricocheted back to their point of origin. A vivid example of this is provided by Britain. Over 200,000 people are estimated to have protested in cities, towns and even villages throughout the summer. Arguably the most newsworthy demonstration took place on 7 June when protesters in Bristol tore down a statue of slaveholder Edward Colston and dumped it in the River Avon. Three days later that symbolic act was referred to by no less a figure than Rev Al Sharpton at the funeral of the very victim whose death had sparked the worldwide uprising. As with the United States, the scale, intensity and diversity of the activities in Britain was far greater than in 2016. What was also clear was that these demonstrations were not simply acts of solidarity with George Floyd. Important though that was, there was also a very clear focus on perceived injustices on the domestic front.

The charity INQUEST was founded in 1981 in the wake of the killing of anti-racist activist Blair Peach. The 33-year-old teacher was bludgeoned by Metropolitan Police Special Patrol Group officers on a demonstration against the far-right National Front in Southall, west London in April 1979 and his death from the injuries he suffered sparked a long-running campaign. Since that time INQUEST has become a widely respected institution providing expertise on state-related deaths and their investigations to bereaved people, lawyers, advice and support agencies, the media and politicians. At the time of writing, INQUEST reported that there had been 1793 deaths "in police custody or otherwise following contact with police in England and Wales since 1990."[8] INQUEST's research suggests that 14 percent of the deaths in police custody over that period have been people of "Black, Asian and Minoritised Ethnicities." This figure is in line with the 2011 census, but INQUEST goes on to note that:

- However, people with Black, Asian and Minoritised Ethnicities (BAME) die disproportionately as a result of use of force or restraint by the police, raising serious questions of institutional racism as a contributory factor in their deaths.
- The proportion of BAME deaths in custody where restraint is a feature is over two times greater than it is in other deaths in custody
- The proportion of BAME deaths in custody where use of force is a feature is over two times greater than it is in other deaths in custody
- The proportion of BAME deaths in custody where mental health-related issues are a feature is nearly two times greater than it is in other deaths in custody[9]

Clearly this level of fatal interaction with the police is not on the same scale as in the United States. It is not insignificant, however, and there was an acute consciousness of this on display in the mobilizations in Britain. Many of those that protested did so with the names of some of those victims displayed on placards, chanted them as they marched and read them out as they rallied. These actions gave the lie to the assertion that they were simply mimicking the US BLM movement and the patronizing suggestion that they neither knew nor cared about victims of injustice in Britain.

There is in fact a history of anti-racist protest in Britain that dates back to before the foundation of INQUEST and the statistics that its research cites. Much of it was recorded contemporaneously by the journal *Race Today*. Originally published by the liberal Institute of Race Relations in 1969, it was transformed into a more radical publication run by a black-led collective from 1973 and edited by Darcus Howe. The Trinidadian-born activist had arrived in the UK in 1962 and soon followed in the footsteps of his uncle, the great Marxist intellectual CLR James, as a writer, commentator and campaigner. Howe's 1988 publication *From Bobby to Babylon – Blacks and the British Police* brought together a series of articles he had written for *Race Today* during a period of heightened tension in the 1980s. The essays chart the changing relationship between Britain's black communities and the police in the decades following the arrival of the Empire Windrush in 1948.

By the 1950s and with the expansion of radio and television to a mass audience in Britain, there was a concerted effort to portray the police as a friendly neighborhood force. The most popular expression of this was the kindly Constable George Dixon in the long running BBC TV series *Dixon of Dock Green*.[10] The term "Bobby" is a reference to Sir Robert Peel, the Home Secretary who founded the first police force, London's Metropolitan Police, in 1829. It has subsequently become widely adopted as an affectionate nickname for police officers. Such ingrained respect for those in authority extended to the growing number of immigrants who arrived from Caribbean islands that had been British colonies. They had been encouraged to regard Britain as their "Mother Country" and anticipated a warm and protective embrace from its institutions when they reached its shores. Instead, they were met with suspicion and hostility despite having come to assist in rebuilding an economy that had been devastated by the Second World War. That ostracism was encapsulated in slogans declaring "No Blacks, No Dogs, No Irish" when they sought accommodation.

On occasion the hostility spilled over into violence, most infamously in the Notting Hill area of west London in 1958. Instead of defending these newly arrived British citizens, the police frequently stood by, ignored or, worse, encouraged the violence. By the time Howe came to write the articles that were eventually published in *From Bobby to Babylon*, the harsh realities of their interactions with the police had led Britain's black communities to classify them in more sinister terms. "Babylon" was a word widely used by the increasingly influential and growing population of Rastafarians and adopted by black youth to classify their experience of oppression generally and those they regarded as responsible for enforcing it specifically, namely the police.

Howe was not simply commentating on these matters, the Race Today Collective was actively involved in community campaigning and he was therefore also speaking from the perspective of a leading participant. Even before the establishment of the Collective, Howe had gravitated toward an old friend and fellow Trinidadian Frank Crichlow, the proprietor of two restaurants in west London, firstly, El Rio and then from 1968, the Mangrove in All Saints Road, Notting Hill. Crichlow's establishments were to become places of great notoriety. The BBC's Television Centre was located nearby in White City and the restaurants were soon frequented by adventurous socialites. The controversial and ultimately disgraced Conservative cabinet monster John Profumo and his lover Christine Keeler were among those that frequented El Rio. Its successor attracted the likes of Nina Simone, Jimi Hendrix, Marvin Gaye, Diana Ross, Bob Marley and Vanessa Redgrave. As Oscar winning film director Steve McQueen's BBC TV series *Small Axe* (2020) illustrated, the racial intermixing that characterized Mangrove and the presence of so-called young, black hustlers was met with deep disapproval by the police. They regarded Mangrove as "a haunt for criminals, prostitutes and ponces" and raided the premises on 12 occasions between January 1969 and July 1970. The rationale for this was that it was being used as a drugs den. No evidence of this was ever found but the police's determination to criminalize Crichlow was relentless. He was eventually pursued for a series of petty licensing irregularities such as allowing dancing and providing food and tea after 11pm. Howe had worked at Mangrove for a period of time, but was back in Trinidad when the raids were at their height. When he returned and found out about the police's activities he persuaded Crichlow that they should organize a protest.

The demonstration took place on August 9, 1970 and was a modest affair which mobilized around 150 vociferous participants. They were confronted by 700 police who proceeded to arrest 19 people. Nine of them, including Crichlow and Howe, were subsequently prosecuted for various offenses including conspiring to incite a riot, affray and assaulting police officers. They became known as the Mangrove Nine and their subsequent trial is widely recognized as one of the great episodes in recent British legal history.

Like his uncle, James, before him, Howe had benefited from a relatively privileged and quintessentially British middle-class education at Queen's Royal College, the most prestigious school in Trinidad. He also had a grounding in English law from a period of study at Middle Temple. Along with co-defendant Althea Lecointe Jones who also had some legal training Howe chose to conduct his own defense at trial though the two did consult and collaborate with Ian Macdonald who was representing other defendants. This was an extremely high-risk strategy given the seriousness of the charges and the lengthy prison terms they could expect if convicted. Howe recalled the episode in an essay entitled *Cause for Concern – In the Public Eye,* and explained that one of the defendants' tactics was to demand an all-black jury on the grounds that only such a panel represented the peers by whom they should be tried. Their tenacity is highlighted by the fact that they argued this preliminary point for 2 days before the commencement of the trial. The court ruled against them, but the tactic succeeded in putting the prosecution on the defensive and highlighting the political nature of the police conduct. Eventually the defendants were able to dismiss 63 prospective jurors and ensure that there were two black people on the jury.

The trial of the Mangrove Nine took place at the Central Criminal Court, Old Bailey, the most senior crown court in England and Wales, and lasted for 55 days. At its conclusion all nine defendants were acquitted of riot. Five of them, including both Crichlow and Howe, were acquitted of all other charges.

The Mangrove Nine trial did not prove to be the end of either Howe or Crichlow's dealings with the police, however. Throughout the 1970s they continued to face surveillance, arrest and prosecution, not least because of their involvement in the Notting Hill Carnival. Ironically the carnival itself had evolved out of a commitment by another Trinidadian socialist, Claudia Jones, to promote positive community relations in the aftermath of the race riots referred to earlier in this chapter. The first event in 1959 had been held at St Pancras Town Hall, but following the organization of an outdoor festival by Rhuanne Laslett, in 1966, a celebration in the streets of Notting Hill became an annual fixture. By the mid-1970s, however, a vocal and influential minority of local residents were expressing their opposition to Carnival and lobbying to have it removed from the streets of Notting Hill. The Mangrove restaurant was at the heart of the community and played a central role in promoting the event. The high-profile involvement of both Howe and Crichlow gave the police an incentive to redress the balance after the infamy of the Mangrove Trial. It was in these circumstances that the 1976 carnival became the scene of a major confrontation between the police and London's black communities. A total of 3000 officers were on duty that August Bank Holiday, a ten-fold increase on previous years. The specific cause of the confrontation is unknown, though an attempt to arrest pickpockets is the most widely cited reason. Whatever the catalyst, it culminated in what is characterized as a riot with over 100 police officers and 60 civilians taken to hospital. Seventeen black youths were eventually charged with a total of 79 offenses. Ultimately just two were convicted of offenses related to the carnival. In the years that followed there were further clashes that have permanently scarred its reputation. By the twenty-first century, Carnival had become widely recognized as Europe's biggest open-air event, but such declarations are always supplemented with expressions of concern about menace and criminality.

New Cross Fire – 1981

The notion that black communities are disproportionately criminalized but marginalized and ignored when they themselves are the victims of crime is highlighted by one of the most notorious and harrowing events that occurred at the start of the 1980s. A fire at a house party in New Cross, southeast London on 18 January, 1981 left 13 young people dead. Party goers, their families and friends were convinced that this was a racist firebombing and that the police should conduct a serious murder inquiry. The investigation that did take place was widely considered to be complacent, dismissive and consequently ineffective. The anger that this generated prompted Howe's Race Today Collective and others to organize a 20,000 strong weekday Black People's Day of Action that rallied around the slogan "13 dead nothing said!" Forty years later a sense of injustice about those events prevails.

1981 Uprisings

Within 2 months of the Black People's Day of Action, the Brixton area of south London, one of the major centers of Caribbean immigration, had erupted in anger at the police. At the beginning of April the force launched an operation in the London borough of Lambeth. Its codename, "Swamp 81," had racial connotations that were not lost on the community. "Swamp" was the very word used by the then opposition leader Margaret Thatcher in a highly controversial 1978 interview to describe the supposedly negative impact of mass immigration. By 1981 Thatcher was in office as prime minister, the UK economy was sinking deep into recession and there were widening social divisions. It was in those circumstances of high tension that over 2000 police swept into Lambeth. The legal basis for Operation Swamp was the Vagrancy Act, a piece of legislation dating back to 1824. Its introductory text states that it is: "An Act for the Punishment of idle and disorderly Persons, and Rogues and Vagabonds, in England"[11]

Section 4 permits police to stop and search people on suspicion of committing an offense:

every suspected person or reputed thief, frequenting any river, canal, or navigable stream, dock, or basin, or any quay, wharf, or warehouse near or adjoining thereto, or any street, highway, or avenue leading thereto, or any place of public resort, or any avenue leading thereto, or any street, or any highway or any place adjacent to a street or highway; with intent to commit an arrestable offence, indictable offence; and every person apprehended as an idle and disorderly person, and violently resisting any constable, or other peace officer so apprehending him or her, and being subsequently convicted of the offence for which he or she shall have been so apprehended; shall be deemed a rogue and vagabond, within the true intent and meaning of this Act; and, subject to section 70 of The Criminal Justice Act 1982, it shall be lawful for any justice of the peace to commit such offender (being thereof convicted before him by the confession of such offender, or by the evidence on oath of one or more credible witness or witnesses,) to the house of correction... for any time not exceeding three calendar months

The antiquated language gives a sense of the provisions, but the Act remains good law and by 1981 "Sus" as it became known was notorious and widely despised in inner-city communities.[12]

As Operation Swamp swung into action 900 people were stopped and 82 arrested. By 10 April resentment was transformed into outrage as officers sought to arrest a black youth called Michael Bailey. The streets erupted in an explosion that lasted for 3 days. Two hundred and ninety-nine police officers were injured as were around 65 members of the public. Two days later the then Home Secretary William Whitelaw commissioned the Law Lord Leslie Scarman to "inquire urgently into the serious disorder in Brixton and to report, with the power to make recommendations." Scarman's report was published in November but the scale of anger is highlighted by the fact that between times further serious outbreaks had occurred in a number of towns and major cities including Southall in west London, Toxteth in Liverpool, Moss Side in Manchester, Handsworth in Birmingham and Chapeltown, Leeds.

From the outset Scarman was challenged to recognize the existence of institutional racism, a concept which, though seemingly academic and hypothetical, has its origins in the radical struggles of the 1960s. The term was first coined by the Black Power activists Kwame Ture (formerly Stokely Carmichael) and Charles Murray. At the start of their seminal publication *Black Power – The Politics of Liberation in America* published in 1967, they distinguish between two types of racism, arguing that:

> Racism is both overt and covert. It takes two, closely related forms: individual whites acting against individual blacks, and acts of the total white community against the black community. We call these individual and institutional racism. The first consists of overt acts by individuals, which cause death, injury or the violent destruction of property. This type can be recorded by television cameras; it can frequently be observed in the process of commission. The second type is less overt, far more subtle, less identifiable in terms of specific individuals committing the acts but it is no less destructive of human life. The second type originates in the operation of the established and respect forces of society, and thus receives far less public condemnation than the first type.[13]

It was suggested to Scarman that it was this latter type of racism that characterized the attitude of the police and which lay behind the toxic relationship that had led to the disturbances. His conclusion was highly controversial. He did not deny the existence of racism and stated very clearly that: "Racial prejudice does manifest itself occasionally in the behavior of a few officers on the streets...Racially prejudiced behavior by officers below the level of senior direction of the force is not common; but it does occur, and every instance of it has an immense impact on the community's attitudes and beliefs."[14] He added, however, that: "I find that the direction and policies of the Metropolitan Police Service are not racist. But racial prejudice does manifest itself occasionally in the behavior of a few officers on the streets."[15]

And specifically on the question of institutional racism Scarman declared:

> It was alleged by some of those who made representations to me that Britain is an institutionally racist society. If by that it is meant that it is a society that knowingly, as a matter of policy, discriminates against black people, I reject the allegation. If, however, the suggestion being made is that practices may be adopted by public bodies as well as by private individuals which are unwittingly discriminatory against black people, then this is an allegation which deserves serious consideration, and where proved, swift remedy[16]

The headline that history has recorded is that Scarman concluded that the problem was simply one of a few rotten apples in an otherwise wholesome barrel. This was an outcome that was met with scorn and derision in the affected communities, not least by Howe who, in a chapter entitled *Scarman: Failing to Grasp the Nettle*, dismissed his package of recommendations as "mere tinkering." The essay concludes with the prophecy that, "Lord Scarman's failure to act...has ensured that those forms which appeared in embryo on the streets of Britain's cities must necessarily develop into full blown manifestations in the not too distant future."[17]

1985 – The return of riots

What happened just 4 years later may not have been quite as dramatic as Howe predicted, but there certainly were further serious outbursts of unrest prompted by the behavior of the police. Once again, Brixton was the site of the initial outburst. On 28 September 1985, police raided 22 Normandy Road, seeking to arrest 21-year-old Michael Groce for armed robbery. The suspect was not present and the allegations against him were eventually abandoned. During the raid, however, a shot was fired that struck his mother, Dorothy "Cherry" Groce, in the shoulder. She was paralyzed from the chest down and confined to a wheelchair for the remaining 26 years of her life. A pathologist ruled that her death was directly related to the injuries she had suffered, and in 2014 an inquest jury concluded that there had been eight procedural flaws in the police operation and that "her subsequent death was contributed to by failures in the planning and implementation of the raid."[18] In the wake of the raid an upsurge lasting 2 days broke out during which 43 civilians and 10 police officers were injured. Less than one week later there was a similar uprising on a notorious deprived estate in Tottenham, north London. The Broadwater Farm riot and its aftermath are widely regarded as one of the seminal episodes in postwar black British history. Without doubt it is one which encapsulates a number of the reasons why the relationship between the police and sections of Britain's black community are so fractious.

On 5 October, 24-year-old Floyd Jarrett was arrested on suspicion of theft and assault, charges which he was later acquitted of. That evening police officers raided the home of his 49-year-old mother, Cynthia Jarrett, in search of the property they believed he had stolen. No stolen items were found but the shock caused by police officers bursting into her home caused Mrs Jarrett to suffer a fatal heart attack. The following evening the estate erupted, leading to the hospitalization of 58 police officers and 24 civilians. One officer, Police Constable Keith Blakelock, was stabbed to death.

In such circumstances, local political leaders are expected to show their mettle. The newly elected Labour Party leader of Haringey council was a forceful figure. Bernie Grant was also black and from an immigrant background. He had been born in what was then British Guiana but moved to Britain in the early 1960s. The exact words that he used in the aftermath of the riots is a matter of dispute, but it was widely reported that he declared that, "The police got a bloody good hiding." Whatever the truth or otherwise of that declaration, three things are indisputable. First, Grant apologized to the family of PC Blakelock for any offense caused. Second and irrespective of his sympathy for the fallen officer, he refused to condemn the young people who rose up. Third and regardless of his words and actions, the press and his political opponents sought to condemn him. Not least among his critics was the prime minister, Margaret Thatcher, who happened to be at the Conservative Party Conference as events unfolded and was engaged in a determined effort to discredit and defund Labour-controlled local authorities. It is a measure of the esteem within which Grant was held, as well as a barometer of the attitude of many toward the police, that the local electorate ignored such attacks and supported a politician who had stood by them. Less than 2 years after the riot and with reminders of his words ringing in his ears on the campaign trail, Grant was voted into parliament in the very same Tottenham constituency that houses Broadwater Farm. He retained the seat right up until his premature death in 2000.

Meanwhile in the wake of the riot the police were determined to secure a conviction for the killing of PC Blakelock. This led to the arrest and prosecution of a high-profile local figure, Winston Silcott, along with five others. The charges against three youths were dismissed by a judge because of the circumstances in which they were interrogated. Silcott, Engin Raghip and Mark Braithwaite were tried, however, convicted and sentenced to life imprisonment in March 1987. After serving over 4 years the Court of Appeal quashed the convictions of all three men in November 1991 after it was found that the notes of the police interrogations – which was the only evidence against them – had been interfered with.

Just one year later, the brutal murder of 20-year-old Lynette White in Cardiff sparked an episode that reinforced suspicion and mistrust of the police. In the immediate aftermath of the crime, the prime suspect was described as a bloodstained and disheveled white man in his mid-30s. Twenty-two months later, with pressure on to progress the case, five black and mixed-race men were arrested and charged. This was despite the fact that no forensic evidence linking them to the scene was ever found. Three of the five, White's boyfriend Stephen Miller, Yusuf Abdullahi and Anthony Paris, were convicted and, like the Tottenham Three, sentenced to life imprisonment. The two acquitted men, John Actie and his cousin Ronnie, had spent 2 years in custody on remand and never got their lives fully back on track.

A three-part BBC TV documentary, *A Killing in Tiger Bay* (2021), also shows that the police investigation was a travesty, motivated by a desire to settle scores with petty criminals and gentrify an area of the city inhabited by poor and marginalized black and white people rather than to deliver justice to the family and friends of Lynette White. Miller was repeatedly interviewed, denied the murder over 300 times but was eventually browbeaten and bullied until he confessed and implicated the others. Meanwhile, the evidence of 13 witnesses corroborating Abdullahi's claim that he was working on a ship 8 miles away from the murder scene was withheld from his lawyers. These facts eventually came out at a Court of Appeal hearing in 1992 at which the convictions of the Cardiff Three were quashed. Despite this, the police continued to defend their actions, claiming that the men had been released because of a legal technicality rather than because they were innocent. The murder investigation was finally re-opened in January 2002. Eighteen months later the real killer, a white man, Jeffrey Gafoor, was arrested, charged, confessed and convicted.

Throughout the rest of the twentieth century there were periodic examples of protest and unrest at the behavior of the police. Further deaths at their hands, including those of Brian and Wayne Douglas (no relation), both in south London in 1995 and that of Roger Sylvester in Tottenham, are testament to the nature of policing in Britain's capital city. But as the case of the Cardiff Five illustrates, examples of aggressive and oppressive policing were not limited to London. Among others, Christopher Alder suffered a violent death in police custody in Hull in 1998. A number of these cases are documented in Ken Fero's 2001 film *Injustice* and led to the establishment of the United Families and Friends Campaign (see Fero's chapter in this volume).

Stephen Lawrence

In stark contrast to the desperate determination to secure convictions for PC Blakelock's killing, the police's response to the death of Stephen Lawrence fueled further suspicion that black victims of crime are treated with contempt. The 18-year-old was murdered while he waited for a bus with his friend Duwayne Brooks on April 23, 1993. The immediate aftermath of a crime is widely regarded as being of critical importance in terms of locking down the scene and securing evidence. Both Brooks and Lawrence's family suggested that instead of conducting the most basic inquiries, the police were initially more interested in establishing why the black youths were out that evening and whether they themselves were involved in some kind of criminality. The police then claimed that they had been met with a "wall of silence" when they sought information from the local community in those critical early hours and days. The real truth was that they were provided with a mass of information, including, repeatedly, the names of a gang of suspects. Stephen Lawrence's mother Doreen, (later Baroness) Lawrence, highlights the wealth of information sent in and the police response to it in detail in her 2006 memoir *And Still I Rise – Seeking Justice for Stephen.*[19]

A delayed inquest was held in 1997 and the five suspects

first identified in the days after the murder were summoned to attend by the coroner, Sir Montague Levine. An inquest is not a trial, but rather an inquiry into the circumstances of a person's death. Nevertheless, all five men claimed the right of privilege against self-incrimination, including in one case, the witness refusing even to confirm his own name when questioned. At the end of the proceedings the infuriated coroner concluded that Lawrence had been "unlawfully killed in a completely unprovoked racist attack by five white youths."[20]

Two years later, the facts of the police investigation were exposed by a public inquiry initiated by the New Labour government. As had been the case with Scarman's inquiry, the chair of the Stephen Lawrence Inquiry, Sir William Macpherson, was challenged to consider the concept of institutional racism. Moreover, that pressure was intensified by the vociferous presence and involvement of the black community, trade unionists and other activists in supporting the Lawrence family and their legal team throughout the course of the proceedings.

As Macpherson prepared to deliver his eagerly awaited report in February 1999 tension was especially high. In particular, Metropolitan Police Commissioner Sir Paul Condon had raised the stakes with a belligerent appearance during which he vociferously defended his officers, dismissed any suggestion of institutional racism and declared that he would resign if any such conclusion was reached.

Macpherson did not capitulate. Having first indicated that: "6.4 'Racism' in general terms consists of conduct or words or practices which advantage or disadvantage people because of their color, culture or ethnic origin. In its more subtle form it is as damaging as in its overt form."[21] He proceeded to declare: "6.34 'Institutional Racism' consists of the collective failure of an organization to provide an appropriate and professional service to people because of their color, culture or ethnic origin. It can be seen or detected in processes, attitudes and behavior which amount to discrimination through unwitting prejudice, ignorance, thoughtlessness, and racist stereotyping which disadvantage minority ethnic people."[22] He then delivered the critical conclusion:

> There must be an unequivocal acceptance of the problem of institutional racism and its nature before it can be addressed, as it needs to be, in full partnership with members of minority ethnic communities. There is no doubt that recognition, acknowledgment and acceptance of the problem by Police Services and their officers is an important first step for minority ethnic communities in moving forward positively to solve the problem which exists. There is an onus upon Police Services to respond to this. Any Chief Officer who feels unable so to respond will find it difficult to work in harmony and co-operation with the community in the way that policing by consent demands.[23]

Macpherson's characterization was far weaker than that which had been proposed by Ture and Murray but it was much stronger than the conclusion Scarman had reached. Most importantly it was a vindication of the dogged determination of the Lawrence family, the advocacy of their legal team and the commitment of the activists who had long campaigned for a more thoroughgoing understanding of the nature, extent and impact of racism. Macpherson himself acknowledged that, far from the idea simply springing fully formed in his own head, he had been educated and impressed by the weight of opinion expressed by those that had contributed to the hearings. His observations about the testimony presented about the tactic of stop and search was particularly stark: "If there was one area of complaint which was universal it was the issue of 'stop and search.' Nobody in the minority ethnic communities believes that the complex arguments which are sometimes used to explain the figures as to stop and search are valid."[24] The inquiry was undoubtedly a landmark moment in British race relations. But it also spoke to the experience of other sections of the working-class community. Neville Lawrence acknowledged that alongside the high-profile endorsement the family received from South African freedom fighter and later president, Nelson Mandela, the financial backing they received from the trade union movement had been crucial in keeping the campaign going in the years between Stephen's death and Macpherson's report. Many organized trade unionists, notably the members of the National Union of Mineworkers who had struck for over a year in 1984/5, and print and dock workers who had also taken sustained industrial action had experienced oppressive treatment by the police during the 1980s. So too had Liverpool football fans at the 1989 Hillsborough stadium FA Cup semi-final during which the lives of 97 were extinguished. As a result of this they were among those who helped ensure that the Lawrence Family Campaign was financially underwritten. One final point to note about the plight of the Lawrence family is that Doreen and Neville always suspected that instead of solving their son's murder the police were more interested in discrediting them and their supporters. In 2013, 2 whole decades after Stephen's death and a year after two of the original suspects were finally convicted of his murder, it was officially revealed that undercover officers had indeed been sent to spy on the Lawrence Family Campaign. Peter Francis's admission that he had carried out such surveillance was one of the primary reasons why the then Home Secretary Theresa May was forced to establish an inquiry into undercover policing.[25] For a period of time in the aftermath of the Stephen Lawrence Inquiry, there was a sense in at least some sections of the BAME community that relations with the police had stabilized if not improved. There was, for example, a decline in the numbers of stops and searches at the start of the new millennium. This was certainly not the case for every minority group, however. The advent of the Labour government's "War on Terror" in the wake of the 2001 attack upon the twin towers of New York's World Trade Center led to a very specific focus upon Muslim communities. That intensified after the London transport network was attacked by a team of suicide bombers in July 2005. The targeting of Muslim communities notwithstanding, it was in these circumstances that the tenth anniversary of the publication of the Stephen Lawrence Inquiry Report was met with confident assertions by law enforcement officers that relations had improved to such an extent that the term institutional racism was "no longer valid." Such claims were always fanciful. A 2009 report, Stop & Think by the Equality and Human Rights Commission, which was timed to coincide with the tenth anniversary of Macpherson's report, noted with regard to that central question of stop and search: "The figures are stark: if you are a black person, you are at least six times as likely to be stopped and searched by the police in England and Wales as a white person. If you are Asian, you are around twice as likely to be stopped and searched as a white person."[26]

2011

Any notion that the new millennium had brought lasting change was shattered by the dramatic events of late summer 2011. On 4 August, police officers pursued a taxi in which 29-year-old Mark Duggan was traveling to an address in east London purportedly to collect a gun. Instead of apprehending him immediately after the alleged exchange, the car was tailed and forced into a highly controversial and risky "hard stop." As he emerged from the vehicle, Duggan was shot and killed by one of the undercover officers. The fact that the incident happened in Tottenham and that Duggan was a well-known figure from the very estate where the 1985 unrest had occurred was portentous. There remained a powerful collective memory of the Broadwater Farm riot and the injustice visited upon the Tottenham Three. The following Saturday tension grew as the Duggan family was given short shrift after marching with a group of supporters to demand an explanation from senior officers at the police station on Tottenham High Road. As the evening wore on, violence flared.

There followed a sustained period of unrest which was not confined to Tottenham but rather spread across the capital and out to a number of provincial towns and cities in England. The primary concern for politicians and much of the press was about the widespread criminal damage and looting that occurred. In response, courts sat through the night to process those who were arrested and charged, and tough custodial sentences were meted out to those who were convicted. This approach was ratified by the Court of Appeal which confirmed in the leading case *R v Blackshaw & Others* that because the offenses had been committed in the context of widespread public disorder, there was a need for exemplary sentences to act as a deterrent to others:

> There is an overwhelming obligation on sentencing courts to do what they can to ensure the protection of the public, whether in their homes or in their businesses or in the street and to protect the homes and businesses and the streets in which they live and work. This is an imperative. It is not, of course, possible now, after the events, for the courts to protect the neighborhoods which were ravaged in the riots or the people who were injured or suffered damage. Nevertheless, the imposition of severe sentences, intended to provide both punishment and deterrence, must follow. It is very simple. Those who deliberately participate in disturbances of this magnitude, causing injury and damage and fear to even the most stout-hearted of citizens, and who individually commit further crimes during the course of the riots are committing aggravated crimes. They must be punished accordingly, and the sentences should be designed to deter others from similar

criminal activity.[27]

The then prime minister, David Cameron, was wrong to describe the events as "criminality pure and simple," however. A similar tone was adopted by his Old Etonian schoolmate and political rival Boris Johnson. In his role as London Mayor, Johnson belatedly flew back from his holiday and wielded a broomstick in the symbolic act of sweeping the perpetrators off the street. Within weeks Theresa May was forced to correct Cameron and fellow cabinet colleague Ian Duncan Smith's assertion that the disorder was primarily the work of a small core of organized gangs. A number of points were clear to serious observers and those of us who practice in the criminal courts. Most of the people involved had nothing to do with gangs. Moreover, a small but significant proportion of those arrested were charged with violent disorder. The focus of attention for these people and many others charged with criminal damage was very specifically the police and those they regarded as figures of authority and authoritarianism, not the acquisition of trainers, mobile phones, widescreen TVs and video games.

In the years that followed the riots there have been a series of reports initiated, influenced by, involving or at the very least informed by the activists and communities that had so vociferously contributed to the Stephen Lawrence Inquiry, and who subsequently spoke out about the divisions that the 2011 uprisings exposed. In 2013 Theresa May commissioned Her Majesty's Inspectorate of Constabulary (HMIC) to conduct a review of stop and search that noted that the police had no legal basis for 27 percent of the encounters. Even the *Daily Mail*, a bastion of support for "law and order" generally and the police specifically, was forced to concede that this was a "blistering report."[28] In 2017 David Lammy, a former Labour government minister in the Department of Justice, but also crucially both black and the successor to Bernie Grant as MP for Tottenham, conducted a review of the criminal justice system. His conclusion was "that BAME individuals still face bias, including overt discrimination, in parts of the justice system."[29] *The Lammy Review* reached this conclusion without even considering stop and search, though it was evident that little progress had been made since the HMIC report. Meanwhile, a review of deaths in custody, demanded and largely influenced by groups such as the United Families and Friends Campaign, was conducted by Dame Elish Angiolini. It is worth quoting her at length:

Deaths of people from BAME communities, in particular young Black men, resonate with the Black community's experience of systemic racism, and reflect wider concerns about discriminatory over-policing, stop and search, and criminalisation. The Government report Police powers and procedures, England and Wales, year ending 31 March 2016 was published on 27 October 2016 and stated that while searches had fallen across all groups (searches on White individuals by 38%, searches on Black and Minority Ethnic individuals by 13%) compared with the previous year, nevertheless: Those from BME groups were 3 times as likely to be stopped and searched as those who are White. In particular, those who are Black (or Black British) were over 6 times more likely to be stopped. In both cases these figures were higher than the previous year, and reflect the fact that although stops of all ethnicities have fallen, stops of White individuals have fallen by more than stops of BME individuals. 5.7 Institutional racism identified in the Macpherson report still appears to be an issue within the police service. This was alluded to by Theresa May on becoming Prime Minister when she said: "If you're Black, you're treated more harshly by the criminal justice system than if you're white." 5.8 Inevitably any death involving a BAME victim who died following the use of force has the capacity to provoke community disquiet leading to a lack of public confidence and trust in the justice system. This can be exacerbated if people are not seen to be held to account, or if the misconduct process is opaque. There is a wider social and political context in which such deaths have occurred, often involving misinformation in the media about the deceased and their family, and the fact that despite Inquest verdicts of unlawful or excessive force, the authorities rarely appear to be held to account.[30]

Arguably it is no coincidence that in the wake of such strident efforts by anti-racist campaigners a police officer was finally convicted of the unlawful killing of former professional footballer Dalian Atkinson in June 2021.

The return of BLM

Mark Duggan's name and that of many of the people mentioned in this chapter appeared on placards, were chanted by protesters and featured prominently in social media posts and chatrooms during the heady summer of 2020. They highlight the fact that the concerns expressed about the police were not simply pointless mimicking of events in America, but rather that they reflect a genuine questioning about their role in modern society by a new generation of British-based activists. Furthermore, it should be noted that as with the United States, the British BLM protests were broad, diverse and sustained well into the autumn. It is in this context that debates about the role and future of the police should be considered. As is the case in the United States, the demand to defund the police is by no means a majority view. Surveys suggest that most people in Britain maintain the belief that the police play an important role in solving crime and keeping communities safe.

Against this, however, there has long been a minority of activists and observers who have insisted that the role of the police is irretrievably oppressive. This perspective is supported by a number of points. First, it is argued that solving crime was not the primary concern of those who sought to establish a force. The early decades of the nineteenth century were a period of great social unrest, one of the most notorious examples of which culminated in the Peterloo Massacre in 1819 (see Clement in this volume). It was in those circumstances and in order to stifle the growth of collective working-class agitation that calls for a police force of sorts grew and arguably this has remained their primary purpose. Second, the percentage of crimes that the police actually solve is pitifully low. According to the government's own statistics, "compared with the previous year, the proportion of crimes recorded during the year ending in March 2021 that resulted in a charge and or summons in the same year stayed broadly the same." That figure was 7 percent.[31]

Conclusion

Concerns about the police have by no means been confined to Britain's black communities. At the end of the twentieth century the exposure of police misconduct had culminated in the Court of Appeal quashing the convictions of the Guildford Four in 1989 and the Maguire Seven and Birmingham Six in 1991. These cases exposed the history of ill treatment experienced by Irish communities. A number of other high-profile scandals also shook confidence in the police, not least among women who have been angered by the failure to offer protection against serious sexual offenses. A notorious 1982 BBC documentary had long since exposed the bullying and dismissive way that Thames Valley police officers treated a complaint of rape.[32] Since then there has been little to inspire confidence and what progress that had been made has seemingly been reversed. A 2021 report commissioned by the Ministry of Justice (MoJ) found that there were an estimated 128,000 victims of rape (including attempted rape) in the 12 months to March 2020. Of these, just 6 percent of adult victims chose to report the assault to the police. There was in fact a significant increase in reported rapes in the 6 years to 2020, which is an indication of the efforts taken to persuade victims – who are overwhelmingly women – to come forward. However, "only 3 percent of adult rape offences assigned a police outcome in 2019–20 were given an outcome of charged/summonsed."[33]

In the same month as the MoJ report, June 2021, a long-awaited study into the murder of private investigator Daniel Morgan was published. It concluded that the Metropolitan Police had been "institutionally corrupt" and had prioritized protecting its own reputation over allegations that corrupt officers had been involved in the killing.

Even among those who continue to support the police, there has been a growing belief that they are simply ill equipped to address many of the issues that arise in complex modern societies. The cumulative effect of decades of neoliberal austerity and the absence of fulfilling work or affordable leisure facilities means that there are many more distressed and vulnerable people left to fend for themselves in the community. The inevitable result of this is low-level anti-social behavior which cannot properly be addressed by the type of zero tolerance approach that is widely adopted by police forces across the world. It is this concern that explains why there have been calls for a broader "multi agency" public health approach to violent crime and associated issues such as county lines drug offenses. As authors such as Alex Vitale argue in *The End of Policing*, it is not such a giant step to consider more radical solutions. If, as this chapter suggests, the police do little to protect communities and solve few crimes, then arguably the time has come to contemplate a different approach to keeping society safe.

A number of commentators, including Angela Davis, speculated about the extent to which the pandemic influenced the events of 2020. By the summer it was already becoming clear that disproportionate numbers of people from Black, Asian and

Minority Ethnic communities were falling seriously ill or dying as a result of coronavirus. Similarly, disproportionate numbers were becoming increasingly impoverished by the limitations of lockdown. For many, this stark reality shattered the complacent consensus that "we are all in it together." At the same time there was a growing sense that fundamental changes will be required if society is to emerge from the pandemic in better shape. This has led to a widespread questioning of life under capitalism and the role that structural racism plays within it. This heightened concern for the future of humanity helps to explain why the scale and diversity of the BLM protests was so great. They also occurred a year after the spectacular emergence of Extinction Rebellion (XR) catapulted concerns about climate change to the top of the political agenda. Those demonstrations were so widespread and disruptive of "business as usual" that prosecutions of people arrested in relation to those 2019 events continued deep into 2021. Many new activists involved in these protests discovered that the role of the police was to enforce the rules of a society that is delivering environmental catastrophe.

The response of the UK Government under Prime Minister Boris Johnson to concerns about law and order was to introduce a Police, Crime, Sentencing and Courts Bill in the spring of 2021. No secret was made of the fact that a number of its provisions were included as a direct response to the XR and BLM uprisings. Briefing notes published alongside the bill indicate that Metropolitan Police Commissioner Cressida Dick lobbied the government for an increase in police powers to control demonstrations. The bill also proposed a significant increase in penalties for offences of criminal damage to public monuments following concerns raised by Conservative MPs in the wake of the BLM upsurge. Meanwhile, the Cabinet Office appointed Dr Tony Sewell to lead a Commission on Race and Ethnic Disparities (CRED). Published in March 2021, the CRED Report was widely condemned as an attempt to discredit BLM and consign the concept of institutional racism to the dustbin of history.

In one of his final television appearances, Darcus Howe was interviewed about the 2011 uprising and pointedly refused to condemn those that had protested. A decade later the Johnson administration was deeply engaged in culture wars that demonstrate that they had learned little from those dramatic events and cared less about the consequences. The "full blown manifestations" that Howe predicted in the 1980s may have been slower than he had anticipated but in a society where divisions remain deep and the political leaders so opportunistic, they cannot be ruled out.

Chapter 11

The Fight for Black Lives to Matter: Appalachian Social Movement Intersections and the Capitalist Carceral State
Michael J. Coyle and Stephen T. Young

Introduction

The term "capitalist carceral state" is composed of two concepts: "capitalism" (especially its predatory character that is legally obliged to bend to profitability no matter most consequences) and "the carceral state" (the formal institutions of the criminalizing system as well as a continuum of programs and organizations that extend surveillance and social control). Placing these two concepts together in the term "capitalist carceral state" points to work that is done with the cooperation of and for the benefit of both, i.e. work that brings profit to capitalists and simultaneously increases the reach of the carceral state. For example, amid the current push to reform police departments in the US, Lexipol LLC, a private firm that writes policies and trainings for more than one-fifth of law-enforcement agencies in the US, has become one of the most powerful voices against police reform and use-of-force standards (Eagly and Schwartz, 2021).

The importance of such "capitalist carceral state" work becomes clear in the context of modern policing and the social movements that have risen against it. The 2013 acquittal of George Zimmerman for the murder of African-American teen Trayvon Martin gave birth to the hashtag #BlackLivesMatter in the US, and began what is arguably one of the largest social movements since the Civil Rights Era.[1] Rising against the racist criminalizing system and in support of racial justice, the Black Lives Matter (BLM) movement brought into question, on an international scale, police violence and the harms produced by the carceral state – especially as it disproportionately impacts black/brown and indigenous people of Color (BIPOC). As the ever-present carnage and oppression by police has not ceased and as media attention to the often decidedly vicious, brutal and frequently racially motivated nature of their expressions continue, protests, sit-ins and community meetings in support of BIPOC and against the criminalizing system persist.

With the 2014 police murders of African Americans Michael Brown (in Ferguson, Missouri), Eric Garner (in New York City) and the protests and wide civil unrest they sparked across the US, BLM became a nationally recognized movement. In the years that followed, media attention to what has always been a steady stream of African-American police murders increased. The culminating year was 2020, which brought (among many others) the police murders of Breonna Taylor, Daunte Wright and most notably George Floyd. The cumulative effect is a now global BLM social movement.

The growth of BLM is important to the struggle for the abolition of police and the larger carceral apparatus in the US. Following the recent police murders of BIPOC and the highlighting of white supremacy that it brought, the call for defunding and abolishing the police in activist, political and social spaces has grown. This provides ample opportunity for the message of BLM to reach populations and groups once thought to be indifferent or antagonistic to the notion of abolishing the carceral apparatus. One region in particular – Appalachia – has experienced consistent growth in supporting this mission despite its reputation and representation in the media. Appalachians, rich in their own history of anti-capitalist and anti-carceral organizing, have demonstrated a desire to join BLM and work toward a world without the violence of the carceral state. However, Appalachian movements and organizations are often ignored due to the stereotyping of the region's political leadership as possessing conservative and pro-capital leanings (Blizzard, 2010).[1]

This chapter seeks to push back against such stereotypes and provide ample reasoning for why the Appalachian region should be looked at as an area for diverse coalition-building. Specifically, we outline the long history of anti-capitalist and anti-carceral movements in the region. To do this we focus on a number of events over the past 2 centuries. First, we discuss the late-nineteenth century labor organizing behind the events of the Battle of Blair Mountain. Second, we outline the events occurring during the Pittston Coal Company strike in the early 1990s. Third, we focus on the resistance to the construction of US Prison Letcher in 2015. Finally, we outline the recent emergence of BLM in Appalachia as a process of coalition-building and organizing against racial injustice and the carceral state. Due to space limitations, discussions of all these are brief. However, outlining each is important to demonstrate the historic roots of Appalachian social movements and our argument that support for BLM is creating an opportunity for continued coalition-building and abolitionist organizing in the region.

A history of organizing

Appalachia consists of various regional and sub-regional pockets of diverse populations united within both geographical and cultural boundaries (Young, 2017). The region covers more than 200,000 square miles following the Appalachian Mountain range throughout the eastern US, and spans from the states of New York in the north to Mississippi in the south. In total the region includes the entirety of West Virginia and large parts of 12 states: New York, Pennsylvania, Ohio, Maryland, Kentucky, Virginia, Tennessee, North Carolina, South Carolina, Alabama, Georgia and Mississippi (Appalachian, 2015).

The Appalachian region has long been a source of natural resource extraction, especially coal and timber. Capitalists first spread throughout the region in search of these valuable resources in the nineteenth century, creating a long history of economic and social oppression tied to industrial development (Young, 2018). Scholars, politicians and investors since the late 1800s have framed the region as "backwards" and used it as an excuse to dominate both the land and the people. The purposeful nature of the stereotypes has led to a region depicted as the embodiment of poverty while also representing what is "wrong" with poor rural populations (Young, 2017). These stereotypes have also allowed scholars and activists to ignore the rich history of social justice, anti-labor and anti-carceral movements in the region.

Since the beginning of the industrial age, extraction-based industries controlled the economic identity of most of the region. However, many of these industries have experienced significant decline over the past few decades, leaving large swathes of the population facing economic instability (Fabricant and Fabricant, 2019). Continued economic volatility has left much of Appalachia, especially in the coal fields of Central Appalachia, in a precarious financial and cultural position, while also creating a surplus population (Young and Pitman, 2020). As we explore below, the historical reliance on extraction-based industries created vast economic oppression, allowed for little economic diversification, and through the passing of pro-capitalist legislation forced laborers into physically dangerous, low-paying jobs. The persistence of this industrial control was and is rooted in the dehumanization of the labor force and a continued stereotyping of the region as both socially and technologically "backward" (Young, 2017).

Stereotyping has led scholars and activists alike to overlook the existing regional dynamics of culture, class and community that lend themselves to social justice movements and a larger transformative praxis (see Anglin, 2002; Schept, 2014). The region has a long history of such movements, of which the Battle of Blair Mountain is arguably the best-known example.

The Battle of Blair Mountain

The events of the Battle of Blair Mountain are deeply entrenched in a long history of the state using violence to ensure benefits for the elites of capitalism (Nida, 2013). Prior to industrialization, Appalachia was a part of the broader market economy of the nation. The area was rich with natural resources, farming, and local trade dominating until the industrialization of the southern coalfields of West Virginia, which led to massive land accumulation by industrialist investors in the late 1890s (Corbin, 2015). During a period of nearly 40 years, these capitalists worked hard to ensure control over the labor market. This was evident in a number of laws passed throughout West Virginia that prohibited workers from creating or joining existing labor organizations (Nida, 2013). The result of such capitalist politics, for example in the southern coalfields of the state of West Virginia, transformed land, mineral rights, water ways and even housing, into the private property of large well-financed coal companies (Blizzard, 2010). This allowed for the creation of a number of "coal camps," or company towns, in isolated areas across southern West Virginia, eastern Kentucky, Pennsylvania and southwestern Virginia. These company towns provided capitalist operators with control over not only mine production, but also the political and economic spheres of the surrounding communities (Nida, 2013).

At the center of control was the "company store" and the provision of "scrip" currency to miners. By paying miners in this fake currency, operators were able to control all consumption and forced miners to purchase goods at inflated prices (Corbin, 2015). When such political and economic control was not enough to maintain "order" in the camps, operators/companies organized violence against miners and their families. Such violence included public beatings, evictions and forced food shortages (Corbin, 1981; Blizzard, 2010). When even these intimidation tactics failed, the companies would turn to the carceral state, which rather unbelievably would declare and enforce martial law through law enforcement, state militia and even federal troops (Nida, 2013).

The capitalist carceral state system of social and economic oppression described here plagued the Appalachian region. It resulted in a number of labor uprisings that supported the radicalization of many of the miners against their abusers. As early as 1892, miners organized around anti-capitalist and pro-union ideals to fight the coal companies' control of their lives (Nida, 2013). Many of these events ended in violence, resulting in the coal companies hiring of "detectives" from the Baldwin-Felts Agency to act as armed enforcement. Shockingly, and demonstrating the unhinged excesses, many mines were designed with machine gun nests to "protect" the operators' product and to "ensure" work rules were enforced (Blizzard, 2010). Further unrest developed when mining became even more precarious, both economically and physically, as operators cut corners on safety measures to generate more profit (Corbin, 2015). Despite constant strikes and uprisings, miners' demands were rarely met through anything more than extremely small concessions. Most often the miners experienced more violence and further restrictions on their safety and pay (Blizzard, 2010).

By the spring of 1920, the violence led to a large effort by the United Mine Workers of America (UMWA) to organize miners in West Virginia (Nida, 2013). This multi-month campaign resulted in large numbers of miners joining the union in various locations. In one such area, Matewan, West Virginia, coal companies retaliated by forcibly evicting miners and their families, as well as calling on the Baldwin-Felts Agency to violently quell the perceived "rebellion" (Bailey, 2008; Corbin, 2015). The violence used by the agents to evict miners and their families was significant enough that the town sheriff, Sid Hatfield, stepped in to stop the agents. The result of the confrontation was a deadly shootout on the main street of Matewan between the sheriff and a small number of union miners, against the agents. Seven Baldwin-Felts agents, the Mayor of Matewan and two miners were killed (Bailey, 2008). These events would result in many violent skirmishes between organized miners and Baldwin-Felts agents throughout the summer and fall of 1920. In August of 1921, Sid Hatfield was summoned to neighboring McDowell County to stand trial for helping organizers destroy coal mining equipment earlier that spring (Corbin, 2015). Hatfield, while attending court, was assassinated on the courthouse steps by Baldwin-Felts agents (Blizzard, 2010). No charges were ever filed.

The fallout from Sid Hatfield's murder was felt strongly throughout the southern coalfields and led to a strengthening of organizing, marching and uprisings. Responding to the use of martial law throughout the region, miners began to form their own armed patrols to protect their property and families (Blizzard, 2010). On August 24, 1921, miners began gathering near the state capital in Charleston, West Virginia. A large group began a multi-day march to Mingo County to free imprisoned striking miners and organizers detained under martial law. Nearly 10,000 miners armed with stockpiled weapons and machine guns purchased by organizers continued their march near Blair Mountain in Logan County. The miners were met by over 3000 West Virginia State Troopers, Baldwin-Felts agents and company loyalists (Nida, 2013). At this point a battle was inevitable. The Battle of Blair Mountain would last nearly 9 days between the end of August and the beginning of September 1921, with millions of rounds fired.

The fighting finally ended on September 2, when over 2000 US Army troops arrived (Blizzard, 2010). The exact number of deaths during the battle is unknown but some estimate it to be in the hundreds. A number of miners and organizers were charged with treason while numerous others were charged with murder. Nearly all of them were later acquitted (Corbin, 2015). No law enforcement, Baldwin-Felts agents or mine operators were charged with anything. To this day, the Battle of Blair Mountain stands as the largest armed "insurrection" since the Civil War (Blizzard, 2010). Ultimately, the Battle of Blair Mountain was a seminal act for US labor movements and paved the way for the growth of unions as the country entered the Great Depression (Corbin, 2015). Specifically, these organizing actions instituted a cultural heritage of resistance against capitalist carceral state oppression in West Virginia and more broadly Appalachia.

The Pittston Coal Company Miners' Strike

Less than 70 years later a new battle against corporate power, class privilege and carceral state oppression emerged. On April 5, 1989 two thousand miners stepped off the job in West Virginia and parts of southwest Virginia in response to harmful labor practices by the Pittston Coal Company (Anglin, 2002). The company had actively sought loopholes to fire union miners over the previous 2 years and by that April had fired over four thousand union miners while threatening to eliminate another three thousand union jobs. Additionally, in the latter months of 1988, Pittston cut healthcare coverage to fifteen hundred retired and disabled miners and their families before a new collective agreement contract could be signed.

By the end of 1988 the miners had worked for 14 months without a contract as they waited for the National Labor Relations Board (NLRB) to investigate 23 charges of unfair labor practices perpetuated by the Pittston Coal Company. During the deliberation period Pittston restructured the company to create a non-union mining division referred to as Pyxis Resources Company. The point of this restructuring was to strategically funnel more of the company's mining operations to Pyxis in an attempt to bypass the union and certain labor regulations. Pittston also tried to weaken the union's negotiating power through a public media campaign that argued the company needed to better position domestic coal in the global market and that unions were a barrier to doing so successfully. The goal was to force the union to concede on important miner protections, such as pensions, healthcare, job security and the right to set work rules (Anglin, 2002). The results of the NLRB investigation granted that the miners' complaints held merit but allowed Pittston to hire temporary replacements of union workers (Anglin, 2002). These results inspired the miners to begin one of the largest labor strikes in recent US history.

The Pittston strike developed and ended differently than Blair Mountain. The UMWA and other organizers were aware that the Pittston Coal Company would likely try to incite violence as a means of a media campaign against the miners, unions and the labor movement – as they had in strikes earlier in the century (Anglin, 2002). Consequently, organizers decided to follow the lead of Civil Rights Era movements. Specifically, "President Richard Trumka and other leaders of the UMWA worked with peace and civil rights advocates, in addition to a public relations firm in Washington, D.C., to develop a strategy of nonviolent protest" (Anglin, 2002, p. 568). The organizers, with the help of other anti-capitalist and labor organizations, used the news media to their own advantage, constructing the miners in a way that opposed the stereotypical images of the region.

Pittston, following tactics employed by other mining companies, contracted with the security firm Vance International to patrol company property. With the aid of the Virginia State Police, a program of surveilling striking miners began (Anglin, 2002). Additionally, as with previous labor incidents, both sides sought legal means to end the strike. The UMWA was unsuccessful in the US District Court. However, Pittston was granted multiple injunctions and fines of more than $64 million were levied against the union and other organizers – the largest fines in US history at the time (Anglin, 2002). In sum, as with the actions of the state during Blair Mountain, both federal and state-level agencies, including the courts, blatantly supported the mining company as a means of ensuring the safety of capital investments, while completely failing to support the endangered lives and livelihoods of miners.

Throughout the Pittston strike, miners and their families took part in a number of organized non-violent events including picket lines, sit-ins and multiple vigils outside local jails to show support for miners who had been arrested. Many of these events were solely organized and attended by women throughout West Virginia, Virginia and Kentucky (Anglin, 2002). Their actions demonstrate a significant turning point in the heteropatriarchical structuring of organizing in Appalachia and would be a significant factor to the company's eventual concession. However, despite an eventual victory, the organizing of these non-violent events did not come without a cost. As in previous labor actions, throughout the Pittston strike, miners, their families and even supporting protesters endured physical violence by law enforcement, pro-company personnel and Vance International employees (Associated Press, 1989).

The Pittston strike did not end until organizers were able to occupy the Moss 3 Coal Preparation Plant, the company's largest preparation facility (Anglin, 2002). Following 3 weeks of stopped production, the state intervened to ensure production would resume before further assets were seized. The Secretary of Labor, Elizabeth Dole, traveled to the site of the strike to meet with miners. She would later force Pittston into contract negotiations with the miners to quell the growing national support miners were receiving. The non-violent and other organizing lessons of the Pittston strike continue to support organizing throughout Appalachia and the US today. Specifically, laid off women miners and the family members of other striking miners have gone on to organize labor strikes for labor movements across the country (Anglin, 2002) and have ensured the continued use of non-violent organizing in the region.

United States Prison Letcher

The most recent example of large-scale anti-carceral and anti-capitalist organizing in the Appalachian region concerns obstructing the building of a prison in eastern Kentucky. United States Prison Letcher (USP Letcher), in Letcher County, Kentucky, was a proposed $510 million – later changed to $440 million – carceral institution framed as a "job creator" and "solution" to economic precarity in Central Appalachia (Ryerson and Schept, 2018; Young and Pitman, 2020).

The prison had significant support from capitalist and carceral investors, including the support of US Representative for Kentucky's 5th District, Hal Rogers (R), and Kentucky Senior Senator and then Senate Majority Leader Mitch McConnell (R) (Lustbader and Gullapalli, 2019). Rogers, the loudest proponent for building the prison, who previously had successfully advocated for the building of three prisons in his district, made numerous claims that USP Letcher would generate at least 300 new jobs for Letcher County (Hager, 2017). These claims were refuted during the multi-year process of obtaining approval for the construction. Federal Bureau of Prisons' data indicated "that many or perhaps all of those jobs could be filled by existing agency employees" (United States, 2015). Rogers strongly supported the construction of the prison all the while hiding the detrimental environmental and economic effects building it would have on the land and people. His persistent agenda fits neatly with a history of legislative actions, laws and carceral state assistance that further marginalize rural areas and people of color, fuel racial and urban/rural divides and expand carceral capitalism, all in the name of profit (Young and Pitman, 2020).

The lasting negative effects the construction of USP Letcher would have on the environment and society created resistance throughout the region. Drawing on a number of earlier organizing techniques discussed above, social movements in Central Appalachia emerged in response to Rodgers' desire to expand the carceral state. The most active of these was the #Our444Million social media campaign. Started in 2016, the campaign focused on encouraging Central Appalachians to reimagine better uses for the $444 million earmarked to build USP Lecther – especially ones that would strengthen employment and the economy without building a prison (Young and Pitman, 2020). This campaign was later joined by the Letcher Governance Project which protested during Representative Rogers' keynote speech at the Shaping Our Appalachian Region (SOAR) Innovation Summit (Adams, 2016). Shortly after it was announced that the construction would take place on a former strip mine, the Campaign to Fight Toxic Prisons[1] and the Abolitionist Law Center[2] worked together to file an environmental lawsuit on behalf of incarcerated people against the Federal Bureau of Prisons (Lustbader, 2019). These four coalescing movements, along with Kentuckians for the Commonwealth, the Ohio Valley Environmental Coalition, the Center for Biological Diversity and the Kentucky Student Environmental Coalition, worked diligently to defeat the building of USP Letcher (Tuhus, 2019).

The tactics of the social movement that stopped the construction of USP Letcher in many ways resemble those of the generations of organizers before them. The strategies demonstrate an ongoing "strong connection with the region and a desire for a better economic and social outlook for the population – one that does not rely on carceral or exploitative expansion" (Young and Pitman, 2020, p. 587). Importantly, as a social movement with a diverse pool of coalition members (carceral abolitionists, environmentalists, students, healthy local economy proponents, and others), the organizing methods against USP Letcher point to the power of fostering social movement intersectional awareness, i.e. the places where shared goals make for natural allies. For abolitionists it means an opportunity to explore continued resistance to white supremacy and the capitalist carceral state.

Appalachia and Black Lives Matter (BLM)

The momentum from the victory against USP Letcher has reverberated and energized much of the organizing efforts throughout Appalachia. More specifically, this victory brings to light the region's unique ability to cross various social, economic and racial lines in order to stop capitalist and carceral expansion in the region (Smith and Fisher, 2016). Recent protests and organizing in support of Black Lives Matter further demonstrates this.

Organizing around BLM in Appalachia began shortly after the first protests over Michael Brown's murder in 2014 (Barlow, 2014). More recently, following the police murders of George Floyd and Breonna Taylor, the region has experienced a significant increase in anti-carceral organizing. In the year following George Floyd's murder on May 25, 2020, Appalachia has witnessed a number of organizing events in solidarity with BLM. Whether in large protests, such as those of Lexington or Louisville, Kentucky, or even much smaller organizing efforts taking place in rural towns throughout West Virginia (Turner, 2020), Appalachia has opened its arms to abolitionist organizing. Importantly, these events draw needed attention to BIPOC, that are often left out of conversations about the history of the region (Turner and Cabbell, 2014). As was often discussed during demonstrations, Appalachia is the home of educator and reformer Booker T. Washington, as well as of the "Father of Black History Month" Carter G. Woodson – and should be celebrated as such during times of social unrest over the murders of black bodies.

One of the authors of this chapter played various roles in a number of BLM organizing efforts throughout Appalachia. Auto-ethnographically, I (Stephen Young) witnessed abolitionist organizing in small cities and towns throughout West Virginia and Eastern Kentucky. As with the other social movements discussed in this chapter, Appalachians took to the streets – this time to demand racial and economic equality and to fight the oppression brought on by the carceral state (see Blizzard, 2010). The organizers welcomed diverse voices and critiques of the region's role in upholding white supremacy. As Gwen Johnson, an organizer in Kentucky, reflected, "with the help of a professor from South Carolina called Gloria Holmes we continued the conversations with Bridge4Unity...We find common ground, acknowledge and learn from different life experiences and the perceptions we bring, and explore how we can come together beyond the racial, cultural, political, and class divides to learn to heal ourselves and our country" (Westlake, 2020, para. 6).

Multiple regional organizations participated in organizing efforts[2]. Groups such as 100 Days in Appalachia and Appalachian Voices made multiple statements in solidarity with the BLM movement, while groups such as the International Storytelling Center held important discussions with activists such as Alona Norwood, founding member of the New Generation of Freedom Fighters (International, 2020). Appalachian native and Grammy-nominated Americana musician Tyler Childers issued a powerful video directed toward "white rural listeners," asking them to not only see and hear BLM, but to work to achieve structural changes (Hudak, 2020). In a statement, Childers reminds Appalachians opposed to such organizing about the region's history: "I'd venture to say if we were met with this type of daily attack on our own people, we would take action in a way that hasn't been seen since the Battle of Blair Mountain in West Virginia. We wouldn't stand for it, why would we expect another group of Americans to stand for it?" (Hudak, 2020, para. 18-19).

Similar to the organizing efforts discussed earlier in this chapter, BLM marches were met with violent resistance by armed counter protesters. However, unlike some of the above examples of organizing in the region, nearly all the BLM protests were non-violent and many often ended as peacefully as they began (Jones, 2020). The emergence of BLM organizing in Appalachia opens a fertile space in which anti-capitalist and anti-carceral organizers can seek solidarity for organizing around predatory capitalism, racial injustice and the carceral state. Understanding and utilizing the rich history of organizing in the region provides a tool for bridging the gap between Appalachians and abolitionists (Young and Pitman, 2020). The continued history of the people of Appalachia fighting to exist outside of the oppression of the carceral state (Young, 2017; Young, 2018) provides both a cultural and economic starting point to address the larger structural issues, such as white supremacy, that harm families throughout the region and those who stand in solidarity with BLM.

Conclusion

As demonstrated in this chapter, the history of Appalachia is replete with stories of the abuses of the carceral state, its unmitigated support of predatory capitalist interests at the expense of an economy organized for the people, and popular resistance to both of these. Importantly, in Appalachian history, the carceral state's actions to support predatory capitalists and criminalize and control its resisters has laid the groundwork to sustain and endlessly reinvent the enormous race, class, gender and many other identity-inequalities that along with the rest of the US typify the region (Anglin, 2002; Turner and Cabell, 2014). This capitalist carceral state has also created a rich history of resistance that speaks to the power of coalition-building and other successful strategies. While different eras have meant a different focus (labor conditions, civil rights, wages, public spending priorities, white supremacy, etc.), the story remains the same: on the one hand the capitalist carceral state has used law, police and the threat and practice of punishment (which includes death and prison time) to reinforce capitalist and white supremacist control over the people and their social movements that arise in resistance; on the other hand the people have successfully engaged and showed their readiness to combat the capitalist carceral state in all its manifestations.

Studied closely, the intersections of important political and social identities that define Appalachia, such as labor, class, race, etc., demonstrate how the carceral state builds and maintains itself through time as a system of power and privilege on the one hand, and an experience of oppression and discrimination on the other. Our goal has been to show that seen through an intersectional lens (Crenshaw, 1989), Appalachian embrace of social movements, be it Blair Mountain, the Pittston strike, the fight to stop Letcher prison, or Black Lives Matter, reflects the region's continued resistance to the capitalist carceral state.

In a certain sense little has changed. The Blair Mountain tradition of anti-capitalist and anti-carceral resistance that emerges in the late 1800s in the fight against exploitation by extractive industries is just as much the fight of the Pittston miners in the 1980s, as it is the fight against Letcher prison and the fight to have Black Lives Matter in the 2000s. In its work to transform a region as fodder for predatory capitalists the carceral state was as willing to use violence to ensure political and economic control for the benefit of the elites of capitalism (and in the process transform a region into an industrial nightmare reminiscent of a Dickens novel) in Blair Mountain, as it was to support the Pittston Coal Company's attempt to force a union to concede on miner protections such as healthcare, pensions and job security, as it is to indiscriminately daily assault, oppress and end black lives as if they do not matter. The cold-blooded execution mannerisms of the carceral state continue, whether it is of those murdered as obstacles in the midst of the capitalist process in Blair Mountain, or of the BIPOC murdered by police in the midst of the white supremacist process. The lies the capitalist carceral state uses to frame also continue unabated. Blair Mountain imposed martial law "to protect," as the construction of a Letcher prison was to be a "job creator" and "solution" to economic precarity in Central Appalachia. Finally, the resistance to the capitalist carceral state has happened and is happening, and it is always highlighting the discrimination, oppression and the colonialist, white supremacist and racial capitalist abuses of the carceral state.

As the victories of the social movements discussed in this chapter demonstrate, there has been an accumulation of knowledge, experience and strategic finesse that is making resistance to the carceral state ever more effective throughout Appalachia. There are many successes in Appalachian history, paramount of which are not only the labor victories of the strikes, the stopped prison-building and the currently developing work to defeat white supremacy, but also the understanding that we all share this capitalist carceral state enemy. Slowly but surely the organized abandonment of the capitalist state (Gilmore, 2020) is being everywhere unmasked, and the monstrosity of the carceral state that knows few limits is being exposed: with each new social movement coalition-building becomes stronger, and importantly, ever-larger swathes of society are identified as impacted, and ever-larger swathes of society are enrolled as participants in the resistance.

Chapter 12

Black Lives Matter and Police Reform: Global Echoes of an American Social Movement
N. Prabha Unnithan

It is customary to connect the origins of American policing to its heritage in England and the work of Robert Peel in the formation of the London Metropolitan Police Force, and, in tracing the history of American policing, to divide it into three eras (Palmiotto 1999; Walker and Katz, 2022). The first, following the introduction of urban policing, the Political Era (1850s-1930s), is generally viewed as a time period driven by patronage and ridden with brutality, corruption and inefficiency. The second, the Reform or Professional Era (1930s-1970s), reduced political interference, raised personnel and performance standards for officers, and imprinted the idea of the police as specialized crime fighters in the public. However, this also resulted in isolating law enforcement from the citizenry they served and exacerbated tensions with now assertive minority communities. The current era that some have called the Community Era has been characterized as actively nurturing "partnerships" between the police and the people through the adoption of practices such as Community-Oriented-Policing (COP) and Problem-Oriented-Policing (POP).

However, two incidents from the 1990s at the height of the rhetorical popularity of COP and POP involving major police agencies lead us to question the depth of commitment American law enforcement has to these practices. The first was the Rodney King incident when Los Angeles police officers on March 3, 1991 used excessive force by beating Rodney King with their batons. A private citizen's videotape of the beating found its way to CNN where it was shown repeatedly (http://

archievescnn.com/2001.law/3/02/beatinganniversary.king02). The second incident occurred on December 13, 1999 when New York City police officers responded to a fight outside a club in Brooklyn. By the time the officers arrived, Abner Louima, apparently trying to break up the fight, had been drawn into the melee. In the scuffle, Officer Justin Volpe was sucker punched; he believed Louima was the culprit. Louima was arrested and taken to the precinct where Volpe rammed a 2- to 3-foot stick into the former's rectum (Frey, 2001: 232-234), resulting in severe physical injuries. Needless to say, both King and Louima are African Americans. The almost routine infliction of physical abuse seen in these incidents that occurred in the two largest cities of the US remind us that even during the heyday of community policing, an ugly history and a persistent thread of violence targeting African Americans exists in the US.

Most conventional histories of American policing tend to leave out these matters in the progression of eras they describe while trying to characterize them as a series of improvements over time. Following deaths resulting from terrorist attacks on New York, Washington, DC and in Pennsylvania on September 11, 2001 (often simply referred to as 9/11), federal government support for COP declined with priority being placed on homeland security. With the new emphasis on homeland security, the militarization of the police (Kraska, 2007; Balko, 2021) through the adoption of military weapons, strategies and equipment received higher priority. The juxtaposition of community problem-solving along with the spread of the "warrior cop" mentality that has come to characterize current policing has resulted in the moniker "The Iron Fist in the Velvet Glove" to describe contemporary American law enforcement (Koslicki and Willits, 2018). The next section delineates some of the gaps.

Historical roots of Police-African-American Conflict

Legal slavery (Heuman and Burnard, 2018) was present in North America from before the US declared independence in 1776 and until the promulgation of the 13th Amendment to the constitution (which ended it officially) in 1865 after the Civil War. Enslaved people were deemed to be the property or chattel of slave owners under law, denying and depriving the former of the rights and privileges accorded to free people. Enslaved African Americans worked under harsh, unsparing and abusive conditions for white slave owners in southern states.

Historically, law enforcement and criminal justice personnel were often at the forefront of treating enslaved African Americans unfairly and unequally beginning with the system of slavery. Slave patrols (Reichel, 1988) organized expressly for policing enslaved people, in particular those who tried to escape or were defiant and disobedient, were common in all the southern states. River patrols also existed to prevent boats being used for escaping the brutal conditions. Some scholars have argued that these slave patrols, formed expressly for the purpose of controlling and punishing African Americans, ought to be included as a forerunner of American policing along with urban and northern police departments based on Peelian principles. For example, Hassett-Walker (2021) traces the connection by noting that, "After the Civil War ended, the slave patrols developed into southern police departments. Part of the early police's post-Civil War duties was to monitor the behavior of newly freed slaves, many of whom, if not given their own land, ended up working on plantations owned by whites and to enforce segregation policies."

Following Reconstruction (mid-1860s to late 1870s) Jim Crow laws codified white supremacist and segregationist practices until the mid-1960s Civil Rights Era. During this period, the lynching of African Americans suspected of crimes or those who had merely violated norms of racial separation were often ignored by many local police agencies. During race riots of the early twentieth century and the civil rights movement of the 1960s, the police were visible and ferocious defenders of a criminal justice system structured for the continued segregation and marking of African Americans for unequal treatment. Penn (2003) notes (in promoting an African American-centered criminology) that, "The unique history of over 240 years of slavery, life in the antebellum South, migration, Black Codes and Jim Crow laws, migration, segregation, affirmative action and disproportionality in the criminal justice system provides clear evidence for a criminological perspective that encompasses the history and culture of the Black people in the United States." Notice how many of the issues mentioned by him are related to the police and law enforcement.

It should not surprise us then that even with the rise of the homeland security policing paradigm supposedly focusing on international terrorism, African Americans continued to be targets of the rough and ready tactics of militarized policing. The very same police departments were also seeking almost simultaneously to partner with the communities they served to assist in tackling major crime problems.

Black Lives Matter

Around the same time as the emergence of Black Lives Matter (BLM) protests targeting police violence against African Americans, Chauncey DeVega (2015) remarked bitterly, "Black Americans are shot, abused, and beaten up by America's police...while surrendering, sleeping, seeking help after being in a car accident, walking down the street, with their hands up, showing identification, standing in a crowd, listening to music, riding bicycles, playing in the park, and being totally submissive and compliant."

Consider the following quote from two sociologists (Andersen and Taylor, 2002: 326) that summarizes the sorry state of affairs pertaining to racial minorities and American criminal justice: "African Americans and Hispanic people are arrested by the police considerably more often than Whites and Asians. In fact...an African-American or Hispanic wrongdoer is more likely to be arrested than is a White man who commits the same crime even when the White man shares the same age, socioeconomic environment, and prior arrest record as the Black or Hispanic. Once in custody, an African-American or Hispanic is more likely to be detained without bail, more likely to go to trial, and more likely to receive a stiffer sentence at the end of the trial than is a White man of similar social background and criminal record."

BLM is an anti-racist social movement that began after the acquittal of George Zimmerman, a neighborhood watch coordinator, who was charged in the death of a black teenager, Trayvon Martin, in Twin Lakes, Florida on February 26, 2012 (see Fasching-Varner, Reynolds and Albert, 2014). The eponymous association styles itself as "a global organization in the US, UK, and Canada, whose mission is to eradicate white supremacy and build local power to intervene in violence inflicted on Black communities by the state and vigilantes" (Black Lives Matter, 2021). The movement began picking up steam during street protests that followed police killings of Eric Garner in New York, by choking (on July 17, 2014) and of Michael Brown (on August 9, 2014) by shooting in Ferguson, Missouri (see Potter and Pohl, 2018).

It gained national and eventually global prominence in mid-2020. Even though there were lockdowns as the COVID-19 pandemic raged, large-scale demonstrations broke out reflecting outrage at the following deaths that summer: the March 13, 2020 shooting of Breonna Taylor at her home in Louisville, Kentucky, during a "no-knock" police raid; the May 25, 2020 asphyxiation of George Floyd at the knee of a police officer in Minneapolis, Minnesota; and the shooting of Rayshard Brooks, who was running away from the police in Atlanta, Georgia on June 12, 2020. A wave of public protests against systemic racism followed these well-publicized events that again highlighted the shameful centuries-long trend of police violence against African Americans.

These largely peaceful protests of 2020 were met with higher levels of force by law enforcement than that used against a largely white mob that attacked the US Capitol on January 6, 2021 in an attempt to prevent Congressional certification of the election of President Joe Biden. Perhaps in dealing with the nationwide BLM protests, there was fear that an unending spiral of violence and counter-violence may have been unleashed. As Legewie (2016) noted: "Incidents of extreme violence against police officers can lead to periods of substantially increased racial disparities in the use of police force." Subsequently, demands to "defund the police" became common, if not exactly mainstream. Given the reluctance of both Democratic and Republican political parties to literally "defund the police," reform efforts have taken this demand as shorthand for shifting money spent on the police to other social services and community priorities.

The push for police reform in the US

The US has one of the most decentralized forms of law enforcement in the world (Bayley, 1990) with police organizations at the federal, state and local (county, municipal) levels. Following the nation-wide protests against the police in summer 2020, reform initiatives began in earnest at all levels. Here we will concentrate on the reform efforts affecting federal and state policing. Local police agencies, while they may carry out changes and improvements on their own, are constrained by policies and procedures imposed by the states they operate in. At the federal level, it should be noted that a President's Task Force on 21st Century Policing (2015) was initiated by the administration of President Barack Obama. Among its major recommendations was the need to re-embrace community policing in terms of philosophy and strategy while also ensuring "fair and impartial policing" by specifically focusing on procedural justice (Lind and Tyler, 1988). This was supposed to mark a shift from the pervasive police militarization and "warrior cop" mentality mentioned earlier following the terrorist attacks of 9/11. The Task Force's recommendations were ignored by President Donald Trump's government.

In early 2021, the George Floyd Justice in Policing Act was passed by the House of Representatives. It contained provisions that would prohibit police use of chokeholds which restrict breathing and holds of the carotid arteries which severely limit the flow of blood to the brain. The deployment of "no-knock" search warrants (common in drug enforcement to prevent suspects from destroying evidence) by federal law enforcement agencies would be restricted. The Act would also tie federal funding for state and local police agencies to implementing this measure, banning the practices mentioned earlier. In addition, a national database that would make police misconduct prosecutions easier was to be created. "Finally, it directs the Department of Justice to create uniform accreditation standards for law enforcement agencies and requires law enforcement officers to complete training on racial profiling, implicit bias, and the duty to intervene when another officer uses excessive force" (H.R.1280 – George Floyd Justice in Policing Act, 2021).

However, negotiations before attempted passage in the Senate fell apart due to opposition from some (though not all) police organizations to the removal of the doctrine of *qualified immunity*. This doctrine currently prevents individual officers from being sued civilly over a claim of excessive force if the use of force was objectively reasonable. As of this writing, national police reform resulting from the BLM movement appears stalled and is not being pursued by Congress. There has been more progress in individual states. According to a New York Times (2021) analysis that utilizes a National Conference of State Legislatures database, as of April 18, 2021, more than 140 police reform bills have been passed in 30 states. The most significant changes have come on three fronts: restrictions on no-knock warrants; requiring and providing funding for body-worn cameras; limiting the aforementioned immunity provisions; and restricting chokeholds. One early and prominent example of police reform at the state-level is Colorado, where bipartisan legislation was passed within a month of the death of George Floyd (Denver Post, 2020). The comprehensive reform bill first stipulated that officers are required to wear body cameras and eliminated chokeholds completely along with the use of deadly force in non-violent situations. It mandated that police officers should intercede when they observe their colleagues using excessive force. It also removed police officer immunity from accusations of civil rights violations, so that these claims can be litigated in state courts.

In 2021 the Colorado legislature added more changes meant to increase transparency and accountability for police agencies (Denver Post 2021a). The new rules regulate a controversial practice of asking eyewitnesses to identify suspects in so-called "showups" wherein "police detain someone matching the description of a criminal and ask a witness if that person is the person they saw committing a crime. Unlike a lineup or an array of photos of different people, witnesses don't have the option of picking someone else during a showup" (Denver Post, 2021b). Other major reforms include more funding for alternatives to police to respond to cases involving mental illness or homelessness, maintaining a public database of officers with a history of lying, and requiring the release of body camera footage to the public within 3 weeks.

We can safely say that while police reform resulting from the BLM movement remains shaky at the federal level, several states have taken steps to change the nature of police-public interaction. This is important in that short of abolishing the police (Chua, 2020), changes at the state-level are likely to have greater long-term effects in that they affect the far more numerous state and local American police agencies.

Echoes in other countries

Criminal justice and policing have generally been thought of as systems vested in national and sun-national units. However, one of the more intriguing developments resulting from the US BLM movement is the resonance that it has had in other countries, many of which may not have experienced the long and fraught history of racial conflict described above in the case of whites and African Americans in the US. The internationalization of social movements (della Porta, Dieter and Rucht, 1999) is a topic that has been of interest to scholars recently. In this section, I briefly survey 12 countries where protests which were reported as having been influenced by the BLM movement took place and how those efforts may have targeted police reform (see Diphoorn, Leyh, and Slooter, 2021). The following is by no means an exhaustive list (see C-NET, 2020).

Australia: Protests which occurred in many major cities associated with BLM, while expressing solidarity with African Americans, have also focused on Australia's history of violence against aborigines and suppression of their rights. Australia's indigenous people constitute around 2 percent of the population but have historically been over-represented in terms of incarceration and deaths in custody. Therefore, much of the scholarship and writing on this topic frames BLM and police reform against the backdrop of continuing mistreatment of the aboriginal Australians. Calls for the implementation of 339 recommendations from a nearly 30-year-old Royal Commission into Aboriginal Deaths in Custody were again made in 2020. To observers conversant with the problematic nature of police treatment of racial minorities world-wide, demands for an end to violence perpetrated against aboriginal people by the criminal justice system, especially the police, have a familiar and frustrating ring (Anthony, Gainsford, and Sherwood, 2020).

Brazil: The police in Brazil are one of the most violent in the world and are estimated to have killed 6416 people in 2020 (Unicorn Riot, 2021) with the vast majority Afro-Brazilian youth (Alves, 2018; Stanford Freeman Spogli Institute for International Studies). Even as BLM-inspired demonstrations took place in some cities, studies cite a rise in police violence against darker-skinned Brazilians who have historically been subject to prejudice and discrimination. More recently, such violence has been linked to far-right politics and "law-and-order" policing practices (Ramos and Volker, 2020). Cesar Munoz (2021) writes despairingly, "Sustained reform can't happen if police officers continue to treat Black Brazilians like suspects and the neighborhoods like hostile territory. The cycle of violence will not end if leaders continue to employ torturers as commanders and police killings go unpunished."

Canada: The visible minority population of Canada include the following (in alphabetical order): Aboriginal (or indigenous) people, Arabs, Blacks, Chinese, Filipinos, Japanese, Koreans, Latin Americans, south Asians, Southeast Asians and west Asians. The official BLM organization has a noticeable presence in Canada and was involved in organizing several protests even before 2020. Protesters expressed outrage over deaths at the hands of US police but also highlighted police violence visited upon black, indigenous and people of color in Canada. BLM, police violence and reform are often discussed in terms of Canada's "veneer of multiculturalism" (Maynard, 2017) and its international reputation as a tolerant and diverse nation.

This serves to whitewash serious issues involving police and people of color and indigenous populations in Canada. Calls to "defund the police" and the intention to hold Canadian police accountable for violence or death resulting from their interactions with people of color appear to mirror what we have seen above in the US. For the BLM organization, 2021 will bring "continued collaboration with Canada's indigenous community. BLM is looking to build partnerships with Indigenous people" (Toronto City News, 2021). Previous research on police reform and change suggests that key barriers and resistance exist within Canadian police agencies (Duxbury, Bennell, Halinski, and Murphy, 2018) to such efforts. This leads Oriola (2020) to conclude pessimistically that, "Police accountability remains low in Canada despite incidents of civilian abuse and death," thus suggesting that police reform is unlikely.

Denmark: More than 86 percent of the population of Denmark identify as Danes. In addition, there are significant numbers of people from other parts of Europe while around 6 percent of Denmark's population is estimated to have origins in African and Asian countries. An organization named BLM Denmark (BLMD) exists with a reported focus on assisting those seeking asylum and individuals charged with crimes. BLMD's connection to the BLM organization in the US is vague and it has experienced splits from within. In any case, demonstrations took place in June 2020 in several cities with a large one outside the American embassy in Copenhagen.

Research and periodical publications highlight the denial or "ignorance" of racism or racist treatment of people of color by the Danish white majority. There have been attempts to educate Danes about the country's history as a conduit for slavery in the Caribbean (The St. Thomas Source, 2020). An initiative to reform the Danish police took place in 2007 which "centralised the police system: the national commissioner substantially strengthened his position vis-à-vis the local district chiefs, while the number of police districts decreased from 54 to 12" (Schaap, 2021). Police reform in Denmark is often framed by invoking human rights, human rights conventions, and the exclusion or denial of equitable treatment to its visible minority residents (Nebeling and Bissenbakker, 2021). Mishra (2020) argues that reform is needed in Denmark given the law enforcement's "poor track record when it comes to policing minorities."

France: In general, France does not identify its own citizens formally along racial lines. However, semi-formal estimates suggest that around 15 percent of the country's population are from Africa (primarily from the North) and Asia, and thus not of European origin. Celestine and Martin-Breteau (2019) note that there was an attempt to create a "Ferguson in Paris" movement after Michael Brown's death in 2014 in Missouri. Thus, even before the events involving George Floyd in June 2020, "as a large-scale social movement aimed to expose and dismantle the systemic violence against racial minorities in the United States, BLM has indirectly raised awareness about racial tensions in France—namely the structures of racism affecting post-colonial sub-Saharan and north African immigrants and their children" (Celestine and Martin-Breteau, 2019).

There have been a significant number of BLM-linked protests against violence perpetrated by police officers who are heavily armed as a result of increased militarization in the 1990s. Research and writing link the BLM protests and police reform movements to France's colonial past as well as discrimination, violence and systemic bias directed at Muslims and north Africans. "Researchers say that there is a long history of racism and violence in the police that goes back to the colonial era" (DW, no date). Regardless, police reform has been stymied by pushback from powerful French police unions which counter that government needs to do more to protect their safety.

Ironically, "While Floyd's death has in other parts of the world led to a reckoning with police violence and impunity, in France, new laws have so far increased police power" (BBC, 2021). The new laws, while banning choke holds, also included an attempt to discourage the filming of public interactions with the police. In France, it is safe to say that increased awareness of bias and victimization by the police has not translated into reforming their practices.

India: BLM protests in the US have attracted attention and resulted in small demonstrations in India, often by leftist groups. Research and reporting have tended to look inward into the failings of Indian society (e.g., colorism, in terms of a preference for lighter skin tone) and its criminal justice system, and especially the police. The latter have a well-deserved reputation for the use of brutal, high-handed and arbitrary tactics against Muslims and Dalits (formerly referred to as "Untouchable" and belonging to a group below the four major castes). "The issue of police violence against minority populations resonates with the situation in India. The Indian police deploy methods such as 'encounter killings,' the targets of which are largely Muslim and low-caste men. Custodial death and torture is rampant in India" (The Wire, 2020). Police reform and change, despite many decades of reports from national commissions and decisions from the Supreme Court of India urging the same, remains elusive (Verma and Subramanian, 2009; Unnithan, 2013; Singh, 2021).

Israel: Around 76 percent of Israeli residents are Jews (descendants of or migrants from various parts of the world), with Arabs (around 21 percent, including those who are Palestinian) constituting the major minority. Given the circumstances surrounding the creation of Israel after World War II and subsequent conflicts involving its neighbors, tensions between the state and Arabs have been a continuing historical thread. Thus, assessing BLM's influence in Israel has to be situated against the backdrop of religion and the political struggle for a Palestinian state [The US BLM condemned actions of the Israeli government and police against Palestinians and expressed support for the latter—see also, Naber, 2017].

In terms of policing minorities, both Ethiopian Israelis (Abdallah, 2020) and the Arabs (Ben-Porat and Yuval, 2019) are discussed in ways similar to African Americans and the

American BLM movement. While demonstrations protesting police violence against Palestinians (and, to a lesser extent, Ethiopian Israelis) are common it is difficult to determine if these are BLM-linked. At the same time, police reform inasmuch as it also involves dealing with minority groups seems to be of interest. A RAND (2014) report mentions a desire among Israelis to reform the police due to "concern over quality of police service" (p.iii). While acknowledging police abuse of power and violence against demonstrators and marginalized populations, reports also indicate political difficulties in creating objective oversight mechanisms or achieving meaningful change. In the case of Israel, given its history of protracted conflict between the state and Arabs, any police reform that may take place may only be linked to BLM rhetorically.

Italy: While most of Italy's residents identify as Italian (92 percent) the country contains significant minorities from Eastern Europe and north Africa along with an undetermined number of Roma. More recently, political and economic crises in countries on the other side of the Mediterranean have given rise to massive migration. Along with other European countries, Italy was the site of BLM-inspired protests in mid-2020. According to Dellaporta and Lavizzari (2021), "In Italy, the protest wave was significant, with almost 150 events, showing variation in terms of geographical distribution across the territory – from small cities and villages to big cities and metropoles – forms of the events given the pandemic restrictions, and the composite nature of organizations involved."

These protests occurred while, "Black people in Italy are not recognized as Italians and are not fully represented in politics nor the arts, including in cinema," notes Muvumbi (2021), who remarks on the irony of Italians being "angrier about racist episodes happening on another continent while it also happens *here*" (emphasis in original). Due to publicized earlier events that involved excessive force, there have been renewed calls for police accountability (Zamperini, Siracusa, and Menegatto, 2017) especially in response to harsh treatment of migrants at the borders (Campesi, 2020). It appears unlikely that BLM-related protests will be linked specifically with police reform efforts if or when they occur.

Japan: With the overwhelming majority (98 percent) of residents of Japan identifying as Japanese and holding a generally positive view of the police (Parker, 2015), BLM-inspired demonstrations which took place in some cities were few in number. Thus protests in Japan in mid-2020 appeared to be more focused on expressing solidarity and concern for the treatment of African Americans by police in the US, rather than with emphasizing similar issues within the country. This is not to say that bias against certain small groups does not occur in Japan. Generally, these groups include the Burakumin (descendants of an underclass historically involved in "unclean" occupations such as butchers and undertakers, nowadays also associated with membership in organized crime); Koreans (descendants of earlier waves of migration from Korea); the Ainu (indigenous people of the island of Hokkaido who possess a distinct culture and language but who are socially marginalized); and Okinawans; along with foreign citizens living in Japan.

Regarding the last group, "Protesters said racial discrimination and the treatment of foreign people in Japan are topics often avoided by the media and in public discourse" (Japan Time, 2020). The Diplomat (2020) noted that young BLM protesters in Japan were concerned with issues of police violence against minorities in Japan. Japanese police reform is described in relation to strong oversight mechanisms. While juxtaposed with BLM, police reform in Japan is not explicitly tied to the movement.

New Zealand: A number of BLM-related protests occurred in major cities in New Zealand in mid-2020 (RNZ, 2020). New Zealand, as a country, has long struggled with bias against and unequal treatment of its native Maori population. Maoris constitute around 17 percent of the population and along with Pacific islanders (around 8 percent) are New Zealand's most visible minorities. The country also has a centralized national police force which may make reform practices easier to implement. BLM and police reform in New Zealand should also be contextualized against the backdrop of a White Nationalist attack on several mosques in Christchurch which killed 51 people.

After that event, New Zealand police decided to arm officers who "are not routinely armed but carry OC spray (pepper spray), batons and Tasers" (O'Brien, Thom, Gordon, McKenna, Kidd, Quince and Exeter, 2021) and carried out a pilot program to test the same (NPR, 2020). This was resisted as it was thought the firearms would be turned against the Maori, who have been disproportionately targeted in incidents involving police use of excessive force. Protests against arming the police coincided with George Floyd's death in Minnesota, which then led authorities to walk back the new policy and continue with unarmed policing. The country's police force had begun conducting a study of "unconscious bias" by police against the Maori, which acquired greater urgency during the BLM protests. The situation in New Zealand suggests that tangible changes in reforming police practices do take place that can be tied, albeit indirectly, to the BLM-inspired protests.

Nigeria: Given the African-American and numerical minority origins of the BLM movement, one would not expect to see it develop in an African majority country such as Nigeria, particularly one where "Organized public protests against police organizations are a rare occurrence" (Ojedokun, Ogunleye, and Aderinto, 2021). But BLM did spark major protests in Nigeria in mid-2020. These were synced to the still-ongoing Nigerian police reform movement called #EndSARS, which began on social media and sought to modify or disband the country's national Special Anti-Robbery Squad (SARS), a unit of the Nigeria Police Force (NPF). This squad is widely regarded as engaging in "brutality, human rights violation, sexual abuse, torture, and extrajudicial killings" (Akinyetun, 2021, Aye this volume) and widely reviled for the same.

Some reports stated that the SARS unit was disbanded after a recent confrontation with protesters which resulted in the deaths of many civilians. However, The Africa Report (2021) characterized the situation as follows: "The protests stopped after 20 October 2020, when the military and police officers shot and killed unarmed protesters in Lagos. A judicial panel was formed to look into the atrocities, but to date, their findings have not been made public. The infamous Special Anti-Robbery Squad (SARS) has not been disbanded, and on the surface, it appears nothing has changed." Scholars have traced the repressive positioning of the NPF through earlier periods of military rule and democracy to its British colonial origin (see Alemika and Chukwuma, 2000) when it was set up and freely used for such purposes. If police reform is defined minimally as involving the dissolution of one brutal arm of law enforcement, we have to judge it as having little success in Nigeria.

United Kingdom: Whites constitute more than 87 percent of the population of the UK. Most of the UK's other residents are drawn from former British colonies in Asia, the Caribbean and Africa. The BLM movement in the UK intersects with calls for greater oversight of police and for paying attention to the treatment of black and brown communities both by police and British society. Racial disparities in the UK's policing are widely cited in the literature with Joseph–Salisbury, Connelly and Wangari-Jones, P. (2021) stating that in the matter of a "predisposition towards police brutality and disregard for Black lives" the UK is similar to the US.

BLM-inspired protests took place in mid-2020 in several cities in England, Scotland, Wales and Northern Ireland eliciting expressions of official and public support (see, for example, Coalition for Racial Equality and Rights, 2021). At the same time there are disagreements among protesters about what reforms should be asked for and how to achieve them. Some factions support radical change (BLM UK being one) and have clashed with those suggesting gradual or moderate approaches (see Reuters, 2020). Reforms, as they exist, are at an early stage: "The National Police Chiefs' Council (NPCC) said it aimed to address concerns over stop and search, the use of force and under-representation of black and minority ethnic officers" (Independent, 2020). While a beginning appears to have been made, determining the overall net effect of BLM-linked protests on police reform will have to wait for now.

There are, of course, other countries where BLM-related protests have occurred, though not necessarily only about police reform, which are not included here. For example, in Indonesia, BLM-inspired demonstrations against the biased treatment of people of Papuan origin took place and were connected with support for the independence of the west Papua region (see Time, 2020). In Belgium, where the statue of a monarch identified with mistreatment of Congolese people was taken down, voices urging the country to acknowledge its imperialist past more clearly have also surfaced (UCLA Global, 2021).

A Discursive Summary

Based on the criterion of whether the BLM movement was able to achieve its goal of reforming the police in the countries and jurisdictions where protests were organized, we have to either say that they did not, or that there was minimal, almost negligible, movement. Some countries saw partial (in some states of the US) or very limited change (Australia, New Zealand and the UK). While we have focused our attention on the link between BLM and police reform, perhaps that may not be the only way to assess what BLM has been able to accomplish. A social movement that was grounded in the lived history and experience of African Americans, a minority group in the US, suddenly caught fire and took global form with responses from many continents. Awareness was raised of the plight of African Americans, but also a diverse set of subjugated groups (e.g., Afro-Brazilians, Indian Dalits, Israeli Arabs and Ethiopians, New Zealander Maoris, etc.).

In this sense, BLM may best be described as a transnational movement that affected national and subnational movements (Rucht, 1999) as opposed to a transnational movement that focuses on transnational problems (e.g., climate change, trafficking, etc.). This may be because, as noted earlier, policing is an intensely national or subnational pursuit. Some of this is also aided by the relative dominance of American culture and approaches to issues internationally (Shimemura, 2002) and the world-wide prevalence of the English language. Note, for example, the number of adaptations of the BLM slogan wherein Black is replaced by the name of a subjugated group in a given country (Dalits, Papuans etc,).

We also note that, to varying degrees, the countries we have considered practice democracy and allow for governments to come to power through electoral politics. It would be difficult, if not impossible, to envisage a movement analogous to BLM in China (which has difficulties with its own persecuted groups, the Uighur, Falun Gong and Tibetans) or Russia (involving say, Chechens or Jehovah's Witnesses). At the same time, the slow pace of police reform in these democracies does speak to the messiness of bringing about change in such polities as opposed to in more authoritarian contexts. However, it is also true that authoritarian governments often depend on their police forces to keep them in power and are thus unlikely to want to change structures that help them retain it.

Even for democracies, BLM and the movements it inspired when considered along with the glacial pace of change and reform of admittedly biased and discriminatory police practices ought to raise troubling questions. First, what are the functions of the police as a group within societal systems of differentiation and stratification and what is the police role in oppressing the weakest sections of that society? Second, we must ask about the repeated involvement of police personnel in encounters with subordinate group members that result in the many tragedies that have unfolded in all of the countries examined here.

Ultimately, it is these tragic encounters that give rise to protest movements such as BLM. Is it possible to police without maiming or killing members of powerless groups? Finally, the many cycles of police reform (witness the historical evolution of police forces as diverse as in the US and Nigeria) appear to lead to eventual retrenchment and retreat. Are we destined to witness this again with the police reforms that began with BLM in the 2020s?

My thanks to Chris Moloney for research assistance. This paper is based on a presentation made to a Plenary Session, "Reflecting on Criminal Justice in the Context of Black Lives Matter," of the British Society of Criminology's Annual Conference in July 2021.

Chapter 13

#EndSARS: Struggle against police brutality in Nigeria
Baba Aye

Tens of thousands of young people took to the streets to protest police brutality across all regions of Nigeria in October 2020. This youth rebellion was sparked by the alleged killing of a young man by operatives of the Federal Special Anti-Robbery Squad (FSARS) on 3 October. For 2 weeks, rallies, processions, sit-ins and other forms of demonstrations were organized in at least 25 of the country's 36 states. The primary demand of the protesters was the disbanding of the notorious elite police squad.

SARS, as the squad which was established in 1992 is generally known, had earned notoriety for extortion, torture and extrajudicial killings. It was thus emblematic of police brutality. However, the history of police brutality did not start with SARS. It goes back to the nineteenth-century origins of the police force, where it served to maintain colonial law and order, often in the most bestial of manners.

After a century of the colonial police's development, Nigeria was granted independence in 1960. Nevertheless, police brutality never became a thing of the past. It remained a force for domination of the poor and settling intra-class scores by the section of the ruling class wielding state power at different times.

Police officers equally saw the uniforms they wore, or more aptly the guns they carried, as a license for impunity. These were used to coerce bribes, dehumanize and kill people. Time and again, these heinous acts faced stiff resistance.

No unit of the police force had ever been faced with such sustained protests over the years as SARS. Moreover, never had there been such intense and widespread protest as the 2020 EndSARS revolt.

This historic mass movement was drowned in blood on 20 October 2020. The police and military acted together as Operation MESA, a joint internal security task force. When the dust settled, about one hundred people had been killed in Lagos state alone.

Before the supposedly leaderless movement's denouement, two wings had taken more apparent shape with the alternatives they put forward. The dominant liberal wing called for police reforms based on a five-point demand. A radical wing that gained ascendancy as the revolt deepened situated the police and police brutality in the political economy of exploitation and called for revolutionary transformation.

EndSARS thus condensed cogent questions on the nature of policing and police brutality, inspiring a young generation for subsequent struggles ahead.

Colonial origins and development of the Nigeria police

The roots of the police force lie in the soil of colonial development. The trajectory of the force's development thus reflects that of colonization. It served the purpose of smashing early resistance to colonization and was then used as a coercive instrument for consolidating the colonial state. Native authorities were complicit in this consolidation, and the use of the police for brutalizing the poor masses into submission. The working-class movement became a significant force after World War II. Guns and batons of the police were brought to bear to try to smash this movement.

The formal colonization of Nigeria started with the annexation of Lagos in August 1861. Within 2 months, a 25-man police force was constituted to safeguard British trading posts (Ahire, 1991, p. 34). A jail was built in the same period. William McCoskry, a merchant who was appointed as acting governor of the Lagos colony, on annexation, "considered these institutions necessary for the pursuit of the objectives of colonial domination and exploitation" (Alemika, 1993, p. 189).

This police force was reorganized into an "Armed Hausa Police Force (AHPF)" 2 years later by Henry Freeman, the first substantive governor. Freeman quadrupled the number of men and was unabashed in his view that this armed body was meant to serve the purpose of colonial expansion and domination.

Manipulation of ethnic differences was built into the development of the force at this time to ensure this aim further. The ranks of the Armed Police Force were escaped or freed slaves, most of whom were Hausa, a different ethnic and linguistic stock, from the northern parts of what would become Nigeria.

They were alien to the communities and loyal only to the colonial power. Their rabid impunity, which was at the very least condoned by the British, drove the wedge between them and the communities which grew to hate them deeper, furthering the divide and rule logic of British colonialism.

In 1864, for example, Hunkain Abujoko, a local chief and trader who had become a thorn in the British merchants' flesh, was accused of violence and robbery by the colonialists. And without any trial, 60 AHPF men were ordered to march on his village. He was killed, supposedly for resisting arrest, and Ajido, his village, was razed to the ground.

Similarly, Governor Denton of the Lagos colony also sent in a force of 500 armed police officers drawn from the AHPF and a West Indian Regiment to attack the Ijebu people who served as middlemen in trade with the hinterland. This force, led by a handful of English officers, conquered the Ijebu to establish free trade and freely looted their properties to boot (Ahire, 1991, p. 35-36).

However, it was not enough to have armed rank and file police whose allegiance was solely to the colonial masters. Notable local chiefs in the Lagos colony who were happy to collaborate were equally appointed as "Very Respectable Constables" or "Stipendiary Chiefs" by the late 1860s (Tamuno, 1970, p. 21).

As colonization expanded, first to the palm-oil rich coastal areas, then to the northern reaches of the territory, constabularies were established in each "protectorate" and used to suppress resistance to the foreign occupation. These armed bodies of men, as McCallum, a governor of the Lagos colony at the time, noted in 1897, were noted for lousy behavior, "looting, stealing and generally taking advantage of their positions."

This was a general phenomenon across British colonial Africa. "A uniform often provided a license to loot," and the "employment of uniformed aliens housed in barracks and police lines emphasized the coercive nature of the forces of law and order" (Killingray, 1986, p. 423-4). Thus, while there were a few crocodile tears by some colonial administrators, brutal violence in looting as much as in smashing anti-colonial resistance fitted perfectly into the design of colonial policing.

The West African Frontier Force was created from the police as a colonial army in 1898. Nonetheless, the police continued to function partly as an army. Internally, it remained central to the pacification project, being organized to carry out punitive expeditions and patrols until the last outpost of resistance to colonial rule was defeated in 1906. Furthermore, externally, its men fought in both world wars as WAFF battalions.

The police and consolidation of colonialism

The 1900-30 period was an "era of steady consolidation" of the police force (Tamuno, 1979, pp. 41-69). This was in sync with the consolidation of colonial rule in the wake of smashing all indigenous resistance to colonization. And indirect rule became the touchstone of colonial administrative policy (Cowan, 1958, p. 12). This enabled a handful of British to effectively colonize a vast territory of some three hundred kingdoms and city-states with a combined population of about 20 million people.

The local ruling class was incorporated into colonial domination of the poor masses. This was effective in the parts of the country which had strong centralized authority in the pre-colonial period, such as the Oyo kingdom in the west and particularly the Emirates in the north.

Two seemingly contradictory developments marked the consolidation of the police force in this context. On the one hand, there was a centralization that resulted in establishing a nationwide Nigeria Police Force (NPF) by 1930. On the other hand, native authorities, which included native courts, were established. These bodies headed by the local nobility wielded control over local police, which were used to ensure taxes were collected by force.

This spurred a wave of anti-taxation revolts as the colonial state ramped up taxation in the late 1920s. Most of these were in the eastern and coastal regions where pre-colonial administration was based on republican values or city-state delegated authority.

In 1927, anti-taxation agitators in the Warri province on the Niger delta organized trade boycotts and rescued prisoners, who had been arrested for not paying taxes, from the police, native prisons and courts (Ikime, 1966, p. 562). During an attempt by the agitators to rescue one of those arrested, police opened fire and killed a man, while several others were injured. The revolt, which revealed intense generalized anti-colonial passions in the region, raged on for months. Nevertheless, it was eventually suppressed by the police.

The Aba Women Wars of 1929 was a watershed moment. Women resisted imminent taxation and unjust rule of the colonial masters through warrant chiefs (Matera, Bastian and Kent, 2012). The first of this series of protests was organized by rural and market women in contiguous eastern and coastal provinces against direct taxation.

More than 25,000 women participated in the uprising. At least 50 of them and one man were killed by the police and army. However, the colonial government was forced to drop its intent to tax women. Inspiration from this revolt inspired similar anti-tax protests in those areas from 1938 to 1956.

Confronting workers' power with police brutality

Curbing workers' power became a central element of the police's role of maintaining "law and order" for the last 3 decades of colonialism. The rather genteel Civil Service Union was the only trade union from 1912 to 1930. In the wake of the Great Depression, unions blossomed in the 1930s. The following decade was marked by mass strikes, which the police did all it could to suppress.

The 1945 General Strike for Cost-of-Living Allowance (COLA) was a watershed inspiring renewed nationalist onslaught against colonial rule. More than 200,000 workers withdrew their services for more than 50 days. The NPF was drafted in but could not break the massive strike.

Two years later, the police moved in on 1500 striking workers demanding improved wages from the United African Company (UAC) at Burutu, in the Niger delta. Thirty-five people were seriously injured as the NPF quelled the strike. Sixty percent of the workers were sacked, while 462 were dispatched to distant locations of UAC operations to weaken combination (Falola, 2009, pp. 162-3).

The November 1949 Iva Valley massacre was the peak of anti-worker police brutality in this period. At least 21 striking miners were shot dead, and 20 were severely beaten up and had to be hospitalized for weeks (Jaja, 1982, p. 86). There was a nationwide outcry, and for the first time, the police responsible were sacked. Events in the aftermath of the massacre accelerated popular resentment (Lakemfa, 2015).

With independence on the horizon, the bourgeois nationalists had no desire to witness the power of the working class. The two fronts of their politics were negotiations with the outgoing colonialists and mobilization of ethnic identities by sections of the class from the three majority nationalities in order to conduct an intra-class struggle for power.

Six decades of flag independence and the police force

Many Nigerians had hoped that the history of "ruthlessness, brutality and the use of violence" (Tamuno, 1970, p. 253), which defined the police during the colonial period, would end with independence on 1 October 1960. It became clear that this was not the case early on in the post-independence period.

The Joint Action Committee of trade unions, which organized a General Strike for improved wages and working conditions in 1964, was one of the first bodies to point this out after police brutally dispersed striking workers' demonstrations in 1963. The unions lamented that the police force "need no longer represent the colonial toga of bloodthirst, Nazi-type troopers" and described police brutality as "a shame on republican Nigeria."[1]

However, they were only witnessing what was the tip of the iceberg of a new beginning of the police being what it is, a coercive force for the subjugation of the laboring masses. In the past sixty-odd years, the force has been used to suppress peasant revolts, mass uprisings, workers' strikes, students' demonstrations and settle scores with political opponents.

Its personnel has also routinely extorted the poor, tortured activists and other citizens, and carried out hundreds if not thousands of extrajudicial murders in their stations, suppressing protests in the most cavalier manner on the streets.

On several occasions, these acts of police brutality have been met with resistance in different forms, including loud outcries, demonstrations and, at times, the torching of police stations. The EndSARS rebellion in 2020 was the peak of such fightback. In the course of the EndSARS revolt and its aftermath, new and rehashed perspectives on what to do with the police to address police brutality came to the fore. Most of these were ahistorical and failed to or chose not to understand the political economy of the police and its consequential brutality.

From the First to the end of the Second Republic

Police reforms and institutional reorganization accelerated in the period leading to independence and immediately thereinafter. These included "Nigerianization" of the top echelons of the force and introduction of a corps of policewomen which focused on "offenses involving juveniles and females," thus freeing policemen for the more "onerous tasks" of repression and, ostensibly, crime control (Tamuno, 1970, p. 283).

Addressing questions related to control of the police was a central contentious point during the transition from colonialism to independence, as Tamuno further highlights.[2] This reflected the "fractious, ethno-centered and self-seeking" character of the ruling class in Nigeria at that point in its evolution (Graf, 1982, p. 119). The resurgence of calls for "state police" in today's Nigeria, marked by its most intense general crisis since the 1967-70 civil war, is a pointer to the unraveling of the country's rulers' vain efforts at forging consensus.

The different sections of the ruling class were and still are united around the primary purpose of the police, which is keeping the poor masses in their place. Like dogs who knew who the enemies of their masters were, police officers did not wait till they were unleashed to brutalize and extort the urban poor and peasants alike. The situation led to the most significant peasant uprising in the country's history and the dynamics of that revolt show these two sides of the same coin.

The *Àgbékòyà Parapọ̀*[3] revolt of 1968-69, in the Yoruba Western Region, was principally against taxation and exploitation by the produce marketing boards[4]. But their ire was also directed against police officers who, as they stated, "spent most of their time harassing us for bribes day and night" (Adeniran, 1974, p.367).[5] Anti-riot police were brought in to quell the revolt as it unfolded. Nevertheless, the peasants fought back. Several police officers were killed, and police stations torched. They also marched on prisons to liberate their comrades who had been arrested and incarcerated. The military could not contain the revolt. Eventually, the government gave in to their demands.

This peasant revolt was one of the first significant theaters where the deadly anti-riot mobile police squadrons were deployed. This mobile police force (MOPOL), which would later become better known as "Kill and Go" during the 1979-83 Second Republic, was established in 1962. It was used with deadly consequences to quell student protests in the 1970s.

A 23-year-old undergraduate of the University of Ibadan was killed on 1 February 1971. The police, including mobile squadrons, had been called in by the university authority to smash a peaceful protest organized by students at the university after several petitions against mismanagement and poor quality of catering services failed to yield any result. This was the first time a Nigerian student had been killed. However, it was just the beginning.

In 1978, the National Union of Nigerian Students (NUNS) organized a nationwide protest over increased school fees and meal tickets. The police and army were brought in by the military government to smash the protest. At least nine students were killed in two universities. The military returned to the barracks the following year. However, police brutality and killings of poor people continued unabated.

The civil government had spent barely half a year in power when it massacred 380 peasants in Bakolori, a community in the northwestern Sokoto state. The poor farmers were protesting the construction of a dam that had left 13,000 families landless and destitute (Yahaya, 2002). The dam project had been initiated by the military junta in 1974. The peasants were dispossessed of their lands and promised compensation. But arable lands were not provided as an alternative, and the compensation never came.

By November 1979, just a month after civil rule was reinstated, they blocked roads leading to the community. They also protected their standing crops while demanding compensation for the crops and trees that had been destroyed to make way for the dam. The state initially seemed conciliatory. However, with no gains forthcoming, the enraged peasants took over the dam in April. The response of the state was with armed troops and anti-riot police, who came to kill and destroy.

While the state reaction was brutal and destructive, the farmers were well organized and carried out their political campaign and self-defense against the rapacious state in a disciplined manner (Beckman,1984).

By the beginning of 1981, there was widespread anger against the civilian government. Corruption stank to the high heavens in its parliament and executive arm. Furthermore, at the same time, austerity measures were introduced in the wake of a sharp fall in oil prices in the global market. There was subtle "hinting at the need for the military to return" which found its way into the mainstream media along with criticisms of the government, which prompted Joe Wayas, the Senate President, to shamelessly express the view that journalists ought to be flogged (Uko, 2004, p. 59).

The MOPOL was restructured and well-armed (including with horsewhips, which were used indiscriminately on poor civilians) "as a safeguard against the return of the military" (Uko, 2004, p.59). Its men went wild and would at times shoot into the air for the fun of it. This was when they acquired the epithet of "Kill and Go." And this paramilitary arm of the police was used effectively to rig the 1983 general elections to ensure "landslide" victory for the ruling National Party of Nigeria.

As a Yoruba adage goes, "the drum sounds loudest just before it gets torn." Months after the rigged elections, the military struck. MOPOL, whose boss, Sunday Adewusi, had boasted would check any would-be coup attempts were nowhere to be found. Fed up with the thieving civilian regime, the popular masses naively welcomed the military with open arms.

Neoliberalism and the peculiarities of SARS

The junta, which came to power on 31 December 1983, was led by Major General Muhammadu Buhari and lasted 20 months. The short-lived regime was nationalist-authoritarian. The military directly policed civil society, institutionalizing a so-called War Against Indiscipline (WAI). An August 1985 palace coup brought in the junta that laid the foundations of neoliberal Nigeria and its discontents.

The junta was led by General Ibrahim Babangida, a self-described "evil genius," whom many also called "Maradona." He dribbled his way into the heart of the nation by calling for a national discussion to decide if Nigeria should access a $2.5bn loan facility that the Buhari junta was negotiating before it was overthrown, with its attendant conditionalities.

He appeared to accept the widespread rejection of that loan. Then he introduced the structural adjustment program (SAP), claiming that it was a homegrown economic program and insisting there was no alternative to SAP. This was, of course, false. The same conditionalities rejected were introduced through the backdoor with the IMF-inspired SAP.

Wage freezes, privatization of state-owned enterprises, large-scale retrenchments and removal of subsidies on commodities such as fuel were all part of the adjustment program. These led to a spiral in the unemployment rates, disillusionment and mass anger. The poverty rate, which was 28.1 percent in 1980, shot up to 48.3 percent with the introduction of SAP. There were massive protests in the late 1980s. The peak of these was the 1989 anti-SAP revolt which was crushed on the Black Wednesday of 31 May by the anti-riot MOPOL and soldiers.

This period also marked increased direct collaboration

of international oil companies with the coercive forces of the state, including the police, in suppressing mass agitations in the Niger delta. The most gruesome manifestation of this was the MOPOL's massacre of at least 80 people in the southeastern village of Umuechem village at the behest of the Shell Petroleum Development Company[6].

While hunger and poverty marked the lives of the popular classes, in the Niger delta and across the country, a "high level of corruption" was associated with the regime (Rasak, 2012, p. 5). However, this was something different from earlier forms of corruption in the country. Corrupt practice was generalized with the seeping of a "settlement" culture into every sinew of social life. Make money or die trying became a mantra for the largely unemployed youth, leading to a spike in crimes, including armed robbery. It was within this context that the regime created the Special Anti-Robbery Squad (SARS) in 1992.[7]

There had been "Anti-Robbery Squads" in different state commands of the police. But SARS was constituted as an elite unit of the police force from the beginning. Its base of operation in the first decade of its existence was the bustling state of Lagos. Its personnel was trained to infiltrate robbery gangs in the state and nip the activities of these gangs in the bud. Undercover SAP operatives were deployed to campuses where some confraternities ran robbery rings on the side.

The 1990s was also a critical decade in the growth and development of new Information and Communication Technology. Many a young unemployed youth seized the opportunity of Yahoo's free email service from 1997 for online scams. They became (and are still) known as *Yahoo boys*. And they became a significant focus of SARS.

SARS was not sparred from the moral decadence of the "settlement" culture. *Yahoo boys* who paid for their crime were mainly those who failed to "settle" SARS operatives. By the twenty-first century, they were casting their fishing nets for victims to fleece as widely as they could. Any young person with a high-end phone or laptop, or who was driving a flashy car, was liable to be harassed as a potential *Yahoo boy*. Young professionals and middle-class elements who might not be bothered by other units of the police thus saw SARS as an enemy.

The poor were not spared. SARS continued its supposedly primary work of fighting armed robbery. The means by which this was done included profiling. Youths in working-class neighborhoods with piercings, tattoos or dreadlocks faced constant harassment as potential armed robbers. Arguing with SARS operatives doing this could and quite often did result in being shot.

The unit was also notorious for torture. False confessions were often extracted through this means. This horrendous trend had been a trademark of SARS from its first year of operation. Ayotunde Adesola, a computer science graduate, was thus tortured after being arrested on the streets on 8 June 1983 (Aye 2020a). Such nefarious practice became more pronounced in the twenty-first century, as SARS operations became nationwide. Between 2009 and 2020, Amnesty International issued three reports which detailed torture and extrajudicial executions by the police, with particular reference to SARS.[8,9,10]

By the end of 2016, anger-fueled coordinated action against SARS occurred for the first time. Furthermore, "after a series of killings in the last quarter of 2017, an online petition was launched and submitted to the National Assembly with 10,195 signatories as #EndSARS protests took place in three major cities" (Aye, 2020b, p. 36).

There was a seemingly positive response by the police. It was announced that SARS "stop and search" activities would stop. However, no concrete action was taken, and SARS activities, including stop and search, continued. There were protests again in 2018 and 2019. In each case, this was after a series of extrajudicial killings by SARS operatives on the streets. In both instances, the government announced halfhearted reforms, which were never implemented, except for a name change from SARS to Federal Special Anti-Robbery Squad (FSARS) in 2019.

This was a rather hollow symbolic act. SARS operatives remained effectively above the law. Despite widely reported violations, the government "failed to prosecute any SARS officer" in those 3 years of repeated protests[11].

This was part of the increasingly authoritarian nature of the ruling All Progressives Congress regime. The APC government, led by Muhammadu Buhari, the former military head of state, came to power in 2015 with promises of fighting corruption, defeating the *Boko Haram* insurgency in the northeast, and revamping the economy. Having failed on all accounts, it sought reprieve in repression. Combined bodies of military and police personnel were routinely used to suppress demonstrations. Moreover, court orders for the release of political opponents were disregarded with impunity. In this context, SARS operatives and police officers generally were emboldened in their brutality.

#EndSARS as a prism

By the time of the COVID-19 lockdown, they had no compunction about killing people to enforce the restrictions on movement. The Nigerian Human Rights Commission reported that police and other security forces killed more people than the SARS-CoV-2 virus in the first month of the lockdown.[12] This included 16-year-old Tina Ezike. Localized protests were organized by the Coalition for Revolution (CORE)[13].

The global movement in the wake of the killing of George Floyd also found an echo in the country. CORE organized protests which drew in just dozens of people in eight towns and cities. However, nothing could have prepared anyone for the 13 days of monumental resistance in October (Aye, 2020c).

The video of SARS allegedly killing a young man in Ughelli,

a town in the Niger delta, on 3 October circulated like wildfire on social media. The following day, an ex-activist and federal minister Festus Kenyamo, who grew up in the town, tried to clear the air pointing out that the said young man was alive and had been brutalized by Operation Delta Safe, a local police unit and not SARS. He urged Ughelli youths who had commenced protests to simmer down, promising to investigate the matter.

But the genie had been let out of the bottle. The protests continued in Ughelli, and nationwide mobilization for action deepened. On 8 October, a policeman was killed in Ughelli, and protests began in the two major cities of Lagos and Abuja, the federal capital territory. Within days, it had become a nationwide rebellion.

From the onset, several forces collaborated and contended within the "leaderless" movement. These could be largely grouped into two categories. On one hand was a liberal wing. This included celebrity actors and musicians, and reformist NGOs. Its presence was amplified with online dominance and capacity to raise funds. The feminist coalition[14] which was formed barely 3 months before the protests became its rallying center, raising over $200,000 to support organizing, medical aid, legal support and sundry purposes in several cities across 31 states[15].

On the other hand was the left-wing of the rebellion, which was represented by CORE. Virtually all other sections of the left were caught flatfooted when the protests started. And few found their way into the dynamics of the rebellion for as long as it lasted. Having fewer resources and "big names" in their ranks, CORE activists were not as visible as the liberals. However, they were influential on the ground, particularly in working-class quarters within the protests, which drew in working-class and professional middle-class elements alike.

There were confrontations between the two sides in the two main cities of Abuja and Lagos. CORE activists highlighted the interconnectedness of police brutality and policing in general with the systemic exploitation and oppression of the poor masses. They tried to fan the embers of the movement into flames of revolution from the beginning. The liberals, on their part, insisted on limiting the struggle to simply ending SARS and for police reforms that would curb brutality.

Copies of the CORE Charter for Total Liberation[16] were torn up by supporters of the liberal wing. They pulled out of the sit-in in front of the Lagos state house of assembly on 10 October to protest the influence of CORE at that site. The occupation, however, grew stronger until the rebellion was quashed.

On 11 October, the police headquarters announced the disbandment of SARS and issued a "five (5) things to know about the dissolution of SARS" bulletin. This seeming concession was aimed at ending the rebellion. And government urged protesters to leave the streets. But drawing from the lessons of earlier so-called reforms and ban of the elite unit, which had been empty words, and with confidence in its growing power, the rebellion stood its ground.

A "5for5" set of demands was immediately issued and signed by "a Nigerian Youth."[17] These demands were:

1. Immediate release of all arrested protesters
2. Justice for all deceased victims of police brutality and appropriate compensation for their families
3. Setting up an independent body to oversee the investigation and prosecution of all reports of police misconduct (within 10 days)
4. In line with the Police Act, psychological evaluation and retraining (to be confirmed by an independent body) of all disbanded SARS officers before they can be redeployed
5. Increase police salary so that they are adequately compensated for protecting lives and property of citizens

These demands were formulated that day, at the barricades in Lagos by CORE comrades, in the heat of the daily assembly they organized at the Alausa front of the movement. But the liberal wing of NGOs in the rebellion appropriated them with the aim of negotiating with the government.

Drawing lessons from announcements of reforms or even the banning of SARS which had turned out to be empty words over the years and buoyed by confidence in the growing power of the mass movement, protesters stood their ground.

The police responded with increased repressive tactics. Water cannons and tear gas were used to disperse protesters in Abuja, who immediately regathered. Dozens of people were arrested. But the protesters persevered. Thugs were also used to confront protesters violently. Some of these, as captured in videos posted online, were ferried by state security officials.

In an attempt to deescalate the mounting pressure, the federal government constituted a presidential panel on police reforms which, in collaboration with the National Human Rights Commission, immediately summoned a "multi-stakeholders forum" on 13 October. This brought together liberal figures within the *massquake* – including celebrities, local NGOs and international NGOs, and philanthrocapitalism bodies like the MacArthur Foundation and the Open Society Foundations.

The Inspector-General of Police accepted the 5for5 demands. But just a few hours after, he announced that SARS was to be immediately replaced with a Special Weapons and Tactics (SWAT) unit. Not surprisingly, this deepened the angst of protesters, further radicalizing the rebellion.

Demands which underpinned the systemic cause and nature of police brutality gained currency as well as a call for the fall of the regime. Attacks by the state also intensified, directly by the police and also through thugs, some of which were driven down to sites of occupations in government-owned coaster buses.

This situation reached a climax on 19 October. Several police stations were torched, police rapid response squads were chased on the streets, and in the mid-western Benin City, protesters stormed two notorious prisons, freeing prisoners – many of whom had been awaiting trial for years – at least for a while.

The following day, the rebellion was drowned in blood. Lagos State, which was the epicenter, was the main target. There was a massacre at the Lekki Tollgate in the city. This was a prominent site of the struggle. Upwards of 5000 protesters, most of whom spent the night there, had gathered at this site for 13 days.

The massacre was carried out by Operation MESA, "a joint Internal Security Operational platform made up of the Army, the Navy and the Air force"[18] established in 2004. This dastardly action could not immediately douse the fires of anger. It quenched those of peaceful protest but sparked violent retribution on the streets for at least another week. During this period, more than 200 police stations were set ablaze, and at least 22 police officers were killed. The hashtag #EndPolice joined #EndSARS and #EndPoliceBrutality in the Nigerian blogosphere as the liberal wing of the movement declared its exit.

Malls were looted, cars burned in the road safety corps office as well as government buildings like that of the Nigeria Ports Authority. The television station and newspaper houses of Bola Tinubu, a key leader of the ruling party, were also torched, while the palace of the King of Lagos was plundered.

But the crackdown was massive. Sweeping arrests were made, and more blood spilled. Thus, order was reinstalled within a week from the massacre. Accompanying the crackdown was the demonization of the violence that took place by the liberal wing of the EndSARS movement and the state alike.

The state repeatedly claimed that a massacre never took place. Under the pressure of public opinion and international condemnation, judicial panels of inquiry were set up in states across the country. Autopsy reports presented to the Lagos state judicial panel confirmed that at least 99 bodies of killed protesters were deposited at the Lagos State University Teaching Hospital's morgue alone between 19 and 24 October 2020[19].

Thus ended a historic moment in the struggle against police brutality in the country. But, while it was crushed, it renewed confidence in mass struggle against police brutality and the system which generates it.

Conclusion

Police brutality is rooted in the colonization of Nigeria. But "post-colonial police forces have not been qualitatively different from their colonial predecessors in terms of organization and orientation" (Alemika, 1993, p 205). The police remained as much an instrument wielded by different sections of the elites to intimidate and oppress their opponents after independence as during colonial rule (Balogun, 2013).

At different times in its evolution, working through different institutions and various dimensions of the bestiality of policing have been reflective of the force's actions. The role of pacification for colonization was primary during early colonialism. SARS arose and gained prominence as a reflection of both economic and technological changes marking the period of neoliberal globalization. It appeared to place crime at the center of policing. But in doing this it revealed the crime that policing itself is.

Maintaining order has been a constant feature of the force. This has consistently been done alongside the military from the colonial era, where the army emerged from the police to OP MESA. This underlines the continuum of police-military as two hands of the same coercive body of the state.

Law and order as well as the dynamics of resistance are not simply localized. There are international dimensions to both sides of this class struggle, in several ways. For example, despite the notoriety of the Nigeria Police Force penchant for brutality, it had been funded and its operatives trained by advanced capitalist states. The British *Independent* newspaper for example revealed that the "College of Policing has worked with Nigerian authorities to train security officers" (Forrest, 2020).

The international dimension on the part of resistance was the inspiration from the global spread of the Black Lives Matter protest in the wake of the murder of George Floyd.

Mass resistance has always commenced spontaneously, as in that case. While the socio-economic situation's relationship with the readiness to confront the system is not a linear one, it is often a contextual enabler. Another enabler, this time political, is the recent demonstrable capacity of confrontations with the state.

These two contextual elements can be seen clearly in the period leading to the EndSARS rebellion. The unemployment rate in the second quarter of the year was 27.1 percent, and the underemployment rate was 28.6 percent. By the second quarter, the unemployment rate was 28.2 percent. And by the fourth quarter, it was 33 percent[20]. The proportion of working poor had also increased. Workers in the formal sector suffered significant wage cuts. And those in the informal economy found it increasingly difficult to make ends meet.

The regime had become increasingly repressive to dam the tide of simmering mass anger. But on 5 August 2019, the Coalition for Revolution (CORE) launched a nationwide #RevolutionNow campaign[21]. This marked a rebirth of radical confrontation by a critical mass. And this was sustained with a series of nationwide protests up to 1 October 2020, just on the eve of the EndSARS conflagration. With the powerful trade union movement shying away from frontal confrontation with the state, the #RevolutionNow campaign inspired confidence in mass action.

The working and living conditions of working-class people and youth continue to worsen amid generalized insecurity. Kidnapping, banditry and wanton killing worsens the frustration of the masses. The school of struggle of CORE equally marches on.

A former presidential spokesperson described #EndSARS as

"almost a revolution" (Abati, 2020). Moreover, indeed, it was such. A pitched battle with the state's attack dogs revealed the state in its utter nakedness. The likelihood of more massive movements than EndSARS emerging in the next few years is high. It will seek much more than "justice" as the epigones of the colonial masters define it.

Chapter 14

Formed from the Colonial Model: Prospects for Reforming the Mexican Police?
Fernando Tenorio Tagle and Vincenzo Scalia

Introduction

All the academic discussions about such issues as crime, security and policing are usually built upon the European and North American context, thus neglecting the need for a wide ranging comparative analysis. Whereas we appreciate that neoliberal hegemony (Harvey, 2007) has brought about similar trends across the world in sharpening social inequalities and political marginalization, these processes have been mediated by national and cultural peculiarities.

In the case of Mexico we are facing sharp contradictions between its status as the fifteenth largest world economy, more and more dynamic and fast-growing, and such serious problems as migration and the rise of organized crime. How these aspects are reflected in the security policies, as well as in the dynamics of policing in Mexico, can add to the domain of criminological knowledge, as well as helping to take a step forward in the process of decolonizing the curriculum that has been developing across US and UK universities in recent years.

Here we propose an analysis of the Mexican police based on a critical criminology-approach. Mexican police forces contain some specific peculiarites (Karam, 2012). As well as being part of the Institutional Revolutionary Party (PRI) party-state government from 1929 to 2008, the police are usually divided between federal and state forces, with central government facing difficulties in maintaining control of them all. Moreover, private police forces and security firms have been thriving in Mexico, as in other Latin American countries (Tavares and Barrera, ed., 2016), This is a consequence of sharp inequalities that make the affluent part of society feel secure through the hire of extra protection supplied by private forces which often turn out to be vigilante squads. This paper will reflect upon all these contradictions.

A criminological framework

In a recent work (Tenorio Tagle 2018), one of the authors came to the conclusion that the Mexican criminal justice system sustains the balance of political forces in a way that does not necessarily correspond to the constitutional framework of other Western countries, as is the case with almost every culture on the planet. In this regard, the specialized literature based on labeling theories and later called critical criminology does not neatly fit the situation in southern Europe and in our Latin American region. In all cases there is evidence of a punitive selectivity that makes it possible to appreciate that criminal punishment, especially jail, is designed for the government of poverty, that is, for the government of the lower classes of society.

Even the contributions of anthropology such as René Girard (2005) show that the struggle that gave rise to the state formation process was brought about at the cost of the weakest of the original archaic societies. Hence the need to enact a system of criminal punishment against those qualified or constructed as "Other": As often happens, few recipients of punitive violence belong to a higher social stratum. Raúl Zaffaroni has constructed the agnostic theory of punishment (2013), where the purpose of punishment is to keep the state's enemies in their place, an issue very evident in economically depressed regions such as Latin America. When other institutions are linked to the criminal justice system, such as the army and the navy in the Mexican case, they will come to act according to this latent function, according to the description of the same by Robert

Merton in his "structure of social action" (1980).[1] Therefore the first interventions in the "fight against crime" are the actions of such an armed body in conjunction with the police forces.

But as in any "struggle" or "war" of this nature, violence grows along with its lethality, as in the Italian, Colombian and indeed Mexican cases. Wars, all of them against so-called "organized crime," began with its central activity in drug trafficking, and later moved into other illegal areas such as trafficking of the goods and human trafficking, kidnapping and "flat renting," that is, charging money for security. This brand of special criminality will have two distinctive elements: First, it is extremely instrumental and, secondly, the rationale that the goal is the accumulation of capital and is organized because members of the penal system are part of it, ensuring the success of the enterprise. Consequently, we find ourselves in a deep cesspit of corruption which transcends all areas of the criminal justice system: the police, the prosecutors and even the judges.

Dario Melossi's insights when interpreting the development of democracy in the United States are revealing:

In the cultural heart of the United States – even today, in my opinion, New England Protestantism, beyond what the representatives of the current fashions of postmodernism and multiculturalism tell us – there was no room for the disorienting, authoritarian and deeply conservative indulgence of the Catholic tradition. Right or wrong, black or white: whoever is or is perceived to be on the wrong side of the law will be punished. And even those who break the law but are powerful (economically, ethnically, racially, culturally or politically) will be able to afford full use of the guarantees that a democratic legal system confers on them – they can be bought – so to speak, the entire stock of guarantees available in the market (Melossi 1997).

If we add to the above, which seems to be a current practice, that with the Spanish colonization of what is now Mexico, "Justice" was incorporated into the category of "salable trades" (Lafaye 1992), which created large profits for all those involved in the criminal justice process: The Crown; the mayor, the magistrates, those in charge of confinement while cases were being solved, etc. It can be conjectured that after Mexico's independence, the new justices that followed the formal norms continued to develop their activities based upon the repealed norms, as if it were a salable trade.

A colonial police?

Although there are important differences between the pre-modern and modern colonizations of the British Empire and those developed by the Spanish Crown, both colonization policies were implemented to impose the formal and informal order of their cultural tradition, as well as other European colonization processes and in all cases with large social costs for the invaded population, including mass slaughter: In Mexico alone, of the 25.2 million indigenous population in 1418, in the wake of the Spanish colonization by 1622 that population was reduced to 750,000 (Borah Woodrow 1985). The epidemics carried by the Spanish population also impacted the death of millions of indigenous people who added to the deaths in what were later called "pacification" wars.

In this regard, Brogden, using the contributions of Johnson (1982), focuses on the issue of indigenous medicine that were delegitimized in order to impose British criteria and the characteristics of those who can practice it. In the autochthonous case of what is now Mexico, medicine was called in the Nahuatl language "Tiziotl" and the doctor "Tizitil." Once the conquest was established, the original medicine was known as "curandería" and by virtue of the autochthonous medicine appealing to its own gods, it was ruthlessly persecuted to the point of its elimination. However, given that to be a doctor in the Spanish tradition, purity of blood was required and therefore there were very few doctors, quackery was formally persecuted but informally tolerated in practice to care for the population that fell ill. By the end of the colonial period, Spanish medicine came to impose itself in the sense that we know it when passing to modernity through the establishment of the universities (Tenorio Tagle 1991).

In all other cultural spheres there is no doubt of the colonial success in imposing the Spanish tradition in the region. An accurate reading can be seen in Jacques Lafaye's text "Quetzalcóatl y Guadalupe," translated as "The formation of the national conscience of Mexico" (1992). The conquest of Mexico like those of other cultural traditions, especially the pre-modern ones, appealed to the superiority of the promoters of invasions (Tenorio Tagle 1999) and, in the case of the Hispanic invasion of what is now Latin America, also leading to the salvation of the conquered population to incorporate it into the "one true religion."

This led to an iron stratification of society, at the top of which were the peninsular – those born in Spain – followed by the Creoles; the various castes of blood mixing with the black and indigenous population, totaling 16 strata (Aguirre Beltrán 1989). However, the way the Catholic Church used the fictitious appearance of the Virgin of Guadalupe in the sixteenth century would not only trap the lower strata within the Spanish Catholic tradition, but would also serve as a tool for the war of independence: "America for the Americans" was a slogan employed years before the Monroe doctrine, because the mother of God had supposedly appeared in America.

In this way, the castes and the natives joined the Creoles to fight against those not born in America, that is, the peninsular (Lafaye 1992). After the military victory, the foundations of the new order were the same as those of the conquest, not only did

Mexican independence begin with an empire but also with the endorsement of Catholicism as the one true religion, which led the old castes to maintain the qualification of superiority over of the Creole population that would later come to form the bourgeoisie. The iron social control in New Spain was maintained during the first century of independent Mexico and would lead to the revolution at the beginning of the twentieth century, in which the social exclusion of the old castes continued, although to a lesser extent, until today.

Focusing on the field of interest here: the criminal justice system and especially the police forces, there is not the slightest doubt of the colonial heritage and its influence in independent Mexico. The reasons for this, somewhat atypical compared to other countries, are related to the successive internal wars between conservatives and liberals, and international ones such as the invasions by the United States and France that Mexico suffered during the nineteenth century.

To demonstrate the political and governmental crisis in this period, consider that from 1822 to 1911 Mexico had two emperors and 48 presidents, one of whom, Porfirio Díaz, was president for the second time from 1884 to 1911. This meant Mexico was an autonomous country but with laws borrowed or inherited from the colonial period. This is demonstrated by the compilations of the laws that governed the Mexican courts during that period of crisis until the restoration of the republic by President Benito Juárez (1867).

This is evidenced by the "Hispanic – Mexican Pandectas," compiled by the jurist Juan N. Rodríguez de San Miguel (1980) and which included many sections which still endure.[2] They were, in reality, copies of the old Hispanic laws from which the processes in the courts were developed. A good example of this are the laws relating to "Riots, Shocks and Popular Strikes" which first appeared in 1432, the second version dating from 1462 and so on, entrusting to the police their prevention and prosecution with the help of the military institutions based in the outskirts of towns or cities. Maybe that is the origin of the criminalization of social protest in our region. The chapter on the organization and functions of the police contains various rules and regulations that, in the opinion of its promoter, the Governor of Mexico City in 1836, stated that the previous regulations of the 1730s, 1790s and others are more than sufficient and, therefore, instead of proposing new legislation, the old rules were retained.

In this same regard, the social control delegated to the police in the case of "masters and servants" is interesting, and on the basis of this, the item "Domestic Servant" is derived. It came from the constitutional laws of the 1830s, where it was decreed that citizenship is lost when becoming a servant. Laws that were in force until 1901 in the country stated when a domestic servant (according to the regulation of "Amos y Criados") moved from one town to another, they had to carry a notebook signed by their Master indicating the reason for the trip; the servant was required to take it to the police for the respective stamp. On arrival at their destination, the new Master should sign the book and take it to the police to be similarly endorsed. In this sense, not only is citizenship lost but also freedom of movement or roaming is restricted (Salazar 1978). As is evident, from the colony to the present day, domestic servants originated from the "lower castes," mainly indigenous people, and currently their social heirs.

Mexican police from 1917 to neo-liberalism

The Mexican revolution at the beginning of the twentieth century gave rise to the current constitution of 1917, which in addition to its liberal court added the agrarian rights of the peasant and the social rights of the working class, in order to eliminate the social stratification of the Colony that persisted in independent Mexico until this time, together with the strong punitive influence of the Victorian law known as "Less eligibility" which promoted the criterion that conditions in the jail must be worse than the worst place in freedom (Melossi D. and Pavarini M. (1981)). However, the institutions of such a system maintained the colonial heritage of the "salable office" in the informality amounting to corruption, which is most cynically displayed in the Mexican police apparatus.

Focusing on the Mexico City police (Elena Azaola 2006) has shown that the corruption of policing began in the University of the Police of Mexico City (formerly the Police School). An example of this is the payment of fees to pass the exams and gain the required qualifications. In addition to this, when the police personnel formally enter their duties, they must pay fees to the bosses, either before starting the working day or at the end of it. The fees are higher if the policeman uses a motorcycle and more if he uses a patrol car. The dominance of Mexico City, where the federal powers are based, over all the Mexican provinces should be appreciated – the provinces gradually follow the legal reforms as well as the forms of action in all fields of public administration. An example of the above can be seen in the "Ayotzinapa" and "Atenco" cases, to which we will refer later. Likewise, if the elucidations of Massimo Pavarini (1997) regarding the prison are followed, proving that such an institution is building its own rules of action independently of the laws, it is highly probable that the same will happen with the laws of other institutions within the criminal justice system, who are caught in the web of corruption regardless of the laws that formally regulate their actions.

This special form of police action that persecutes and simultaneously tolerates crime has its origin in the "informal economy," which ranges from so-called "piracy," that is to say, the sale of signature products but clandestinely and falsely elaborated, up to all the actions of illegal trafficking, without neglecting various forms of theft and other crimes. It is understood that those who commit crimes and are tolerated pay the bribes, as happened in the liberal stage of capitalist society: However, in the current neoliberal stage, it seems that the relations between crime and the police forces are being reversed, with the forces of law and order being under the control of criminality itself. In this regard, consider the large amounts of money that organized crime raises every year. As an example, Luis Astorga has shown in the Sinaloa case that:

> Carlos Morán Cortés, former president of the Eustaquio Buelna Bar Association, proved that the main criminals were the police themselves, who engaged in assault, kidnapping and murder. He also said that senior state officials and those of the Attorney General's Office were in collusion with the traffickers. Other authorized voices from various political parties and even the Church, although in a less forceful way, concurred with these remarks (Astorga 2016. p. 166).

Furthermore, he also claims: "In Mexico, the central government has its own security forces, but most of the political corporations depend on the states and municipalities where all political parties hold government positions and, therefore, are able to combat or protect criminal organizations" (Astorga 2015). Whichever political party governs the federation or its member states is irrelevant. The linkage of state institutions, such as the criminal justice system and in general the political sphere, as members of the private sector, are participating in the field of corruption. It is interesting that sometimes the political system and its forces of order are in command and other times the process is reversed. Then organized crime itself gives the orders (Astorga 2015, 2016).

Another form of corporate crime is what Raúl Zaffaroni and Ílison Dias dos Santos describe as the era of "financial totalitarianism," where financial institutions on the global stage are developing a more aggressive activity with negotiations in regions such as Latin America that lead to a serious deterioration of their wealth and a powerful enrichment of the service providers and of the corrupt politicians – the representatives of the countries that sign the economic agreements (Zaffaroni and Dias dos Santos (2019)).

Both actions can be seen in the cases known as "Atenco" and "Ayotzinapa." The government demanded the eviction of people to construct a new airport, partly in retaliation for them preventing the establishment of the airport earlier in 2006. They tried to evict street vendors from the town, leading to bouts of extreme violence that culminated in multiple arrests where people were tortured, harassed and sexually violated. After various legal disputes that reached the international arena, the Inter-American Court of Human Rights decided in 2018 to condemn the Mexican State for their actions.

In the second case, Ayotzinapa, regarding the kidnapping of students and their subsequent disappearance in 2014, the PRD governed the municipalities involved and the State Government and the PAN in a federation. The stories and investigations certify the participation of police officers from the different orders of government and organized crime. To this day the case has not been resolved and only a few student corpses have been found in clandestine graves located in other states of the country.

Both actions can be seen in the cases known as "Atenco" and "Ayotzinapa": The Atenco case demonstrates the authoritarianism of the state, while the Ayotzinapa case illustrates the controlling influence of organized crime. In the first of them, the National Action Party governed the country, the PRI the State of Mexico and the PRI, in conjunction with the Green Party, the municipality. The immediate antecedent that contextualizes the Atenco case dated May 3 and 4, 2006, is the federal government demand to build the Mexico City airport on lands of the Municipality of Atenco, State of Mexico, which were expropriated for these purposes. However, in 2001 the Front of Peoples in Defense of the Land (hereinafter "FPDT") was formed with the "initial objective of opposing the expropriation of their lands. Having achieved its objective, it survived as a social organization, claiming its own claims and supporting the causes of other social movements. Shortly after, they joined seventeen social organizations."

Subsequently, the 2003-2006 municipal development plan of Texcoco established as one of its objectives "the relocation of informal commerce located in the municipal seat in order to recover common use areas and improve the urban image."

By virtue of the foregoing, on October 21, 2005, an agreement was signed between the government and the representatives of the florists who traded in front of the Belisario Domínguez market in order to be relocated to the Centro de Abasto de Productos del Campo y Flores de Texcoco, where the municipality gave space for each florist to be assigned a position. However, eight florists had not relocated and continued to sell in front of the Belisario Domínguez market. On April 11, 2006, elements of the municipal police tried to prevent flower growers from locating their positions. However, said authority remarked that, shortly after, approximately thirty or forty people with machetes showed up, including florists from Texcoco but also members of the FPDT, leading to a confrontation, which damaged vehicles of the aforementioned General Directorate.

On May 2, 2006, in a new meeting, with the presence of Patricia Romero Hernández (leader of the florists) and Ignacio del Valle Medina (leader of the FPDT) and of authorities of the government of the state of Mexico, but without the presence of the authority in the municipality of Texcoco, the Director of the Interior agreed to the request to withdraw the public force from the vicinity of the market, "so that the next day they would install their posts in that place, because it was celebrated on the day of the Holy Cross." However, that same day the Municipal

Police of Texcoco reinforced the security device that had been installed since April 12, 2006. Municipal, state and federal police participated in the operations of May 3 and 4, 2006. On May 3, the police forces prevented the installation of flower stalls as agreed and clashes broke out between the FDPT and the police forces, causing both parties injuries. Some policemen were detained by members of the FDPT and part of the civil population in solidarity with the flower sellers took refuge in a building. Reinforced, the police forces detained several people, including those who had taken refuge in the building, who were transferred to the prison authorities.

Simultaneously in Atenco, the FDPT closed a highway in order to free the detainees. On May 4, meeting representatives of the State of Mexico, including its governor (who would later become the President of the Republic), and of the Federation, it was agreed to use force to rescue the detained police officers, their weapons and patrols and detain those who acted in flagrante delicto. As is evident, they fulfilled their objectives by violating the human rights of the civilian population, arresting people who were in their homes and the detainees were transferred to official bodies for prosecution. Some seriously injured were taken to hospital. Notwithstanding, in addition to various human rights violations, the Atenco case shows various practices of torture against detainees and especially against women based on various forms of harassment and rape. After various legal remedies that reached the international arena, the Inter-American Court of Human Rights decided in 2018 to condemn the Mexican State for such events. What has been narrated up to here is found in the aforementioned link to the rulings of the Inter American Court of Human Rights (corteidh. or.cr <contentious cases.Mexico> Women victims of sexual torture in Atenco VS Mexico).

In the second case related to the kidnapping of students and their subsequent disappearance in 2014, the PRD governed the municipalities involved and the State Government and the PAN governed in the federation. The stories and investigations certify the participation of police officers from the different orders of government and organized crime. To this day the case has not been resolved and only a few bodies of students have been found in clandestine graves located in other states of the country.

Some parts taken from the report of the interdisciplinary group of independent experts "GIEI" reveal that the events of September 26 and 27, 2014 were an action attributable to the Mexican State, understanding as such, the group of organs of the three levels of government that by action and omission intervened and allowed the events that caused the effects of disappearance, death and serious injuries, together with criminal groups, in particular "Los Rojos and Los Guerreros Unidos."

The Ayotzinapa report published by the "GIEI" highlights the following:

1. The scale of the attack and number of victims: During these events, the direct victims of different human rights violations were more than 180 people, the vast majority of them young people and many minors:

   a) Six people were extrajudicially executed (including a normalista with clear signs of having been tortured, and another two with point-blank shots, that is, less than 15cm away; and with three fatalities in the attack on the Hornets, including a minor), in four different settings: the intersection of Juan N. Álvarez and Periférico Norte streets (in this case in two different episodes), the Andariego road in the industrial area of Iguala, the road leaving Iguala in front of the Palace of Justice, and the Santa Teresa junction 15 km from the city on the way to Chilpancingo.

b) More than 40 people were injured, some of them extremely serious and underwent surgery, and one of them is still in a coma and / or stupor. These victims were injured in the events referred to in the initial scene on Juan N. Álvarez and Periférico Norte streets, in the second attack 3 hours later in the same place and at the Santa Teresa intersection where there were two consecutive attacks.

c) About 80 other people, including Ayotzinapa students and teachers and other people who mobilized in their support, suffered different forms of persecution and attempts on their lives in at least three settings, including the drivers of the affected buses: the street Juan N. Álvarez and Periférico norte; the area before the Palace of Justice and the Pajaritos neighborhood; and the area of Colonia 24 de Febrero in Iguala.

d) Another 30 people in the Los Avispones bus case at the Santa Teresa crossing scene suffered attacks on their lives and survived.

e) 43 Ayotzinapa normalistas were detained and forcibly disappeared from two different places and buses, one in the center of the city and the other on the outskirts of Iguala.

f) Among the victims, we must also consider the relatives of these direct victims, at least 700 people, considering only the direct relatives, and especially the relatives of the 43 disappeared normalistas.

Although the level of aggression and violence cannot be summarized in numerical data, these figures show both the extent of the violence, the different times and scenarios in which it occurred, and the scope of its consequences that persist today.

List of missing students: 1) Felipe Arnulfo Rosa, 2) Benjamín Ascencio Bautista, 3) Israel Caballero Sánchez, 4) Abel García

Hernández, 5) Emiliano Alen Gaspar de la Cruz, 6) Doriam Gonzales Parral, 7) Jorge Luis Gonzales Parral , 8) Magdaleno Rubén Lauro Villegas, 9) José Luis Luna Torres, 10) Mauricio Ortega Valerio, 11) Jesús Jovany Rodríguez Tlatempa, 12) Abelardo Vázquez Peniten, 13) Adan Abraján de la Cruz, 14) Christian Tomás Colón Garnica, 15) Luis Ángel Francisco Arzola, 16) Carlos Lorenzo Hernández Muñoz, 17) Israel Jacinto Lugardo, 18) Julio César López Patolzin, 19) José Ángel Navarrete González, 20) Marcial Pablo Baranda, 21) Miguel Ángel Mendoza Zacarías, 22) Alexander Mora Venancio, 23) Bernardo Flores Alcaraz, 24) Luis Ángel Abarca Carrillo, 25) Jorge Álvarez Nava, 26) José Ángel Campos Cantor, 27) Jorge Aníbal Cruz Mendoza, 28) Giovanni Galindes Guerrero, 29) Jhosivani Guerrero de la Cruz, 30) Cutberto Ortiz Ramos, 31) Everardo Rodríguez Bello, 32) Christian A Alfonso Rodríguez Telumbre, 33) Martín Getsemany Sánchez García, 34) Jonás Trujillo Gonzales, 35) José Eduardo Bartolo Tlatempa, 36) Leonel Castro Abarca, 37) Miguel Ángel Hernández Martínez, 38) Carlos Iván Ramírez Villarreal, 39) Jorge Antonio Tizapa Legideño, 40) Antonio Santana Maestro, 41) Marco Antonio Gómez Molina, 42) César Manuel Gonzales Hernández and 43) Saúl Bruno García.

The point called level of aggression suffered reveals the capacity for armed violence that the attack on students and other people entailed, as referred to below:

2. The level of aggression suffered

The aforementioned data shows the level of aggression suffered, its indiscriminate nature (shooting at civilians, unarmed and fleeing), as well as the progressive increase in the level of aggression since the start of the bus seizure (persecution and shots into the air) until the blockade, shots to kill, beatings, preparation of ambush actions, or persecution for a long time that were experienced at different times. The attack with firearms in the very center of the city involved shooting at buses filled with young people who had taken them from the bus station, and at a large group of people who were in the street or at a concert in the zócalo in large numbers. The deployment of agents around the city appearede was absolutely disproportionate and meaningless, given the level of risk that a bus seizure or an eventual confrontation with stones thrown could pose at some point. The *normalistas* were not armed, nor did they boycott any political act, nor attack the population as indicated in different accounts.

The GIEI has had to face an enormous level of fear, even today, in order to carry out its investigation in Iguala. Many witnesses did not want to speak, others did so in the midst of great fear and requesting confidentiality, others provided information only after numerous previous contacts made through trusted networks. Fear is not only a response to the level of aggression suffered, but to the degree of control perceived in the area by the perpetrators or their accomplices, and the lack of protection that witnesses feel against possible actions against them. Witness protection is key in this process and its importance has been pointed out to state authorities.

In other parts of the report, it is noted that at least nine attacks took place in different places and at different times, which shows the coordination capacity of those who perpetrated them, authorities and members of a criminal group. The time in which the action took place ranges from 5:59 pm to 8:00 pm of prior surveillance in which the movement of the normalistas is monitored, and the attack lasted from 9:40 pm to 12:30 am. The monitoring was carried out by state, federal and army police, with direct attacks by Iguala, Cocula and other aggressors.

The coordination system between state, municipal and federal police, in addition to the Mexican army known as C-4, operated during the night of September 26 and 27, 2014.

The communications which the GIEI has been able to access show that there were people who reported acts of violence or asked for help through the emergency telephone number 066 and two periods in which no communications appeared in C4 (provided to the GIEI), and that there were times when the communications were intercepted by the National Defense Secretariat (SEDENA).

The presence of federal, state and army police is documented in different places where the events occurred. In one part of the report the following is related:

> In addition to the municipal police of Iguala and Cocula who were the direct aggressors, in the two scenes of Juan N. Álvarez and the Palace of Justice where normalistas were detained and disappeared, there was the presence of agents from the army, federal and ministerial police at different times. After the arrest of the normalistas, an army patrol visited the guardrail police station where a group of arrested normalistas apparently had been taken, and later the same patrol went to the Cristina Hospital where a group of surviving normalistas and one of the wounded had taken refuge. He also guarded the crime scene where two normalistas were killed on Juan N Álvarez and Periférico Norte streets after the second attack. Later, another army patrol arrived between 6 and 7 am and guarded the place where the lifeless and tortured body of Julio César Mondragón appeared, before the civil authorities arrived.

What can be said is that the direct acts of aggression were committed at least by municipal police from Iguala and Cocula and by members of criminal groups. Although state and federal police may have acted at various times, in any case, they and the army were present in the scenes of the violence and participated in the coordination of it, among other means, through the C4. The GIEI report analyzes the issue of the direction and coordination of attacks in the following terms:

3. Direction and coordination of attacks and / or responses to them

The level of intervention of different police officers and scenarios and of the attacks at different times shown by the documents, testimonies and expert opinions evaluated by the GIEI, shows the existing coordination and command to carry out said action. The operational need for coordination between forces from two different municipal police forces (Iguala and Cocula), and at least 18 municipal patrols and one from civil protection that intervened that night indicate the need for a central coordination level that gave the orders.

On the one hand, according to a protected witness, a state patrol participated in transferring a detained and later released driver. On the other hand, one of the surviving drivers indicates that he was taken to a safe house in the center of Iguala, and presented to a man who was directing the operation or making decisions about the actions to be carried out with detainees. This modus operandi indicates a command structure, with operational coordination. This testimony also suggests that the decision of what to do with the bus drivers, who were detained with the later disappeared *normalistas*, was not taken at that time and that the objective of the action was not directed against them but against the *normalistas*. Notwithstanding the fact that the content of the communications is not known, at the time the attacks were taking place there was communication between two of those accused of being responsible for these events, the Municipal President and the Secretary of Public Security, Felipe Flores. One of the antennas that picked up a call from this phone is near the scene of the Palace of Justice. Mr Abarca indicated that he had communicated with members of the Guerrero government's security secretary, the federal police, and the 27th Battalion. If the content of these conversations was information on the events or other coordination circumstances, this is part of what must be investigated.

The textual parts have been taken from the Ayotzinapa report, relating to the first six months of the GIEI's investigation, from pages 311 to 318. The second part of the GIEI report includes a set of observations that show the shortcomings and successes in the investigation. From the selected parts of the Ayotzinapa report it can be convincingly inferred that it was an attack of such proportions that it required a coordinated action in which different state, federal, Guerrero State, Cocula and Iguala forces intervened – alongside the Mexican army; and the report concludes that although it was the municipal police and criminal groups who carried out the actions constituting homicide, the disappearances and torture, it can also be inferred that other federal and state authorities directly intervened, and had a presence, observation and knowledge of what was happening, and – of course – did not prevent it. The same can be inferred from the presence and performance of the army.

The GIEI originated from an agreement between the Mexican Government and the Inter-American Commission on Human Rights to communicate to Mexican citizens and the Mexican State the precautionary measure 409-14, granted by the commission in favor of the students of the Rural Normal School "Raul Isidro Burgos de Ayotzinapa" pursuant to Article 25 of the commission's regulations regarding Mexico. Because the Mexican State allowed the GIEI to act for only two periods of six months each, the Inter-American Commission on Human Rights created a Special Follow-up Mechanism to the Ayotzinapa Matter (MESA) in whose final report of November 25, 2018 is the GIEI report that was derived from Precautionary Measure 409-14, whose purpose was to search for the students, investigate the facts and care for the victims. In turn, the Special Mechanism was created by the Inter-American Commission to monitor compliance with the precautionary measure and the recommendations of the GIEI. Due to the mechanism's presence in Mexico, Mexican investigations have been directed at different municipal police forces, such as the municipal police of Huitzuco de los Figueroa, Tepecoacuilco de Trujano, Tilcaya, Eduardo Neri, and Buena Vista de Cuéllar and Apaxtla de Castrejón, as well as the state police of Guerrero, the federal police, the ministerial police of the local prosecutor's office and the investigation of the 27th infantry battalion. The investigations denote the intervention of a complex and organized police and military apparatus.

The report reveals police intelligence activities in telephone analysis. What has not happened is an investigation regarding the possible criminal intervention of higher authorities of a police, military and political nature. In its conclusions, the mechanism presents different recommendations to prosecute the perpetrators and to investigate the allegations of torture that are currently better documented in accordance with the Istanbul Protocol methodology. The mechanism also recommended that the Mexican State put into practice the general laws recently approved on torture, forced disappearance and disappearance committed by individuals, as well as on the search for persons. The General Law to Prevent, Investigate and Punish Torture and Other Cruel Inhuman or Degrading Treatment or Punishment was published in the Official Gazette of the Federation on June 26, 2017, and the General Law on Forced Disappearance of Persons, Disappearance committed by Individuals and the National System for the Search of Persons was published in the Official Gazette of the Federation on November 17, 2017. It can be said that both laws are the result of activism of victims and of civil society, in particular, of national campaigns and international non-governmental organizations. Various cases, including Ayotzinapa, constitute a fundamental precedent for the approval of these laws.

Finally, in March 2018 the United Nations High Commissioner for Human Rights published the Double Injustice Report on human rights violations in the investigation of the Ayotzinapa case, in which it accounts for the confessions obtained through torture, the lack of access to an adequate defense and violations to the detriment of the persons to whom the Mexican State attributed responsibility in the case. Currently the Office of the Attorney General of the Republic has created a Prosecutor's Office for the Ayotzinapa case, derived from the Truth Commission that the current Federal Executive created in this regard. These horrifying examples of state crimes carried out by agents of social control indicate that we are in a new stage of colonialism in which the police forces of various countries participate, such as the cases of Mexico and other Latin American countries and also the United States. We are also in a process of economic invasion where the promoters of the same enrich themselves along with multiple negative consequences for the inhabitants of the invaded countries. In all cases evidence of corruption is overwhelming: in order for these actors to get away with this special form of criminality the presence and active collaboration of the corrupter and the corrupted is required: No one is exempt from responsibility although, as mentioned above, the powerful – racially, ethnically, economically and politically – can buy the entire stock guarantees that an apparent democratic state offers in the market. The question posed is whether to fight or to protect crime. Perhaps if neocolonialism were suppressed, which seems an idealistic notion, all social problems, such as those presented here, could be reduced by appealing to the title of the book by Nils Christie, "A suitable amount of crime" (Chrisitie 2004), where the police instead of protecting the state and its institutions, saw their duty as to protect the still weak sovereign, that is the citizen.

Conclusions

Can neo-colonialism, as an articulation of neoliberalism, be suppressed? What would be in this case the implication for police forces? These questions should be reflected upon at the end of this paper, although there is no straightforward answer to them.

Apparently, neo-colonialism in policing thrives more than ever in Mexico, with the US government constantly attempting to seek collaboration with Mexican police forces in stopping illegal immigration and fighting organized crime. The 2016 Merida plan, where Mexican special forces were trained, equipped and paid by the USA government, looks like an articulation of this neo-colonial model of policing. On the other hand, there are many growing counter-tendencies to this. Mexican civil society has become more and more reactive against neo-colonialism, as well as mobilizing against organized crime and the many and varied brutalities of local police forces. The activism of civil society, as well as the mobilization of local populations, can be the first step toward changing Mexican police and policing, by promoting a different training and recruitment criteria, as well as through enforcing the institution of independent authorities to investigate police crimes. These changes need to be incorporated at the institutional stage, through the adoption of uniform governance criteria both at the level of the federal and the state governments. Only in this fashion can a way out of neo-colonialism be drawn.

Chapter 15

The Police in Neoliberal Greece: Toward a Radical Confrontation?
Stratos Georgoulas and Georgios Papanicolaou

Introduction

As the first several weeks of 2021 passed in lockdown Greece, few would have suspected that Nea Smyrni, a quiet residential area in the southeast of Athens, would become the epicenter of protest against police abuse and excessive force. In the afternoon of March 7, 2021, a group of police officers from DIAS, a fast response unit of the Hellenic Police featuring heavily equipped personnel on motorbikes, forcibly dispersed a group of young people taking a stroll in the square. The group had allegedly violated the restrictions of movement in public spaces which the Greek government had introduced as part of the country's Covid-19 response. Videos of the incident emerged rapidly on social media and left very little doubt that this was yet another incident of unnecessary and excessive force – one of many featuring this particular police unit. As popular discontent with the heavily policed curfews and restrictions had been brewing for a while, Nea Smyrni became the location of a sizable spontaneous demonstration later that Sunday. Then on 9 March a large rally and demonstration took place, this time an explicit protest against police abuse and excessive force, particularly in the context of the counter-pandemic measures. As protesters marched, a group of young people attacked a police officer belonging to another police motorbike unit, "Drasi" – the successor of the notorious "Delta" unit that had established a reputation for violent tactics during the anti-austerity mobilizations of the first half of the 2010s (see, e.g., BBC News, 2011). The group reacted against the unit's trademark tactic of riding on bikes through the crowd; a young person emerging from the crowd caught up with the last motorbike, pulled the rider to the ground and a melee followed. Having recovered their colleague, the police in turn escalated their response throughout the evening, performing acts of violence and arrests, particularly targeting young people returning home from the march (Papanicolaou and Rigakos, 2021). In the wake of the incident, the police abducted and arrested 21-year-old Aris Papazacharoudakis, a member of the local anarchist collective Masovka, who was then allegedly tortured while in police custody. Following his release, as no charges were brought against him, Papazacharoudakis presented publicly his allegations of police torture, which the police and the leadership of the Ministry of the Protection of Public Order dismissed. The 21-year-old is currently preparing to pursue a legal case against the police.

The incidents during and after the protest at Nea Smyrni very much reflect several key tactical, organizational and institutional developments in Greek policing. There is now a renewed emphasis on the policing of public spaces, particularly targeting political dissent and social protest, generally by means of specialized, mobile and heavily militarized public order units. This development is driven by the policies of the New Democracy party, elected in 2019 with an emphatic "law-and-order" agenda. These policies fuel known authoritarian and militaristic tendencies in the Hellenic Police, as the government actively invests in new specialist units and new equipment targeting public space and vocally defends their deployment rationale and tactics. At the same time, the government has proceeded with the introduction of a series of controversial legislative acts, regarding, for example, the policing of public assemblies and protest, or the policing of university campuses. In 2020-21, these initiatives were also complemented by increasingly restrictive police measures allegedly addressing the Covid-19 pandemic, but used in practice to target political protest on several occasions, such as the commemoration of the November 1973 student uprising against the military junta or the murder of teenager Alexandros Grigoropoulos by a police officer in 2008.

What looms large in the backdrop of this development is the government's economic policies furthering the neoliberal restructuring of Greece's economy and labor market superintended by the EC-ECB-IMF "Troika" (Sakellaropoulos, 2019). The wider relevance of the Greek context is that it offers a template for the study of the evolving police role and increasing authoritarianism within the framework of the country's intensive neoliberalization. This invites reflection on both the ongoing police transformations as well as the possible political strategies challenging this process: amid increasing popular discontent directed against the police, there is now increasing public exposure of police actions, particularly police violence, on social media, as well as a growth in public debate concerning police reform and even abolition, echoing the demands of the BLM and Defund movement in the USA and elsewhere.

Thus our primary aim in this short chapter is to assess the prospects of moderate and/or radical police reform against the backdrop of Greece's current political situation. Inevitably this exercise involves a brief stock-taking of some key aspects of and developments in Greek policing, as well as related government policies, and we discuss these in the first part of our text. Then in the second part we survey the potential of those political forces and voices challenging the present outlook of the police in Greece. Our main argument is that while police reform currently appears unlikely to be initiated by Greece's political establishment, increasing popular discontent with the role the police are assuming in Greece's public life may be opening up the prospect of a more direct and radical movement challenging that police role.

The Hellenic Police: praetorians meet authoritarian neoliberalism

It is no surprise that the history of the police in Greece is one of unambiguous allegiance to the country's establishment and of deep-rooted connection with the political right. Since the emergence of the modern independent Greek state in 1832, the police have remained fiercely loyal to the assortment of authoritarian regimes that have marked the country's turbulent history, from the nineteenth-century monarchy to Cold War regimes featuring the political surveillance and suppression of the large groups of the population associated with the political left after the end of the civil war in 1949, up until the collapse of the military junta in 1974.

Throughout this long history, attempts at reform have only succeeded in modernizing the police apparatus, consolidating its militaristic and bureaucratic outlook. The coming of socialist PASOK to power in 1981 also resulted in a major organizational reshuffle of Greece's police forces alongside an attempt to establish some form of democratic control over the police. While not insignificant in terms of challenging the right's traditional grip on the police, the results of reform under PASOK in the 1980s have failed to moderate, let alone reverse, the established historical patterns of suspicion and hostility between police and the people, particularly the political left and the worker and student movements that became increasingly militant in the 1970s and early 1980s.The very same PASOK, having assumed a much more moderate social-democratic profile and embarking on the process of neoliberal reforms, was instrumental in setting the police on the course of neoliberal organizational restructuring internally and of the adoption of much more aggressive policing strategies in the mid-1990s and after (Rigakos and Papanicolaou, 2003; Vidali, 2007).

In the wake of those developments, the police assumed a prominent active role in suppressing the anti-austerity movements and political activism during the introduction and implementation of the extreme austerity programs (the notorious "memoranda") in the 2010s. In the process, the historical connections of the police with the right were reaffirmed, most dramatically in the light of increasing levels of far-right influence among front-line police personnel. The criminal trial leading to the conviction of the leadership of the neo-Nazi Golden Dawn party in 2020 also offered unambiguous evidence of police complicity with the far right, including attempts to obscure the circumstances of the murder of musician and activist Pavlos Fyssas by a member of Golden Dawn in September 2013.

The Hellenic Police, Greece's single national police force, is responsible for public order, criminal law enforcement as well as state security functions in Greek territory (except ports and coastal areas which are under the jurisdiction of the Coast Guard). It incorporates border control and other special guard units under the organizational umbrella of the Ministry for "the Protection of the Citizen," which is a branch of the executive separate from the ministries of defence and of justice. The origins of this body are to be found in the former gendarmerie, Greece's first and largest police force. Another force, the Police of the Cities, specializing in policing Greece's capital, Athens, and a few other major cities was merged with the gendarmerie in 1984 under PASOK. While there were differences between those two forces, with the city police developing a more professional police outlook during the years it existed between 1920 and 1984, ultimately the militaristic, bureaucratic and hierarchical structure and ethos of the gendarmerie survived the reform and continues to characterize the operation and mentality of the Hellenic Police. The gendarmerie had been key in consolidating state sovereignty and the pacification of the countryside, particularly with the suppression of local revolts and banditry. In the twentieth century, both forces assumed an active role in administering political surveillance and suppression of the population in the post-civil war period (Rigakos and Papanicolaou, 2003).

Reform under PASOK placed the single national police force under the political control of the Ministry of Public Order and abolished the previously existing headquarters structure in a move to expunge right-wing clientelism and patronage over the police. The neoliberal restructuring of the force under PASOK in the 1990s, while involving a major modernizing change in the system of personnel selection, requiring cadets to join the force via the system of a national university entry exam, left intact the traditional militaristic characteristics of police training and personnel career progression. Ultimately, PASOK was responsible not only for restoring traditional structures of command by reinstating the police headquarters staff structure, but also for the development of different tiers of police units by means of the introduction of special units drawing ex-army personnel serving under employment terms and conditions that differ from those of regular police graduating from the police academy.

These Border and Special Guards were introduced as a lower-cost solution to border controls and for the protection of vulnerable infrastructure and other facilities, yet they were subsequently incorporated into regular police personnel, albeit with limited career progression prospects. As a result, second-tier police personnel have been instrumental in shoring up the Hellenic Police's militaristic outlook, since over time a significant proportion of serving police officers (about one in five currently) have been recruited based on the Special Guards qualifications and selection criteria. Equally, there has been a clear tendency toward the development of additional strategic units both centrally and regionally, while at the level of front-line policing, several units specializing in motorized patrol, public order and riot control, immigration controls, organized crime and anti-terrorism were created, upgraded or restructured. Controversially, some of these units assigned to public order policing and patrol have been populated by second-tier personnel, while new intrusive and wide-ranging powers were assigned to units dealing with "organized crime" and "anti-terrorism" under consecutive legislative initiatives since the 1990s.

The changes in police deployment, appearance, equipment and operational tactics of the different types of either riot police or fast response units rolled out by the "modernizing" PASOK in the late 1990s meant that the Greek police were ready to assume the openly reactionary role assigned to them at the onset of the financial crisis and the implementation of the economic adjustment and restructuring programs imposed by the EC-ECB-IMF "Troika" in the 2010s. The dawn of a new era had been emphatically announced by the murder of teenager Alexandros Grigoropoulos by a Special Guards officer in December 2008 and the brutal police response to the riot that followed this incident. The outlook of Greek police has since been marked by their heavily militarized presence and violent response in the country's increasingly restless public spaces, with protesters, leftist political dissidents and migrants being the primary target of police action.

This is not to say that in previous times since the restoration of parliamentary democracy in 1974 the police had not spearheaded the state's violent suppression of workers, students and other social movements and political activism. It was, however, in the 2010s that the increasingly militaristic and reactionary characteristics of the Hellenic Police became pervasive to such an extent that one may recognize the signs of blatant institutional failure even by modest liberal standards.

The impossibility of police reform

The suffocation of public spaces by mobile militarized police, the systematic recourse to heavy-handed action, including unnecessary force and lethal violence, embedded in a regime of failing or absent accountability structures, growing connections with para-institutional centers (Christopoulos, 2014) and absence of meaningful public debate on policing, all account for the Greek police's disturbing record since the 2010s.

Beyond observations and analyses of organizational structures and dynamics (Rigakos and Papanicolaou, 2003; Vidali, 2007), the reactionary role and activity of the police has been amply documented by a series of reports by academic observers as well as Greek and international human rights watchdogs (e.g., Amnesty International, 2009; 2012; 2014; 2021). In the 2010s, the most prominent development was the renewed convergence between the far right and the police, particularly the mass of militarized front-line units. The neo-Nazi party Golden Dawn's public presence developed alongside police action against migrant populations and popular resistance against austerity, and was clearly indicating the emergence of practical alliances between the far right and front-line police units. Whether these connections have extended among higher-ranking police officers is a moot point; however, the proceedings of the trial of Golden Dawn's leadership for the murder of musician and leftist activist Pavlos Fyssas left little doubt about the extent to which Golden Dawn was allowed to interfere with and influence police activity (Kampagiannis and Human Rights 360, 2021).

Even though the criminal conviction of Golden Dawn's leadership in 2020 has meant that this party is now effectively defunct, significant far- and populist-right forces remain active within the large conservative party of New Democracy, resulting in the perpetuation of links between the police and reactionary right-wing politics. New Democracy's law-and-order policies since 2019 very much serve to amplify aggressive police militarism, well in line with the approach of the political leadership of the Ministry for the "Protection of the Citizen" under the Samaras 2012-15 New Democracy-led coalition government, a period during which New Democracy politicians tolerated if not effectively condoned reported police abuse and violence (Margaronis, 2012).

The dominance of New Democracy in the government currently, and the reinstatement of PASOK's political mastermind of neoliberal police reform Michalis Chrysochoidis as the minister in charge of the police, not only offers no prospect of any police reform along conservative political lines, but in fact serves as a legitimizing factor for police counter-reform. In fact, the consolidation of an aggressive police outlook is very much in tune with New Democracy's policies accelerating neoliberal restructuring in Greece, particularly as the government is now preparing further sweeping "reforms" in the economy, the labor market and a range of public services, including education and health.

The present reactionary regression of Greek policing is further encouraged by Syriza's own regression to much more modest ("responsible") positions toward the police. This development essentially means that there remains no credible alternative plan for police reform from within Greece's political establishment. Syriza's original positions for police reform were very much in tune with the party's radical manifesto for sweeping changes in the way the state and public services operate and interact with the citizenry; a major policy goal while Syriza remained in opposition before 2015 was "police democratization," meaning not only police organizational reform toward a loosening of bureaucratic and hierarchical structures, but also decisive steps toward the reversal of the trends toward militarization. For example, Syriza's 2012 election manifesto made explicit reference to the necessity of disbanding the assortment of militarized public order units, particularly of the notorious "MAT" riot control units, whose presence and activity has punctuated Greek public spaces since their inception. Syriza continued to develop these positions up until late 2014 (Papanicolaou and Rigakos, 2014; Rigakos, 2016), but as the party ascended to power in January 2015, the bulk of these proposals were shelved in favor of a strategy aimed at appeasing the police.

Syriza's capitulation to the austerity demands of the Troika in July 2015 and the policies of the Syriza-led coalition government that emerged from the September 2015 election further sidelined plans for radical (or even liberal) police reform, despite the fact that Syriza can be credited with ameliorative moves, such as the disbandment of the "Delta" mobile riot control unit, whose extreme violent tactics against protesters during the anti-austerity mobilizations of the first half of the 2010s were fiercely criticized by the left. Syriza's political disarray following their 2019 electoral defeat, and the party's ongoing move toward more centrist positions in matters of "law and order" mean that voices for police reform even along social-democratic/liberal lines in the event of Syriza returning to power lack political credibility and gravitas.

Beyond the "mainstream" left, represented by Syriza currently, there remains a whole history of confrontational relations between the police and the extra-parliamentary left and oppositional social movements, which the present conservative government carefully prepares to inflame, by means of delivering legislatively and practically some highly symbolic blows to civil liberties, particularly the right to protest and the well-established patterns of youth political mobilization in Greece's universities (Dimou, 2021). These policies have already sparked mass protest against the government's legislative initiatives toward the regulation of the right to protest, higher education reform and the police-led Covid-19 pandemic control measures (including the imposition of curfews, the policing of the lockdown and other measures restricting life and expression in Greece's public spaces.

Conclusion: what prospects for resistance?

As our brief discussion of the outlook of the police in Greece suggests, Greece is rapidly becoming the setting for acutely confrontational relations involving the police, not dissimilar to those experienced in other countries. Popular discontent with the police was drastically amplified during the Covid-19 pandemic as the conservative government not only implemented an assortment of restrictive measures, but also pushed ahead with not only restrictive policies under the banner of "law and order," but also accelerated neoliberal reforms in the economy, potentially preparing a new round of austerity measures to address the economic impact of the pandemic and deteriorating public finances. The right's true aim is, of course, to advance neoliberal economic restructuring. As part of this strategy, the police will be assigned the task of suppressing active resistance on one hand and, on the other, of instilling fear in the wider population. The heavily militarized presence of the police and the increasingly frequent provocative shows of brute force are instrumental to this strategy, and Greece appears once again likely to become the setting of disturbing incidents of police repression and abuse. Here lies the danger: with little opposition from within the established political formations of the left, much will depend on the capacity of the forces of resistance not only to confront police violence with creativity and resolve, but equally to address the core of the right's strategy and to organize popular struggles around a vision of a post-capitalist future.

Endnotes

Introduction

1. Younge, Gary (2021) "Out Hunting" *London Review of Books*, July 29
2. Callinicos, Alex, Stathis Kouvelakis and Lucia Pradella (2021) *Routledge Handbook of Marxism and Post-Marxism*. Abingdon: Routledge
3. von Tunzelmann, Alex (2021) *Fallen Idols: Twelve Statues That Made History* London: Headline
4. Bowling, Ben, Robert Reiner and James Sheptycki (2019) *The Politics of the Police (5th edition)* Oxford: Oxford University Press

Chapter 1

1. (Platt, 1982)
2. (Schrader, 2019)
3. (Harring 2017 15)
4. (Bunyan 1977 2)
5. (Bunyan 1977 3)
6. (Weiner 2012)
7. (Harring 2017 15)
8. (Bunyan 1977 302)
9. (Reiner 2010 6)
10. (Hibbert 1958, Rogers 2012)
11. (Clement 2014, Emsley 1985)
12. (Wells 1983)
13. (Carlyle in *Chartism* [1843], in Clement 2016 120. See also Emsley 2010)
14. (Cohen 2011, Frederiksen and Harboe 2022)
15. (Hall *et al* 1978 320)
16. (Sparks 2021 429)
17. (Hall *et al* 1978 323)

18. (Hall 1979)
19. (Friend and Metcalf 1981 148, also Darlington and Liddle 2001 for the full story of the trade union victory in 1972)
20. General Frank Kitson's *Low Intensity Operations* (1971) advocates extra-parliamentary violence – state 'security' measures for social control
21. Clement and Scalia 2020
22. Ganser 2005, Weiner 2012, for the Europe and the US, Bevins 2020 covers Indonesia, Brazil and the fate of the 'third world'
23. Peter Hain's collection *Policing the Police* (1979), also Bunyan (1977, 1981) and Hillyard (1987)
24. (Friend and Metcalf 1981 146-147)
25. (Friend and Metcalf 1981 148)
26. (Hain 1979 5)
27. (Friend and Metcalf 1981 65-66 and Rollo 1980 179-185)
28. (New York Times 2020 3, For a longer view of Black Lives Matter and its predecessors see Taylor (2016))
29. (Chapman 1970 96)
30. (Reiner 2010)
31. (Whyte 1943)
32. (Scraton 1985 48)
33. (Ferrell 2019)
34. (Maynard 2017 6-7)
35. (Scraton 1985 37, 80)
36. (Vegh Weis 2018)
37. (Baker 2016 and 2021)
38. (Sandhu 2021)
39. (Hall *et al* 1978 38)
40. (Wodak, 2015 67)
41. (Smith 2021)
42. (Gilmore *et al* 2016 196-7)
43. (cited in Gilmore *et al* 2016 175)
44. (Davis 2016 cited in 2020 Verso Radical Diary)

45. (Hall *at al* 1978 395-395)
46. (Davis 2013 cited in Lamas 2021 414)
47. (Kamat 2016 73)
48. (Fenton 2021 152)
49. (Fenton 2021 81-2)
50. (Fenton 2021 254)
51. (Scalia 2017, Ruggiero 2018 contain examples and references)
52. (Basketter 2021a 11)
53. (Basketter 2021b 10)
54. (Ibid)
55. Sandhu, Serina. "Female crime victims 'belittled and not believed on police chief's watch'" *The Independent* September 10, 2021 p.15
56. BBC News 1 February 2022. "Met Police: Misogyny, racism, bullying, sex harassment"
57. (e.g. Duff 2021, Elliott-Cooper 2021, Coyle and Nagel 2021)
58. (Zola 1958 140 and 221-222)
59. (Elias, 2007 141 discussed in Clement and Mennell 2020)
60. (Elias, 2007 142)
61. (Elias, 2007 114)

Chapter 3

1. Buchanan, L., Q. Bui and J.K. Patel (2020). "Black Lives Matter May Be the Largest Movement in U.S. History," The New York Times, 3 July. Available at: https://www. nytimes.com/interactive/2020/07/03/us/george-floyd-protests-crowd-size.html (Accessed: 10 September 2020).
2. See Maher, G. (2021). *A World Without Police: How Strong Communities Make Cops Obsolete*. Verso Books; McDowell, M.G. and Fernandez, L.A., 2018. 'Disband, Disempower, and Disarm': Amplifying the theory and practice of police abolition. *Critical Criminology*, 26(3), pp.373-391; and Vitale, A.S., 2017. *The end of policing*. Verso Books.

3. Maher, G. (2021). *A World Without Police: How Strong Communities Make Cops Obsolete*. Verso Books.

4. Muhammad, K.G. (2019). *The condemnation of Blackness: Race, crime, and the making of modern urban America, with a new preface*. Harvard University Press; Monkkonen, E.H., 2004. *Police in urban America, 1860-1920*. Cambridge University Press.

5. Hadden, S.E. (2003). *Slave patrols: Law and violence in Virginia and the Carolinas*. Harvard University Press; Reichel, P.L. (1988). Southern slave patrols as a transitional police type. *Am. J. Police, 7*, p.51.

6. Swanson, D. J. (2020). *Cult of Glory: The Bold and Brutal History of The Texas Rangers*. Viking Press, Page 10.

7. Neocleous, M. (2000). *The fabrication of social order*. London: Pluto Press

8. The Center for Popular Democracy (2020). "Freedom to Thrive: Reimagining Safety & Security in Our Communities." Available at: https://www.populardemocracy.org/news/publications/freedom-thrive-reimagining-safety-security-our-communities (Accessed: 15 October 2021).

9. Reuters, (February 16, 2021). "Biden Suggests More Police Funding, No Jail for Drug Offenders." Available at: https://www.reuters.com/article/us-usa-biden-police/biden-suggests-more-police-funding-no-jail-for-drug-offenders-idUSKBN2AH0C6 (Accessed: 10 September 2021).

10. New York City Council, (June 30, 2020). Council Announces Agreement on FY 2021 Budget. Available at: https://www.reuters.com/article/us-usa-biden-police/biden-suggests-more-police-funding-no-jail-for-drug-offenders-idUSKBN2AH0C6 (Accessed: 10 September 2021).

11. Smith, Dakota and David Zahniser, (May 26, 2021), L.A. Cut Millions from the LAPD after George Floyd. Here's Where That Money is Going. *The Los Angeles Times*. Available at: https://www.reuters.com/article/us-usa-biden-police/

biden-suggests-more-police-funding-no-jail-for-drug-offenders-idUSKBN2AH0C6 (Accessed: 10 September 2021).

12. Squires, Camille (29 January 2021). Austin is Funding Homelessness Services by Defunding Police. *City Monitor*. Available at: https://citymonitor.ai/government/budgets/austin-is-funding-homelessness-services-by-defunding-police (Accessed: 10 September 2021).

13. Vitale, Alex (June 3, 2020). How Much Do We Need the Police? NPR Code Switch. Available at: https://www.npr.org/sections/codeswitch/2020/06/03/457251670/how-much-do-we-need-the-police

14. White Bird Clinic, (2021). "What We Do." Available at: https://whitebirdclinic.org/about/ (Accessed: 10 September 2021).

15. Nickeas, Peter (June 4, 2021). More Than a Dozen Cities Push to Minimize or Even Eliminate Police Presence at Mental Health Calls. *CNN*. Available at: https://www.cnn.com/2021/06/04/us/police-alternate-response-mental-health/index.html (Accessed: October 16 2020).

16. Schwartz, Sarah, Stephen Sawchuk, Eesha Penderharker, and Ileana Najarro (June 4, 2021). These Districts Defunded Their School Police. What Happened Next? *Education Week*. Available at: https://www.edweek.org/leadership/these-districts-defunded-their-school-police-what-happened-next/2021/06 (Accessed: 10 September 2021).

17. Community Resource Hub (2021). Resources on School Policing and Youth. Available at: https://communityresourcehub.org/resources/ (Accessed: October 16 2020).

18. This report can be accessed in full here: https://blackorganizingproject.org/wp-content/uploads/2021/07/The-Peoples-Plan-2019-Online-Reduced-Size.pdf (Accessed: 10 September 2021).

19. See this site for the document: https://d3n8a8pro7vhmx.

cloudfront.net/commonjustice/pages/477/attachments/
original/1630695014/Solutions_to_Violence_final.
pdf?1630695014 (Accessed: 10 September 2021).

20. CBC (July 15 2021). Five Fast Facts About the NYPD's Adopted FY 2022 Budget. Available here: https://cbcny. org/research/five-fast-facts-about-nypds-adopted-fy-2022-budget (Accessed: 10 September 2021).

21. Swindoll, J. (2021). "LA County votes for $36M increase in police funding after major crimes surge," Disrn. Access September 27, 2020. Available at: https://disrn.com/news/la-county-votes-for-36m-increase-in-police-funding-after-major-crime-surge/ (Accessed: 10 September 2021).

22. Tucker, E. (2021, July 24). *Minneapolis voters will decide whether to replace the police department with a Public Safety Department.* CNN. Accessed September 17, 2021, from https://www.cnn.com/2021/07/23/us/minneapolis-public-safety-department-measure/index.html

23. Bailey, H. (2020, August 6). *Plan to disband Minneapolis Police halted in city Commission vote.* The Washington Post. Available at: https://www.washingtonpost.com/nation/2020/08/05/plan-disband-minneapolis-police-department-halted-city-commission-vote/ (Accessed: 10 September 2021).

24. Kaba, M., 2014. Police 'Reforms' You Should Always Oppose. In *Prison Culture* – reprinted in Kaba, M. (2021) *We Do This 'Til We Free Us* Chicago: Haymarket

25. NBC Meet the Press (June 7, 2020) Available at: https://www.nbcnews.com/meet-the-press/meet-press-june-7-2020-n1226966 (Accessed: 26 September 2021).

Chapter 4

1. Brenda Weinberg interviewed in *Injustice* (2001) Directed by Ken Fero and Tariq Mehmood. [Film]. Available at: https://vimeo.com/34633260 [Accessed 2 August 2021].

2.   The work of Migrant Media is outlined in Fero, K. (2015) *Migrant Media and the road to Injustice*. Race and Class. Vol 57 N°1. London: Institute of Race Relations.

3.   Getino, O. and Solanas, F. (1971) *Towards A Third Cinema*. Tricontinental 14. La Habana: Organización de Solidaridad de los Pueblos de África, Asia y América Latina. London: Afterimage N°3.

4.   Godard, J. and Gorin, J. (1970) *Manifesto of the Dziga Vertov Group*. London: Afterimage N°1.

5.   Fanon, F. (1963) *The Wretched of the Earth*. London: Penguin Books.

6.   *Justice for Joy* (1995) Directed by Ken Fero. [Film]. Available at: https://www.channel4.com/programmes/justice-for-joy [Accessed 2 August 2021].

7.   Alder, J. *What's the worst that could happen? The death of Christopher Alder*. [Online]. Centre for Crime and Justice Studies. https://www.crimeandjustice.org.uk/publications/cjm/article/what's-worst-could-happen-death-christopher-alder [Accessed 2 August 2021].

8.   Hitchens, C and Said, E. *Blaming the Victims: Spurious Scholarship and the Palestinian Question* (1988) London: Verso Books.

9.   Pascoe Sawyers interviewed in *Justice for Joy* (1995) Directed by Ken Fero. [Film]. Available at: https://www.channel4.com/programmes/justice-for-joy [Accessed 2 August 2021].

10.   *Channel 4 Duty Log* following national broadcast of Justice for Joy. 17 July 1995. Unpublished collection of the author.

11.   Zizek, S. (2009) *Violence*. London: Profile Books.

12.   Sivanandan, A. (1991) *A Deadly Silence*. London: Institute of Race Relations.

13.   BBC News (2001) *Newsroom South East*. [Online]. 6 July. Available from: https://www.youtube.com/watch?v=tQqN4sD5XgE&t=7s [Accessed 2 August 2021].

14.   Campbell, D. (2002) *Same Old Story*. London: The

Guardian. [Online]. 18 April. Available from: https://www.theguardian.com/culture/2002/apr/18/artsfeatures1 [Accessed 2 August 2021].

15. X, M. (1964) *The Ballot or the Bullet.* Full transcript of speech by Malcolm X. April 3 1964. Available from: https://www.rev.com/blog/transcripts/the-ballot-or-the-bullet-speech-transcript-malcolm-x [Accessed 2 August 2021].

16. Angiolini, E. (2017) *Report of the Independent Review of Deaths and Serious Incidents in Police Custody.* London: Home Office. Available from: https://www.gov.uk/government/publications/deaths-and-serious-incidents-in-police-custody [Accessed 2 August 2021].

17. Fero, K. (2018) *Documentary Practice as Radical Process in Challenging Dominant Media and State Narratives.* Sheffield: Sheffield Hallam University. http://shura.shu.ac.uk/23304/1/Fero_2018_PhD_ChallengingDominantMedia.pdf [Accessed 2 August 2021].

18. Gramsci, A. (1971) *Prison Notebooks.* London: Lawrence & Wishart.

19. Cooper, A. (2001) *My Tears Will Catch Them.* Sight & Sound, October. London: British Film Institute. [online]. Available from: http://old.bfi.org.uk/sightandsound/feature/68 [Accessed 2 August 2021].

20. Butler, G. (1999) *Inquiry into Crown Prosecution Service Decision-Making in Relation to Deaths in Custody and Related Matters.* London: Home Office. Available from: https://assets.publishing.service.gov.uk/government/uploads/system/uploads/attachment_data/file/259791/custody.pdf [Accessed 2 August 2021].

21. *Ultraviolence* (2020) Directed by Ken Fero [Film] https://ultraviolencefilm.com/ Available from:https://player.bfi.org.uk/subscription/film/watch-ultraviolence-2020-online [Accessed 2 August 2021].

Chapter 5

1. Matt Clement (2016, 194-5) identifies a similar trend in criminology. He argues that criminologists, since the 1960s, have ignored the underlying political reasons behind anti-police brutality riots in the US and the UK. Just like political theorists, the criminologists assume that the riot is a violent crime, and hence is an illegitimate means of social protest. 1960s black civil rights activists, ranging from King, to Malcolm X, to Stokeley Carmichael (later known as Kwame Ture), however, argued that the inner-city riots of the 1960s had to be listened to as *legitimate* expressions of outrage against the structural racism that made police violence and urban poverty possible.

2. For examples of recent philosophical treatments of political disobedience that drop the requirement of non-violence, see Celikates (2016), Delmas (2018), Markovits (2004) and D'Arcy (2014).

3. For an argument that the conditions of inner-city blacks in the contemporary US violate the basic principles of Rawls's theory of justice and so justify law breaking forms of resistance, see Shelby (2007).

4. For recent philosophical defenses of justified rioting see D'Arcy (2014), Havercroft (2021), Hooker (2016) and Pasternak (2018).

5. During the George Floyd protests in June 2020, Bernice King (Martin Luther King Jr's daughter) posted several tweets in support of the uprising, quoting approvingly King's description of a riot as the language of the unheard. See for example https://twitter.com/berniceking/status/126 8190782042918913?lang=en

6. For a historical sociological analysis of the riot, that argues that throughout history rioters have seen themselves as defending the common law against corrupt elites, see Clement (2016).

7. For philosophical arguments that justify riots in this context see Havercroft (2021) and Pasternak (2018).

Chapter 8

1. The slogan "Another World is Possible" was adopted by the World Social Forum in Porto Alegre in Brazil in April 2001.
2. According to Choonara (2020), the average annual rate of growth has diminished from 5.2 percent p.a. in the period 1961-74 to 2.5 percent p.a. between 2009-2018.
3. Hammond (2003) reports over one hundred thousand attendees in Porto Alegre, Brazil for the third World Social Forum in 2003.
4. The more liberal abolitionist perspectives would suggest that existing state and economic institutions can be re-balanced toward the majority.

Chapter 9

1. https://time.com/4779112/police-history-origins/#:~:text=The%20first%20publicly%20funded%2C%20organized,to%20other%20places%2C%20says%20Potter
2. https://plsonline.eku.edu/insidelook/brief-history-slavery-and-origins-american-policing
3. https://time.com/4779112/police-history-origins/#:~:text=The%20first%20publicly%20funded%2C%20organized,to%20other%20places%2C%20says%20Potter
4. https://socialistworker.org/blog/critical-reading/2014/12/09/main-role-police-protecting-ca
5. https://portside.org/2020-06-19/trading-one-uniform-another-can-police-be-de-militarized-when-so-many-cops-are-military
6. https://www.yesmagazine.org/social-justice/2020/06/02/police-reform-training/
7. https://www.csmonitor.com/USA/Justice/2020/0619/

It-s-way-past-time-to-try-something-new-The-push-to-defund-police

8. https://www.brennancenter.org/our-work/research-reports/state-policing-reforms-george-floyds-murder

9. https://data.census.gov/cedsci/profile?q=United%20States&g=0100000US

10. https://www.bjs.gov/content/pub/pdf/cbpp18st.pdf

11. https://www.pewresearch.org/fact-tank/2020/05/06/share-of-black-white-hispanic-americans-in-prison-2018-vs-2006/ft_20-05-05_imprisonmentrates_2a/

12. https://www.hsph.harvard.edu/news/hsph-in-the-news/blacks-whites-police-deaths-disparity/

13. https://www.bloomberg.com/graphics/2020-city-budget-police-defunding/

14. https://theappeal.org/austin-cut-police-budget-supportive-housing-homelessness/

15. https://www.npr.org/2020/12/10/944938471/minneapolis-shifts-8-million-in-police-funding-but-keeps-force-at-current-level

16. https://abc7.com/defund-the-police-lapd-black-lives-matter-los-angeles-city-council/10384293/

17. https://www.nytimes.com/2020/09/26/us/politics/minneapolis-defund-police.html

18. https://www.startribune.com/minneapolis-to-spend-6-4-million-to-hire-more-police/600022400/

19. https://www.npr.org/2020/10/19/924146486/removing-cops-from-behavioral-crisis-calls-we-need-to-change-the-model

20. https://www.kron4.com/news/bay-area/berkeley-works-to-reform-police-traffic-enforcement/

21. https://www.theguardian.com/us-news/2020/jun/01/minneapolis-public-school-end-police-contract

22. https://www.cnn.com/2020/06/28/us/police-out-of-schools-movement/index.html

23. https://www.cnn.com/2021/03/25/us/nyc-police-reform-ny
    pd/index.html
24. https://www.themarshallproject.org/2020/12/18/colorado-
    tries-new-way-to-punish-rogue-cops
25. https://www.chicagotribune.com/news/criminal-justice/ct-
    chicago-police-civilian-oversight-community-groups-2021
    0723-7ilpalqxine2fphw53hj5jifqa-story.html
26. https://www.brennancenter.org/our-work/research-report
    s/state-policing-reforms-george-floyds-murder
27. https://www.ncsl.org/research/civil-and-criminal-justice/
    law-enforcement-statutory-database.aspx
28. https://www.fbi.gov/services/cjis/ucr/use-of-force
29. https://crime-data-explorer.fr.cloud.gov/pages/le/uof
30. https://leg.colorado.gov/sites/default/files/documents/202
    0A/bills/2020a_217_enr.pdf
31. https://assets.foleon.com/eu-west-2/uploads-7e3kk3/41697
    /pdf_-_chokeholds.d78d7aa1fada.pdf
32. https://www.washingtonpost.com/politics/2021/05/13/its-
    not-just-voting-legislators-have-introduced-100-state-bills
    -targeting-protesting/
33. https://www.vox.com/2021/4/25/22367019/gop-laws-oklah
    oma-iowa-florida-floyd-blm-protests-police
34. https://www.nbcnews.com/think/opinion/seattle-protester
    -hit-car-latest-casualty-dangerous-far right-trend-ncna123
    3525
35. https://www.nytimes.com/2021/04/03/us/george-floyd-der
    ek-chauvin-trial.html
36. https://www.politico.com/news/magazine/2021/04/09/dere
    k-chauvin-cops-george-floyd-480460
37. https://assets.foleon.com/eu-west-2/uploads-7e3kk3/41697
    /pdf_-_duty_to_intervene.6e39a04b07b6.pdf
38. https://assets.foleon.com/eu-west-2/uploads-7e3kk3/41697
    /pdf_-_duty_to_intervene.6e39a04b07b6.pdf
39. https://www.nytimes.com/2020/07/18/us/derek-chauvin-

george-floyd.html

40. https://www.nbcnewyork.com/news/local/new-law-reveal
    s-complaint-history-for-nypd-officer-fired-for-eric-garners
    -chokehold-death/2479606/

41. https://www.nytimes.com/2015/01/23/us/in-tamir-rice-sho
    oting-in-cleveland-many-errors-by-police-then-a-fatal-one
    .html

42. https://www.nbcnews.com/news/us-news/officer-who-kill
    ed-tamir-rice-found-unfit-previous-police-job-n261111

43. https://www.pbs.org/newshour/nation/wandering-cops-m
    oving-from-department-to-department-is-a-roadblock-to-
    police-accountability

44. https://assets.foleon.com/eu-west-2/uploads-7e3kk3/41697
    /decertification.d1229f8ea972.pdf

45. https://fas.org/sgp/crs/misc/IF11585.pdf

46. https://www.ncsl.org/research/civil-and-criminal-justice/
    decertification.aspx

47. https://www.iadlest.org/our-services/ndi/about-ndi

48. https://www.usatoday.com/in-depth/news/investigations/
    2019/04/24/usa-today-revealing-misconduct-records-polic
    e-cops/3223984002/

49. https://www.iadlest.org/

50. https://assets.foleon.com/eu-west-2/uploads-7e3kk3/41697
    /decertification.d1229f8ea972.pdf

51. https://www.npr.org/2021/05/24/999742035/whats-change
    d-and-what-hasnt-in-the-year-since-george-floyd-was-kill
    ed

52. https://www.theguardian.com/us-news/2021/mar/07/us-
    cities-defund-police-transferring-money-community

53. https://www.bloomberg.com/graphics/2021-city-budget-
    police-funding/

54. https://www.interruptingcriminalization.com/defundpolic
    e-update

55. https://co.chalkbeat.org/2020/12/15/22177144/denver-phas

e-out-police-3-schools

56. https://www.theguardian.com/us-news/2020/jun/25/police-schools-oakland-chicago-los-angeles

57. https://www.opb.org/news/article/defund-portland-police-budget-eudaly/

58. https://www.kqed.org/news/11862094/sf-mayor-breed-unveils-plan-for-reinvesting-120-million-from-police-into-black-communities

59. https://www.bloomberg.com/news/articles/2020-12-10/what-s-in-the-2021-minneapolis-police-budget

60. https://www.texastribune.org/2020/08/13/austin-city-council-cut-police-budget-defund/

61. https://www.theguardian.com/us-news/seattle

62. https://www.chicagotribune.com/news/criminal-justice/ct-chicago-police-civilian-oversight-community-groups-2021 0723-7ilpalqxine2fphw53hj5jifqa-story.html

63. https://www.bbc.com/news/world-us-canada-57589416

64. https://www.cnn.com/2020/09/13/us/austin-texas-defund-police-billboard/index.html

65. https://www.texastribune.org/2021/01/21/greg-abbott-police-funding-reforms/

66. https://www.statesman.com/story/news/politics/elections/2020/11/06/fact-check-is-austin-one-of-most-dangerous-cities-in-us/43010523/

67. https://aflcio.org/press/releases/afl-cio-creates-new-task-force-racial-justice

68. https://inthesetimes.com/article/afl-cio-police-reform-unions-black-lives-matter

69. https://www.npr.org/2021/01/18/958120766/at-least-13-off-duty-police-officers-suspected-of-having-taken-part-in-capitol-r

70. https://www.businessinsider.com/31-police-officers-investigated-suspected-capitol-riot-involvement-report-2021-1t Involvementhttps://www.businessinsider.com › Politics

71. Lenin, Vladimir Il'ich, 1870-1924. The State and Revolution: Marxist Teaching on the State and the Task of the Proletariat in the Revolution. https://www.marxists.org/archive/lenin/works/1917/staterev/ch01.htm#s2

Chapter 10

1. https://www.theguardian.com/us-news/ng-interactive/2015/jun/01/the-counted-police-killings-us-database?CMP=Share_iOSApp_Other
2. Buchanan, Bui and Patel, 2020
3. On 17 June 2021, President Joe Biden signed the Juneteenth National Independence Day Act into law. June 19 is therefore now a federal holiday.
4. https://www.wbur.org/hereandnow/2020/06/19/angela-davis-protests-anti-racism
5. https://www.vanityfair.com/culture/2020/08/angela-davis-and-ava-duvernay-in-conversation
6. Dramatically known as "patrolling the pigs," it is captured in vividly spectacular fashion in the cartoons of the Party's illustrator Emory Douglas. See, for example, Black Panther: The Revolutionary Art of Emory Douglas.
7. https://thegeopolitics.com/the-global-impact-of-the-black-lives-matter-movement/
8. https://www.inquest.org.uk/deaths-in-police-custody This figure is at 10 August 2021 and is for England and Wales only as Scotland has its own authority.
9. https://www.inquest.org.uk/bame-deaths-in-police-custody
10. The series ran for 432 episodes from 1955 to 1976.
11. Vagrancy Act 1824 (5 Geo. 4.c. 83).
12. The majority of the Act remains in force in England and Wales today and 573 people were prosecuted under its provisions in 2020.
13. Kwame Ture, Charles V Hamilton, Black Power – The Politics of Black Liberation (Vintage, New York 1992)

https://mygaryislike.files.wordpress.com/2016/12/black-power-kwame-ture-and-charles-hamilton.pdf P 20.

14. The Rt. Hon. The Lord Scarman, OBE, "Report to the Rt. Hon. William Whitelaw CH, MC, MP, Secretary of State for the Home Department, on the Brixton Disorders of 10-12 April 1981," London: HMSO, November 1981, p. 65.

15. "The Brixton Disorders of 10-12 April 1981," 1981, p. 127.

16. "The Brixton Disorders of 10-12 April 1981," 1981, p. 1.

17. Howe, Darcus, From Bobby to Babylon – Black and the British Police, Bookmarks, London 2020 p. 82

18. https://www.inquest.org.uk/cherry-groce-inquest-conclusions

19. Lawrence, Doreen, And Still I Rise – Seeking Justice for Stephen, Faber & Faber, London 2006, Chapter 5 "In the Dark." Her account is corroborated by the evidence presented to Sir William Macpherson's public inquiry in 2008.

20. The Stephen Lawrence Inquiry - https://assets.publishing.service.gov.uk/government/uploads/system/uploads/attachment_data/file/277111/4262.pdf p345

21. The Stephen Lawrence Inquiry - https://assets.publishing.service.gov.uk/government/uploads/system/uploads/attachment_data/file/277111/4262.pdf p41

22. Ibid Section 6.48 p49

23. Ibid Section 4.58 p52

24. Ibid p360

25. https://www.ucpi.org.uk/about-the-inquiry/
The Undercover Policing Inquiry was established in 2015 originally under the chairmanship of Lord Justice Christopher Pitchford. He died in October 2017 and was replaced by Sir John Mitting. As at August 15, 2021, two phases of evidence hearings have been completed. No date had been announced for the completion of the remaining "tranches" of evidence in that module or for the completion

of further modules. The final report is not expected until at least 2023.

26. Stop & Think - https://www.equalityhumanrights.com/sites/default/files/ehrc_stop_and_search_report.pdf p5

27. R v Blackshaw [2011] EWCA Crim 2312 [2012] WLR 1126

28. https://www.dailymail.co.uk/news/article-2358583/A-quarter-police-stop-searches-illegal-250-000-people-stopped-officers-sticking-rules.html

29. The Lammy Review - An Independent review into the treatment of, and outcomes for, Black, Asian and Minority Ethnic individuals in the Criminal Justice System - https://assets.publishing.service.gov.uk/government/uploads/system/uploads/attachment_data/file/643001/lammy-review-final-report.pdf

30. Report of the Independent Review of Deaths and Serious Incidents in Police Custody - https://assets.publishing.service.gov.uk/government/uploads/system/uploads/attachment_data/file/655401/Report_of_Angiolini_Review_ISBN_Accessible.pdf

31. https://www.gov.uk/government/statistics/crime-outcomes-in-england-and-wales-2020-to-2021/crime-outcomes-in-england-and-wales-2020-to-2021

32. Police (1982) - Episode 3 "A Complaint of Rape" BBC http://www.screenonline.org.uk/tv/id/464502/index.html

33. https://assets.publishing.service.gov.uk/government/uploads/system/uploads/attachment_data/file/994817/rape-review-research-report.pdf

Chapter 11

1. While the primary organization that developed during and since that period is known as Black Lives Matter (#BLM), the term Black Lives Matter (BLM) is now broadly used to point to a decentralized social movement that is protesting and organizing against police and the carceral system more

generally for its violent anti-Blackness.

2. https://abolitionistlawcenter.org/Our-Work/Projects/Cam paign-To-Fight-Toxic-Prisons/

Chapter 13

1. Daily *Times*, 19 July 1963 and *Nigerian Post*, 21 October 1963, cited in Tamuno, 1970, p. 255

2. The issue in contention was over scrapping the native authorities and local/regional governments' police formation for a centralized Nigeria Police Force.

3. This roughly translates into League of Farmers Revolting against Sufferation, from the Yoruba

4. These boards were set up toward the end of the colonial era, to generate funds for the state while shortchanging the peasants. With independence, the farmers had high hopes that this situation would change. But "(t)he peasants were soon to discover, however, that it was the men in control of affairs that changed, not the method of control or the mien of the ruling bureaucratic elite." (Adeniran, 1974, p. 366)

5. Quote from the memorandum submitted by the Àgbékòyà Parapọ̀ to the Ayoola Commission constituted by the military junta to look into the remote and immediate causes of the revolt, cited in Adeniran 1974: 367

6. See Amnesty International's 2017 report online: https://ww w.amnesty.org/download/Documents/AFR4473932017EN GLISH.PDF

7. See Chukwuma I. (1994), *Above The Law*, Lagos: Civil Liberties Organization, cited in Aye, 2020d.

8. See www.amnesty.org/download/Documents/44000/afr44 0382009en.pdf

9. See www.amnesty.org/download/Documents/AFR4448682 016ENGLISH.PDF

10. See www.amnesty.org/download/Documents/AFR4495052

020ENGLISH.PDF

11. See Akinpelu 2009 https://www.premiumtimesng.com/news/headlines/399892-despite-violations-nigeria-failed-to-prosecute-any-sars-officer-in-three-years-amnesty.html

12. See BBC report "Coronavirus: Security forces kill more Nigerians than COVID-19" online: https://www.bbc.com/news/world-africa-52317196

13. Segun Ogun 2020: https://socialistworkersleague.org/2020/06/02/justice-for-tina-candlelight-rally-on-4-june/

14. See "In our own words: the Feminist Coalition": https://feministcoalition.medium.com/in-our-own-words-the-feminist-coalition-61bc658446dd

15. For protests supported by the Feminist Coalition during the EndSARS revolt, see: https://www.notion.so/80db6dfd d25f4277a5bc0fbcdc612857?v=027410e7a4784ceaa097e412c a6100f7

16. See CORE Charter for Total Liberation: https://socialistworkersleague.org/2020/10/01/core-charter-for-total-liberation/

17. See online: https://twitter.com/AishaYesufu/status/1318157 843636387840/photo/1

18. See: https://lsstf.lagosstate.gov.ng › operation-mesa-op-mesa/

19. Adediran 2021: "#EndSARS: 99 bodies deposited at Lagos morgue, three from Lekki tollgate – pathologist"

20. National Bureau of Statistics 2021: 3. Available online: https://nigerianstat.gov.ng/elibrary

21. See Aye 2019e "The Actuality of Revolution1: 'this act in itself will not delay their day of judgment'" https://socialistworkersleague.org/2019/08/07/the-actuality-of-revolution now-i-this-act-in-itself-will-not-delay-their-day-of-judgment/

Chapter 14

1. See also the basis of the interpretations of Sigmund Freud in *Psychology of the masses and analysis of the "I"* (2017) and

The interpretation of dreams Volume Two (2017).

2. Known as the 7 Partidas, the Laws of the Indies and The Newest Compilation of the Laws of the Indies and Mexican Laws.

Bibliography

Chapter 1

Baker, David (2016) *Deaths After Police Contact: Constructing Accountability in the 21st Century* London: Palgrave Macmillan

Baker, David (2021) *Police-Related Deaths in the United States* Virginia: Rowman and Lillefield

Basketter, Simon (2021a) "Cover-Up! How the state helped hide the truth about the murder of Daniel Morgan" *Socialist Worker* 16 June 2021 pp.10-11.

Basketter, Simon (2021b) "Why the cops are corrupt to the core" *Socialist Worker* 23 June 2021 pp.10-11

BBC News 1 February 2022 "Met Police: Misogyny, racism, bullying, sex harassment discovered" Met Police: Misogyny, racism, bullying, sex harassment discovered - BBC News

Bevins, Vincent (2020) *The Jakarta Method: Washington's Anticommunist Crusade and the Mass Murder Program that Shaped our World* New York: Public Affairs

Bunyan, Tony (1977) *The Political Police in Britain* London: Quartet

Bunyan, Tony (1981) 'The police against the people' *Race & Class* 23 (2/3) pp.153-171

Camp, J. and C. Heatherton (eds.) *Policing the Planet* London: Verso

Chapman, Brian (1970) *Police State* London: Pall Mall

Clement, Matt (2014) "Mobs versus Markets" in Pakes, F. and D. Pritchard *Riot, Unrest and Protest on the Global Stage* Basingstoke: Palgrave Macmillan

Clement, Matt (2016) *A People's History of Riots, Protest and the Law: The Sound of the Crowd* London: Palgrave Macmillan

Clement, Matt and Vincenzo Scalia (2020) "The Strategy of Tension: Understanding State Labeling Processes and Double-Binds" *Critical Criminology* 29 (3) 569-588 https://

doi.org/10.1007/s10612-020-09494-5

Clement, Matt and Stephen Mennell (2020) "Elias, ultra-realism and doublebinds: Violence in the streets and the state" *European Journal of Criminology* (online first) https://doi.org/10.1177%2F1477370820977889

Cohen, Stan (2011) [1972] *Folk Devils and Moral Panics* London: Routledge

Coyle, Michael J. and Mechtild Nagel (ed.) (2021) *Contesting Carceral Logic: Towards Abolitionist Futures* London: Routledge

Darlington, Ralph and Dave Liddle (2001) *Glorious Summer: Class Struggle in Britain 1972* London: Bookmarks

Davis, Angela Y (2013) "Critical Refusals and Occupy" *Radical Philosophy Review* 31: pp.66-81 cited in Lamas, Andrew T. "Angela Davis" in Callinicos, Alex, Stathis Kouvelakis and Lucia Pradella (eds.) (2021) *Routledge Handbook of Marxism and Post-Marxism* Abingdon: Routledge pp.409-417

Davis, Angela Y (2016) [1973] *If they come in the Morning* London: Verso

Duff, Koshka (ed.) (2021) *Abolishing the Police* London: Dog Section

Elias, Norbert (2007) *Involvement and Detachment* Dublin: UCD Press

Elliott-Cooper, Adam (2021) *Black Resistance to British Policing* Manchester: Manchester University Press

Emsley, Clive (1985) "Repression, 'terror' and the rule of law in England during the decade of the French Revolution" *The English Historical Review*, Volume C, Issue CCCXCVII, October 1985, pp. 801–825, https://doi.org/10.1093/ehr/C.CCCXCVII.801

Emsley, Clive (2010) *Crime in England 1750-1900* London: Routledge

Ferrell, Jeff (2019) "In Defense of Resistance" *Critical Criminology* (online first DOI 0.1007/s10612-019-09456-6)

Fenton, Justin (2021) *We Own This City* London: Faber and Faber

Frederiksen, Martin and Ida Harboe Knudsen (eds.) (2022) *Modern Folk Devils: Contemporary Constructions of Evil* Helsinki: Helsinki University Press

Friend, Andrew and Andy Metcalf (1981) *Slump City: The politics of mass unemployment* London: Pluto

Ganser, Daniel (2005) *NATO's Secret Armies* London: Frank Cass

Gilmore, Ruth Wilson and Craig Gilmore (2016) "Beyond Bratton" in Camp, J and C Heatherton (eds.) *Policing the Planet* London: Verso

Hain, Peter (ed.) (1979) *Policing the Police Volume 1* London: John Calder

Hall, S., Critcher, C., Jefferson, T., Clarke, J., and Roberts, B. (1978) *Policing the Crisis* London: Macmillan

Hall, Stuart (1979) "Drifting into a law and order society" *Cobden Trust Human Rights Lecture*

Harring, Sidney L. (2017) *Policing a Class Society* Chicago: Haymarket

Hibbert, Christopher (1958) *King Mob: The Story of Lord George Gordon and the London Riots of 1780* London: Longmans, Green and Co.

Hillyard. Paddy (1987) "The Normalization of Special Powers: from Northern Ireland to Britain" in Scraton, Phil (ed.) *Law, Order and the Authoritarian State* Milton Keynes: Open University Press

Kamat, Anjali (2016) "The Baltimore Uprising" in Camp and Heatherton (eds.) *op cit*

Kitson, Frank (1971) *Low Intensity Operations: Subversion, Insurgency, Peace-keeping* London: Faber and Faber

Lamas, Andrew T. "Angela Davis" in Callinicos, Alex, Stathis Kouvelakis and Lucia Pradella (eds.) (2021) *Routledge Handbook of Marxism and Post-Marxism* Abingdon: Routledge pp.409-417

Maynard, Robyn (2017) *Policing Black Lives: State violence in*

Canada from slavery to the present Fernwood Publishing: Manitoba CA.

New York Times (2020) "Black Lives Matter May Be the Largest Movement in US History" 3 July

Platt, Tony (1982) *Iron Fist and the Velvet Glove: An Analysis of the US Police* New York: Synthesis

Reiner, Robert (2010) *The Politics of the Police* Oxford: Oxford University Press

Rogers, Nicholas "The Gordon Riots and the Politics of War" in Haywood, Ian and John Seed (eds.) (2012) *The Gordon Riots: Politics, Culture and Insurrection in Late Eighteenth-Century Britain* Cambridge: Cambridge University Press

Rollo, Joanna "The Special Patrol Group" in Hain, Peter (ed.) (1980) *Policing the Police Volume 2* London: John Calder

Ruggiero, Vincenzo (2018) *Dirty Money* Oxford: Oxford University Press

Sandhu, Serina "Female crime victims 'belittled and not believed on police chief's watch'" *The Independent* 10 September 2021 p.15

Scalia, Vincenzo (2017) *Crime, Networks and Power* Basingstoke: Palgrave Macmillan

Schrader, Stuart (2019) *Badges without Borders: How Global Counterinsurgency Transformed American Policing* Berkeley: University of California Press

Scraton, Phil (1985) *The State of the Police* London: Pluto

Smith, Mikey (15/3/2021) "Minister defends harsher sentences for attacks on statues than on women" Mirror.co.uk https://www.mirror.co.uk/news/politics/minister-defends-harsher-sentences-attacks-23721534

Sparks, Colin (2021)) "Stuart Hall" in Callinicos, Alex, Stathis Kouvelakis and Lucia Pradella (eds.) *Routledge Handbook of Marxism and Post-Marxism* Abingdon: Routledge pp.426-435

Taylor, Keeanga Yamatta (2016) *From #blacklivesmatter to Black Liberation* Chicago: Haymarket

Vegh Weis, Valeria (2018) *Marxism and Criminology: A History of Criminal Selectivity* Chicago: Haymarket
Weiner, Tim (2012) *Enemies* London: Allen Lane
Wells, Roger (1983) *Insurrection: The British Experience 1796-1803 Gloucester*: Alan Sutton
Whyte, William Foote (1943) *Street Corner Society* Chicago: University of Chicago Press
Wodak, Ruth (2015) *The Politics of Fear* London: Sage
Zola, Emile (1958) *His Excellency* London: Elek Books Ltd

Chapter 2

Aspinall, P. J. (2021). BAME (black, Asian and minority ethnic): the "new normal" in collective terminology. *J Epidemiol Community Health*, 75(2), 107.
Bacchini, F., and Lorusso, L. (2019). Race, again: how face recognition technology reinforces racial discrimination. *Journal of information, communication and ethics in society*.
Beaman, J. (2020). Underlying Conditions: Global Anti–Blackness amid COVID–19.
Bowling, B., and Phillips, C. (2003). Policing ethnic minority communities.
Brunson, R. K., and Stewart, E. A. (2021). In Search of a Critical Mass: Do Black Lives Matter in Criminology and Criminal Justice Programs?
Cain, M. E. (2015). *Society and the Policeman's Role*. Routledge.
Christie, N. (1986). The ideal victim. In *From crime policy to victim policy* (pp. 17-30). Palgrave Macmillan, London.
Delsol, R. (2006). *Institutional racism, the police and stop and search: a comparative study of stop and search in the UK and USA* (Doctoral dissertation, University of Warwick).
Demie, F. (2021). The experience of Black Caribbean pupils in school exclusion in England. *Educational Review*, 73(1), 55-70.
Donnelly, E. A. (2017). The politics of racial disparity reform: Racial inequality and criminal justice policymaking in the

states. *American Journal of Criminal Justice, 42*(1), 1-27.

Dunham, R. G., and Petersen, N. (2017). Making Black lives matter: Evidence-based policies for reducing police bias in the use of deadly force. *Criminology & Public Policy, 16*, 341.

Fatsis, L. (2019). Policing the beats: The criminalisation of UK drill and grime music by the London Metropolitan Police. *The sociological review, 67*(6), 1300-1316.

Ghandnoosh, N. (2015). Black lives matter: Eliminating racial inequity in the criminal justice system.

Gunter, A. (2003). The Trouble with Black (Male) Youth. *Criminal Justice Matters, 54*(1), 22-23.

Height, Dorothy available at Dorothy Height quote: Civil rights are civil rights. There are no persons who...(azquotes.com)

Hetey, R. C., and Eberhardt, J. L. (2018). The numbers don't speak for themselves: Racial disparities and the persistence of inequality in the criminal justice system. *Current Directions in Psychological Science, 27*(3), 183-7.

Home Office 2020: https://www.ethnicity-facts-figures.service. gov.uk/crime-justice-and-the-law/policing/stop-and-search/ latest

Institute of Race Relations 2014: https://irr.org.uk/research/deat hs/bame-refugee-and-migrant-deaths-in-custody-2014-2020/

Joseph–Salisbury, R., Connelly, L., and Wangari-Jones, P. (2020). "The UK is not innocent": Black Lives Matter, policing and abolition in the UK. *Equality, Diversity and Inclusion: An International Journal.*

Palmer, S. (2012). "Dutty Babylon": policing Black communities and the politics of resistance: Suzella Palmer charts the history of policing Black communities. *Criminal Justice Matters, 87*(1), 26-27.

Reiner, R. (2010). *The politics of the police.* Oxford University Press.

Robertson, L., and Wainwright, J. P. (2020). Black Boys' and Young Men's Experiences with Criminal Justice and Desistance in

England and Wales: A Literature Review. *Genealogy*, 4(2), 50.

Warmington, P. (2014). *Black British intellectuals and education: Multiculturalism's hidden history*. Routledge.

Weitzer, R., and Tuch, S. A. (1999). Race, class, and perceptions of discrimination by the police. *Crime & delinquency*, 45(4), 494-507.

Williams, P., and Clarke, B. (2018). The black criminal Other as an object of social control. *Social Sciences*, 7 (11), 234.

Chapter 5

Arendt, H. (1972) "On Violence", in *Crises of the Republic*. New York: Harcourt Brace Jovanovich, pp. 103–198.

Celikates, R. (2016) "Rethinking Civil Disobedience as a Practice of Contestation—Beyond the Liberal Paradigm," *Constellations*, 23(1), pp. 37–45. doi: 10.1111/1467-8675.12216.

Clement, M. (2016) *A people's history of riots, protest and the law: the sound of the crowd*. London: Palgrave Macmillan.

D'Arcy, S. (2014) *Languages of the Unheard: Why militant protest is good for democracy*. 1 edition. London: Zed Books Ltd.

Delmas, C. (2018) *A duty to resist: when disobedience should be uncivil*. New York: Oxford University Press.

Havercroft, J. (2021) "The British Academy Brian Barry Prize Essay. Why Is There No Just Riot Theory?", *British Journal of Political Science*, pp. 1–15. doi: 10.1017/S000712342000085X.

Hooker, J. (2016) "Black Lives Matter and the Paradoxes of US Black Politics: From Democratic Sacrifice to Democratic Repair", *Political Theory*, 44(4), pp. 448–469. doi: 10.1177/0090591716640314.

King Jr, M. L. (1968) *The M.L. King Speech*. Available at: http://www.gphistorical.org/mlk/mlkspeech/ (Accessed: 19 July 2018).

King, M. L. (2002) *The autobiography of Martin Luther King, Jr* Edited by C. Carson. London: Abacus.

Markovits, D. (2004) "Democratic disobedience," *Yale LJ*, 114,

p. 1897.

Pasternak, A. (2018) "Political Rioting: A Moral Assessment", *Philosophy & Public Affairs*, 46(4), pp. 384–418. doi: 10.1111/papa.12132.

Rawls, J. (1999) *A Theory of Justice*. Revised edition. Cambridge, Mass: Harvard University Press.

Rudé, G. (2005) *The Crowd in History: A study of popular disturbances in France and England, 1730-1848*. 2nd edition. London: Serif.

Shelby, T. (2007) "Justice, Deviance, and the Dark Ghetto", *Philosophy & Public Affairs*, 35(2), pp. 126–160. doi: 10.1111/j.1088-4963.2007.00106.x.

Thompson, E. P. (1971) "The moral economy of the English Crowd in the eighteenth century," *Past & Present*, 50, pp. 76–136.

Walzer, M. (1982) *Obligations: Essays on Disobedience, War, and Citizenship*. New Ed edition. Cambridge, Mass: Harvard University Press.

Chapter 6

Amnesty International (2018) *Trapped in the Matrix: Secrecy, stigma, and bias in the Met's Gangs Database,* London, Amnesty International United Kingdom Section.

Banks, J. (2011) "Foreign National Prisoners in the UK: Explanations and Implications," *Howard Journal of Criminal Justice* 50:2, pp. 184-198.

Barker, M. (1981) *The New Racism: Conservatives and the Ideology of the Tribe,* London, Junction Books.

Barker, M. (1992) "Stuart Hall, PTC", in Barker M. and Beezer, A. (eds) *Reading into Cultural Studies,* London, Routledge, pp. 83-103.

BBC (2018) "Windrush: How do you prove you've been living in the UK?", *BBC News* 18 April. Available at www.bbc.co.uk/news/uk-43795077 (accessed 23 July 2021).

Bourne, J. (2001) "The life and times of institutional racism", *Race & Class* 43:2, pp. 7-22.

Bradford, B. and Tiratelli, M. (2019) *UK Justice Policy Review Focus 4: Does stop and search reduce crime?* London, The Centre for Crime and Justice Studies.

Brown, J. (1982) *Policing by Multi-Racial Consent: The Handsworth Experience,* London, Bedford Square/NCVO.

Bunce, R. and Field, P. (2010) "Landmark Court Case Against Police Racism," *Diverse Magazine,* 1 December.

Burnett, J. (2012) "After Lawrence: racial violence and policing in the UK", *Race & Class* 54:1, pp. 91-98.

Cameron, D. (2005) "Full text of David Cameron's Victory Speech," *Guardian,* 6 December. Available at www. theguardian.com/politics/2005/dec/06/toryleadership2005. conservatives3 (accessed 23 July 2021).

Cameron, D. (2011) *PM's speech at Munich Security Conference,* 5 February, London, Cabinet Office. Available at www.gov. uk/government/speeches/pms-speech-at-munich-security-conference (accessed 23 July 2021).

Cathcart, B. (1999) *The Case of Stephen Lawrence,* London, Penguin, 2000.

Commission on Race and Ethnic Disparities (2021) *The Report [The Sewell Report],* London, UK Government.

Counter Terrorism Policing (2020) *Safeguarding young people and adults from ideological extremism,* Counter Terrorism Policing South

Dick, C. (2012) "Stephen Lawrence murder: nothing in the Met's history had a greater impact," *Guardian,* 3 January. Available at www.theguardian.com/global/2012/jan/03/cressida-dick-stephen-lawrence-verdicts (accessed 23 July 2021).

Evans, R. (2019) "Black undercover officer who spied on Stephen Lawrence campaign named", *Guardian,* 16 July. Available at www.theguardian.com/uk-news/2019/jul/16/ black-undercover-officer-who-spied-on-stephen-lawrence-campaign-named (accessed 23 July 2021).

Fekete, L. (2013) "Total Policing: Reflections from the Frontline," *Race & Class* 54:3, pp. 65-76.

Ferguson, R. (2020) "Challenging Prevent: Building Resistance to Institutional Islamophobia and the Attack on Civil Liberties," in Hart, E. L., Greener, J. and Moth, R. (eds) *Resist the Punitive State,* London, Pluto, pp. 232-254.

Foot, P. (1969) *The Rise of Enoch Powell,* London, Penguin.

Gilroy, P. (1982) "Police and thieves" in CCCS, *The Empire Strikes Back: Race and Racism in 70s Britain,* London, Hutchinson, pp.143-182.

Gilroy, P. (1987) *There Ain't No Black in the Union Jack,* London, Hutchinson.

Gramsci, A. (1971) "The Study of Philosophy: Some Preliminary Points of Reference" in *Selections from the Prison Notebooks,* London, Lawrence and Wishart, pp. 323-343.

Gupta, P. S., and Bhattacharya, S. (2002) *Power, Politics and the People,* London, Anthem.

Hall, S., Critcher, C., Jefferson, T., Clarke, J., and Roberts, B. (1978a) *PTC, Mugging, the State and Law & Order,* Basingstoke, Palgrave Macmillan (this edition 2013).

Hall, S., Critcher, C., Jefferson, T., Clarke, J., and Roberts, B. (1978b) "The New Challenge of the Right," in Hall, S. *The Hard Road to Renewal: Thatcherism and the Crisis of the Left* (London: Verso, 1988).

Hall, S. (1985) "Cold Comfort Farm," in Hall, S. *The Hard Road to Renewal: Thatcherism and the Crisis of the Left* (London: Verso, 1988).

Hall, S. (1999) "From Scarman to Lawrence," *History Workshop Journal,* No. 48 (Autumn, 1999), pp. 187-197.

HM Government (2011) *Contest: The United Kingdom's Strategy for Countering Terrorism,* London, HM Government.

Home Office (2011) *An overview of recorded crimes and arrests resulting from disorder events in August 2011.* Available at www.gov.uk/government/publications/an-overview-of-recorded-crimes-and-arrests-resulting-from-disorder-events-in-august-2011 (accessed 23 July 2021).

Home Office (2013) *Tackling illegal immigration in privately rented Accommodation. The Government's Response to the Consultation,* 10 October. Available at www.gov.uk/government/consultations/tackling-illegal-immigration-in-privately-rented-accommodation (accessed 23 July 2021).

Home Office (2015), *Prevent Duty Guidance,* 12 March. Available at www.gov.uk/government/publications/prevent-duty-guidance (accessed 23 July 2021).

Home Office (2020a) *Trends and Drivers of Homicide,* Research Report 113, March.

Home Office (2020b) *Group-based Child Sexual Exploitation: Characteristics of Offending,* December.

Honeycombe-Foster, M (2020), "Boris Johnson launches fresh review into racial inequality in wake of Black Lives Matters protests", *Politics Home,* 15 June. Available at www.politicshome.com/news/article/boris-johnson-launches-fresh-review-into-racial-inequality-in-wake-of-black-lives-matters-protests (accessed 23 July 2021).

House of Lords (2018) "Impact of 'Hostile Environment' Policy," *House of Lords Library Briefing,* 11 June.

Howe, D. (1988) *From Bobby to Babylon, Blacks and the British Police,* London, Bookmarks, 2020.

Jaitman, L. and Machin, S. (2013) "Crime and immigration: new evidence from England and Wales," *IZA Journal of Migration,* 2:19.

King's Fund (2015) "What do we know about the impact of immigration on the NHS?" *The King's Fund verdict.* Available at www.kingsfund.org.uk/projects/verdict/what-do-we-know-about-impact-immigration-nhs (accessed 23 July 2021).

Kirkup, J. and Winnett, R. (2012) "Theresa May Interview, 'We're Going to Give Illegal Migrants a Really Hostile Reception,'"

Telegraph, 25 May.

Liberty (2021) *Misuse of Extreme Powers Latest Threat to Rule of Law, Says Liberty Following Shamima Begum Ruling*, 26 February.

Macpherson, W. (1999) *The Stephen Lawrence Inquiry*, London, The Stationary Office.

Mills, H. (1992) "Police pay £50,000 to settle case," *Independent*, 12 October. Available at www.independent.co.uk/news/uk/police-pay-pounds-50-000-to-settle-case-an-action-for-damages-by-a-civil-rights-leader-has-ended-but-without-an-apology-heather-mills-reports-1557060.html (accessed 23 July 2021).

Ministry of Justice (2019) *Statistics on Race and the Criminal Justice System 2018*, London: Ministry of Justice.

Olende, K. (2020) "The 'Hostile Environment' for Immigrants, The Windrush Scandal and Resistance", in Hart, E. L., Greener, J. and Moth, R. (eds) *Resist the Punitive State*, London, Pluto.

ONS (2021) *Homicide in England and Wales: year ending March 2020*, London, Office for National Statistics, 25 February.

Powell, E. (1968), "Speech at Birmingham 20th April, 1968," *EnochPowell.net* www.enochpowell.net/fr-79.html (accessed 23 July 2021).

Lord Scarman (1981) *The Scarman Report, The Brixton Disorders 10-12 April 1981*, Harmondsworth, Pelican.

Silvestri, A., Oldfield, M., Squires, P. and Grimshaw R. (2009) *Young People, Knives and Guns*, London, Centre for Crime and Justice Studies.

Sivanandan, A. (1976) Race Class and the State: The Political Economy of Immigration, *Catching History on the Wing*, London, Pluto, 2008, pp. 65-89.

Sivanandan, A. (1985) "RAT and the Degradation of Black Struggle," *Communities of Resistance, Writings on Black Struggles for Socialism*, London, Verso, 1990, pp. 77-122.

Sivanandan, A. (1990) "All that Melts into Air is Solid," *Communities of Resistance, Writings on Black Struggles for Socialism*, London, Verso, pp. 19-59.

Sivanandan, A. (2006) "Britain's shame, from multiculturalism to nativism," *Institute of Race Relations.* Available at www.irr.org.uk/news/britains-shame-from-multiculturalism-to-nativism

Syal, R. (2021) "Home Office failing Windrush generation again, spending watchdog finds," *Guardian,* 27 July. Available at www.theguardian.com/uk-news/2021/jul/27/home-office-failing-windrush-generation-again-spending-watchdog-finds (accessed 17 August 2021).

Taylor, D. (2021) "UK deportation flight to Jamaica leaves with just seven people on board," *Guardian* 11 August. Available at www.theguardian.com/uk-news/2021/aug/11/uk-deportation-flight-jamaica-leaves-seven-people-onboard (accessed 17 August 2021).

Thatcher, M. (1978) *TV Interview for Granada World in Action ("rather swamped"),* 27 January. Available at www.margaretthatcher.org/document/103485 (accessed 23 July 2021).

Ture K. and Hamilton, C. V. (1967) *Black Power: The Politics of Liberation in America*, New York, NY, Vintage, 1992.

UK Government (2021) *Nationality and Borders Bill 2021*, London, UK Government. Available at bills.parliament.uk/bills/3023 (accessed 23 July 2021).

UK Government (2021) *Police, Crime, Sentencing and Courts Bill 2021*, London, UK Government. Available at bills.parliament.uk/bills/2839 (accessed 17 August 2021).

Virdee, S. (2014) *Racism, Class and the Racialized Outsider,* Basingstoke: Palgrave Macmillan.

Walker, P. (2021) "Disproportionate targeting of Jamaicans for deportation from UK, data suggests", *Guardian,* 25 July. Available at www.theguardian.com/uk-news/2021/jul/25/disproportionate-targeting-of-jamaicans-for-deportation-from-uk-data-suggests (accessed 17 August 2021).

Williams, P. (2015) "Criminalizing the Other: Challenging the Race-gang Nexus," *Race & Class* 56:3, pp. 18-35.

Chapter 7

Abdalla, P. (2020) "'People want to stand up for what's right': in Wilkes-Barre, teens raise their voices in peaceful protest". *Pennsylvania Capitol-Star*. 3 June.

Barker, K., Baker, M., and Watkins, A. (2021) "In city after city, police mishandled Black Lives Matter protests". *The New York Times*. 20 March.

Buchanan, L., Bui, Q., and Patel, J. (2020) "Black Lives Matter may be the largest movement in US history." *The New York Times.* 3 July. Available at https://www.nytimes.com/interactive/2020/07/03/us/george-floyd-protests-crowd-size.html

Collins, R. (2008) *Violence: A Micro-sociological Theory,* Princeton: Princeton University Press.

'Corona, W. (2020, June 03) Carrollton police officers dance with protestors during rally. Retrieved January 13, 2021, from https://www.wsbtv.com/news/local/atlanta/carrolton-police-officers-dance-with-protestors-during-rally/T6HPEDFD3F G5BE3FOHVFA7DAGM/

Cruz, C. (2020, June 02) Peaceful protest in downtown Lawrenceville Monday night following death of George Floyd ends in prayer. Retrieved January 12, 2021, from https://www.gwinnettdailypost.com/local/peaceful-protest-in-downtown-lawrenceville-monday-night-following-death-of-george-floyd-ends-in-prayer/article_69715722-a42f-11ea-a903-5328ab9d0b1c.html

D'Arcy, S. (2013) *Languages of the Unheard*: *Why Militant Protest Is Good for Democracy*, London: ZED Books.

Davis, S. (1986) *Parades and Power: Street Theatre in Nineteenth-Century Philadelphia*, Berkeley: University of California Press.

Delgado, M. (2016) *Celebrating Urban Community Life: Fairs, Festivals, Parades, and Community Practice*, Toronto: University of Toronto Press.

Dennis, E. (2020) "'It's not over,' protesters vow", *Moscow-Pullman Daily News.* 13 July.

Gajanan, M. (2020) "Protests are being held in small cities and towns across the US – and young people are leading the charge", *Time*, 4 June. https://time.com/5847228/george-floyd-nationwide-protests/

Hettrick, D. (June 7, 2020) Peaceful and uplifting march draws 4,000 people to Shoreline's Black Lives Lost protest. Shoreline Area News. Retrieved from https://www.shorelineareanews. com/2020/06/peaceful-and-uplifting-march-draws-4000. html.

Hinton, E. (2021) *America on Fire*, New York: Liveright Publishers.

Massara, J. (2020, July 15) Want to Protest? Get A Permit: Lawrenceville Police. Retrieved January 13, 2021, from https://patch.com/georgia/dacula/want-protest-get-permit-lawrenceville-police

Monti, D. (1999) *The American City*, Oxford: Blackwell Publishers.

Nassauer, A. (2019) *Situational Breakdowns: Understanding Protest Violence and Other Surprising Outcomes*, Oxford: Oxford University Press.

O'Hehir, A. (2020) 'Protest in a small town: Black Lives Matter comes to rural America – and it matters,' *Salon*, 15 June [Online]. Available at https://www.salon.com/2020/06/15/protest-in-a-small-town-black-lives-matter-comes-to-rural-america--and-it-matters/

Robertson, C. (2020) "What Black Lives Matter has revealed about small-town America", *The New York Times.* 28 August.

Shuler, J. (2020) "Can the white people of small-town America get behind the movement for black lives?" *New Republic*, 2 July.

Tilly, C. and S. Tarrow (2015) *Contentious Politics*, Oxford:

Oxford University Press.

Wikipedia (2020) https://en.wikipedia.org/wiki/List_of_George_ Floyd_protests_in_the_United_States. See also "2020-21 United States racial unrest." https://en.wikipedia.org/wiki/2020%E2%8 0%9321_United_States_racial_unrest.

Chapter 8

Alexander, M. (2010) *The New Jim Crow. Mass Incarceration in the Age of Colorblindness* New York and London: The New Press

Bauman, Z. (1998). *Work, Consumerism and the New Poor.* Open University Press

Black Lives Matter (2021) "About" *Black Lives Matter Website* https://blacklivesmatter.com/about/ [Accessed 29.03.21]

Burgess, C. and Read, R. (2020) "Extinction Rebellion and environmental activism – the XR interviews" *Journal of Human Rights and the Environment*, Vol. 11 Special Issue, pp. 171–80

Campisi, M. C. 2014. "From a Duty to Remember to an Obligation to Memory? Memory as Reparation in the Jurisprudence of the Inter-American Court of Human Rights" *International Journal of Conflict and Violence* 8 (1): 61–74.

Chodor, T. (2015) "Neoliberal Hegemony and the Pink Tide in Latin America" London: Palgrave Macmillan

Choonara, J. (2020) "A new cycle of revolt" *International Socialism Journal* 165 pp. 21-36

Corredor, J., Wills-Obregon, M.E. and Asensio-Brouard, M. (2018) "Historical memory education for peace and justice: definition of a field" *Journal of Peace Education*, 15:2, pp.169-90

Davis, A.Y. (2016) *Freedom is a Constant Struggle* London: Haymarket Books

Delgado, R. and Stefancic, J. (2007) "Critical Race Theory and Criminal Justice" *Humanity and Society*, Vol. 31 pp. 133-145.

Extinction Rebellion (2021) "Act Now" *Extinction Rebellion website* https://extinctionrebellion.uk/act-now/ [Accessed 06.07.21]

Ferrell, J (2001) *Tearing Down the Streets. Adventures in Urban Anarchy* London: Palgrave

Ferrell, J. and Greer, C. (2009) "Editorial: Global Collapse and cultural possibility" *Crime, Media Culture,* 5(1), pp. 5-7

Fleetwood, J. and Lea, J. (2021) "De-funding the Police in the UK" *British Society of Criminology Newsletter* https://www.britsoccrim.org/wp-content/uploads/2020/08/BSCN85-Fleetwood-Lea.pdf [Accessed 05.07.2021]

Fridays for Future (2021) *Website* https://fridaysforfuture.org/ [Accessed 16.06.21]

Graeber, D. (2011) "Occupy Wall Street's anarchist roots" *Al Jazeera* https://www.aljazeera.com/opinions/2011/11/30/occupy-wall-streets-anarchist-roots/ [Accessed 24 June 2021]

Hanley, R.P. (2018) "Rousseau, Smith, and Kant on Becoming Just" in LeBar, M. (ed) (2018) *Justice* Oxford Scholarship Online https://oxford-universitypressscholarship-com.liverpool.idm.oclc.org/view/10.1093/oso/9780190631741.001.0001/oso-9780190631741-chapter-3 [Accessed 26th March 2021]

Hammond, J.L. (2003) "Another World Is Possible: Report from Porto Alegre" *Latin American Perspectives* Vol. 30, No. 3 pp. 3-11

Honig, B. (1993) "Rawls on Politics and Punishment" *Political Research Quarterly* Vol. 46, No. 1 pp. 99-125

Klein, N. (2015) *This Changes Everything: Capitalism Vs. The Climate* London: Penguin Books.

Lashua, B., Johnson, C.W. and Parry, D.C. (2021) "Leisure in the Time of Coronavirus: A Rapid Response" *Leisure Sciences,* Vol. 43 (1-2) pp. 6-11

Lee, E.V. (2021) "Native children didn't 'lose' their lives at residential schools. Their lives were stolen" *The Guardian* https://www.theguardian.com/commentisfree/2021/jul/06/native-children-didnt-lose-their-lives-at-residential-schools-their-lives-were-stolen [Accessed 17.08.21]

Monbiot, G. (2020). "Coronavirus shows us it's time to rethink everything. Let's start with education." *The Guardian*, May 12 https://www.theguardian.com/commentisfree/2020/may/12/ coronavirus-education-pandemic-natural-world-ecology [Accessed 14.07.21]

Naegler, L. (2018) "Goldman-Sachs doesn't care if you raise chicken": the challenges of resistant prefiguration *Social Movement Studies* Vol. 17, No. 5, 507–523

Patriquin, L. (2019) *Permanent Citizens' Assemblies: A New Model for Public Deliberation* Rowman & Littlefield International

Pejcha, C.S. (2020) "Better living through anarchy: Tracking the rise of the temporary autonomous zone" [Accessed 05.04.21]

Piketty, T. (2020) *Capital and Ideology*. Cambridge, MA: Belknap Press of Harvard University Press.

Robins, J. and Newman, D. (2021) *Justice in a Time of Austerity. Stories from a system in crisis* Bristol: Bristol University Press

Sarangi, P. (1991) "Notion Of 'State' in John Rawls' Theory of Justice" *The Indian Journal of Political Science* Vol. 52, No. 2 pp. 195-207

Theodorou, J. (2018) "What Grassroots Groups Can Teach Us About Smart Aid" *The New Humanitarian* https://deeply. thenewhumanitarian.org/refugees/articles/2018/02/19/ living-on-mafia-leftovers-life-in-italys-biggest-refugee-camp [Accessed 29.03.21]

Webb, D. (2019) "Here we Stand: The Pedagogy of Occupy Wall Street" *Australian Journal of Adult Learning* Vol 59 (3) pp 342-64

Chapter 11

Adams, R. (2016). "Group opposing prison holds protest at SOAR Innovation Summit." *WYMT*, 6 June (Online). Available at https://www.wymt.com/content/news/Letcher-Governance-Project-holds-silent-protest-at-SOAR-Summit-in-381971531.

html (Accessed May 2019).

Anglin, M.K. (2002). "Lessons from Appalachia in the 20th century: Poverty, power, and the 'grassroots.'" *American Anthropologist, 104*(2), 565-582.

Appalachian Regional Commission. (2015). *The Appalachian Region. ARC,* 1 July (Online). Available at https://www.arc.gov/about-the-appalachian-region/ (Accessed October 2018).

Associated Press. (1989). "Violence in coal strike is increasing." *AP,* 5 September (Online). https://www.nytimes.com/1989/09/05/us/violence-in-coal-strike-is-increasing.html (Accessed May 2021).

Bailey, R.J. (2008). *Matewan Before the Massacre: Politics, Coal and the Roots of Conflict in a West Virginia Mining Community.* Morgantown, WV: West Virginia University Press.

Barlow, M. (2014). "Protestors peacefully speak out against police culture." *The Appalachian,* 5 December (Online). https://theappalachianonline.com/protesters-peacefully-speak-policing-culture/ (Accessed June 2021).

Blizzard, W.C. (2010). *When Miners March.* Oakland, CA: PM Press.

Corbin, D.A. (2015). *Life, Work, and Rebellion in the Coal Fields: The Southern West Virginia Miners, 1880-1922.* Morgantown, WV: West Virginia University Press.

Crenshaw, K. (1989). "Demarginalizing the intersection of race and sex: A Black feminist critique of antidiscrimination doctrine, feminist theory and antiracist politics." *University of Chicago Legal Forum, 1*(8), 139-168.

Eagly, I.V. and Schwartz, J.C. (2021). "Lexipol's fight against police reform." *Indiana Law Journal* (Forthcoming). https://ssrn.com/abstract=3869120 (Accessed July 2021).

Fabricant, N. and Fabricant, M. (2019). "Cognitive fracture: How disposable bodies and toxic status quo led to the rise of trump in Appalachia." *Journal of Labor and Society, 22*(1), 187-195.

Gilmore, R.W. (2020). "The case for prison abolition: Ruth Wilson Gilmore on COVID-19, racial capitalism & decarceration." *Democracy Now!*, 5 May (Online). https://www.democracynow.org/2020/5/5/ruth_wilson_gilmore_abolition_coronavirus (Accessed May 2020).

Hager, E. (2017). "A timely prison project? Or a GOP. congressman's boondoggle?" *The Marshall Project,* 7 November (Online). https://www.themarshallp roject.org/2017/11/07/a-timely-prison-project-or-a-g-o-p-congr essman-s-boondoggle (Accessed October 2019).

Hudak, J. (2020). "Tyler Childers to fans: 'Stop being so taken aback by Black Lives Matter'." *Rolling Stone*, 18 September (Online). https://www.rollingstone.com/music/music-country/tyler-childers-long-violent-history-black-lives-matter-1062224/ (Accessed July 2021).

International Storytelling Center (2020). "Do Black Lives Matter in Appalachia?" *ISC*, 3 July (Online). https://www.storytellingcenter.net/freedom-stories/do-black-lives-matter-in-appalachia/ (Accessed July 2021).

Jones, C. (2020). "Black Lives Matter protests rarely end in violence: Especially in Appalachia." *100 Days in Appalachia*, 23 July (Online). https://www.100daysin appalachia.com/2020/07/black-lives-matter-protests-rarely-e nd-in-violence-especially-in-appalachia/ (Accessed July 2021).

Lustbader, S. and Gullapalli, V. (2019). "Fighting against a new prison – and winning – in Letcher County, Kentucky. *The Appeal*, 1 July (Online). https://theappeal.org/fighting-against-a-new-prison-and-winning-in-letcher-county-kentucky/ (Accessed August 2019).

Nida, B. (2013). "Demystifying the hidden hand: Capital and the state at Blair Mountain." *Historical Archaeology*, 47(3), 52-68.

Ryerson, S. and Schept, J. (2018). "Building prisons in Appalachia: The region deserves better." *Boston Review*, 28 April (Online). http://bostonreview.net/reading-lists/rosiebusiakiewicz-boston-review-prison-strike-2018   (Accessed October 2019).

Schept, J. (2014). (Un)seeing like a prison: Counter-visual ethnography of the carceral state. *Theoretical Criminology*, *18*(2), 198-223.

Smith, B.E. and Fisher, S. (2016). "Reinventing the region: Defining, theorizing, organizing Appalachia." *Journal of Appalachian Studies*, 22(1), 76-79.

Standing, G. (2016). *The Precariat: The New Dangerous Class*. London, UK: Bloomsbury Academic.

Tuhus, M. (2019). "Broad coalition defeats plan to build federal prison on toxic former mountaintop removal coal site." *Between the Lines*, 10 July (Online). https://btlonline.org/broad-coalition-defeats-plan-to-build-federal-prison-on-toxic-former-mountaintop-removal-coal-site/   (Accessed October 2019).

Turner, B. (2020). Black lives have always mattered in Appalachia. *Lexington Herald*, 1 July (Online). https://www.kentucky.com/opinion/op-ed/article243815142.html (Accessed July 2021).

Turner, W.H. and Cabbell, E.J. (2014). *Blacks in Appalachia*. Lexington, KY: University Press of Kentucky.

United States Department of Justice. (2015). "Final environmental impact statement for proposed United States penitentiary and federal prison camp: Letcher County, Kentucky." *Prison Legal News*, 1 July (Online). https://www.prisonlegalnews.org/media/publications/FEIS_For_Proposed_US_Penitentiary_and_Federal_Prison_Camp_July_2015.pdf   (Accessed November 2019).

Westlake, S. (2020). "Appalachian solidarity with Black Lives Matter." *Art Place*, 15 July (Online). https://www.artplaceamerica.org/blog/appalachian-solidarity-black-lives-matter (Accessed June 2021).

Young, S.T. (2017). "Wild, wonderful, white criminality: Images of 'white trash' Appalachia." *Critical Criminology*, *25*(1), 103-

117.

Young, S.T. (2018). "'Do we really want to go down that path?': Abandoning Appalachia and the Elk River chemical spill." *Social Justice, 45*(2/3), 93-117.

Young, S.T. and Pitman, B. (2020). Total extraction: Exploitative behaviors of the carceral apparatus towards carceral officers in Central Appalachia. *Critical Criminology, 28*(4), 577-593. Black Lives Matter and Police Reform: Global Echoes of an American Social Movement

Chapter 12

Abdallah, S. (2020). Black Lives Matter abroad, too: Proposed solutions to the racialized policing of Ethiopian Jews in Israel. *William. & Mary Journal of Race, Gender & Social Justice,* 27, 2, 515-525.

Akinyetun, T. S. (2021). Reign of terror: A review of police brutality on Nigerian youth by the Special Anti-Robbery Squad (SARS). *African Security Review* 30, 1, 1-18.

Alemika, I. C. C. E. E., and Chukwuma, I. (2000). Police-community violence in Nigeria. Lagos. Centre for Law Enforcement Education (CLEEN)-National Human Rights Commission (NHRC).

Alves, J.A. (2018). *The Anti-Black City: Police Terror and Black Urban Life in Brazil.* University of Minnesota Press.

Andersen, Margaret L. and Howard F. Taylor (2002) *Sociology: Understanding a Diverse Society.* Wadsworth/Thomson Learning.

Anthony, T., Gainsford, A., and Sherwood, J. (2020). Instead of demonising Black Lives Matter protesters, leaders must act on their calls for racial justice. https://theconversation. com/instead-of-demonising-black-lives-matter-protesters-leaders-must-act-on-their-calls-for-racial-justice-143269 [Retrieved on August 22, 2021]

Balko, Radley (2021). *Rise of the warrior cop: The militarization of*

America's police forces. Public Affairs.

Bayley, D. H. (1990). *Patterns of policing: A comparative international analysis.* Rutgers University Press.

BBC (2021). Adama Traore: How George Floyd's death energised French protests. https://www.bbc.com/news/world-us-canada-57176500 [Retrieved September 13, 2021].

Ben-Porat, G., and Yuval, F. (2019). *Policing Citizens: Minority Policy in Israel.* Cambridge University Press.

Black Lives Matter (2021). About. https://blacklivesmatter.com/about/ [Retrieved August 22, 2021].

Chua, Charmaine. (2020). Abolition is a constant struggle: Five lessons from Minneapolis. *Theory & Event* 23, 5, S-127.

C-NET (2020). Global scenes of Black Lives Matter protests show outrage far beyond US. https://www.cnet.com/pictures/scenes-black-lives-matter-protests-around-the-world-show-outrage-beyond-us/ [Retrieved July 7, 2021].

Campesi, G. (2020). Police accountability and human rights at the Italian borders. In Carrera, Sergio and Marco, Stefan (eds). *Fundamental rights challenges in border controls and expulsion of irregular immigrants in the European Union* (pp. 125-147). Routledge.

Celestine, A. and Martin-Breteau, N. (2019). In and beyond the field: Researching black lives matter from France. *American Studies Journal, 68,* 1, 68-96.

Coalition for Racial Equality and Rights (2021). Scotland's response to George Floyd and Black Lives Matter: One year on. https://www.crer.scot/post/scotland-s-response-to-george-floyd-and-black-lives-matter-one-year-on [Retrieved August 22, 2021]

della Porta. Donatella, Hanspeter Kriesi & Rucht, Dieter (Eds). *Social movements in a globalizing world.* (Pp 206-222). Palgrave Macmillan

Denver Post (2020). How Colorado found the political will to pass a sweeping police reform law in just 16 days. https://

www.denverpost.com/2020/06/19/colorado-police-reform-accountability-bill/ [Retrieved July 21, 2021]

Denver Post (2021a). How Colorado lawmakers changed policing in their first full session since George Floyd protests. https://www.denverpost.com/2021/06/20/police-colorado-use-of-force-george-floyd/ [Retrieved July 22, 2021]

Denver Post (2021b). How the wrongful arrest of a Black teen in Denver led to proposed statewide reform of eyewitness identification. https://www.denverpost.com/2021/05/10/eye witness-identification-showups-colorado-legislation/ [Retrieved July 22, 2021]

della Porta. Donatella, Hanspeter Kriesi and Rucht, Dieter (1999). *Social movements in a globalizing world*. Palgrave Macmillan.

della Porta, Donatella and Anna Lavizzari. (2021). The Black Lives Matter Movement in Italy: Diffusion, organization, and resonance. https://ecpr.eu/Events/Event/PaperDetails/59273 [Retrieved September 13, 2021].

DeVega, Chauncey (2015). White killers go to Burger King: Race, Planned Parenthood and our diseased white privilege. https://www.salon.com/2015/12/01/white_killers_go_to_burger_king_race_planned_parenthood_and_our_diseased_white_privilege/

Diphoorn, T., Leyh, B. M., and Slooter, L. (2021). Transforming police reform: Global experiences through a multidisciplinary lens. *Policing: A Journal of Policy and Practice 15*, 1, 340–347.

Duxbury, L., Bennell, C., Halinski, M., and Murphy, S. (2018). Change or be changed: Diagnosing the readiness to change in the Canadian police sector. *The Police Journal, 91*, 4, 316–338.

DW (no date). French protesters call for an end to police violence. https://www.dw.com/en/french-protesters-call-for-an-end-to-police-violence/a-53943165 [Retrieved September 12, 2021].

Fasching-Varner, Kenneth J., Reynolds, Rema E., and Albert, Katrice A. (2014). (eds.) *Trayvon Martin, race, and American justice: Writing wrong.* Sense Publishers.

Frey, Richard G. (2001). Abner Louima case: Idiosyncratic personal crime or symptomatic police brutality? In Michael J. Palmiotto, ed. (Pp 232-242). *Police misconduct: A reader for the 21st Century.*

Hassett-Walker, Connie (2021). How you start is how you finish? The slave patrol and Jim Crow origins of policing. https://www.americanbar.org/groups/crsj/publications/human_rights_magazine_home/civil-rights-reimagining-policing/how-you-start-is-how-you-finish/ [Retrieved August 15, 2021]

Heuman, Gad and Burnard, Trevor (eds). (2018) *The Routledge history of slavery.* Routledge,

H.R.1280 - George Floyd Justice in Policing Act (2021). https://www.congress.gov/bill/117th-congress/house-bill/1280 [Retrieved August 24, 2021]

Independent (2020). Black Lives Matter: UK police leaders announce "plan of action" to address racial inequality after protests. https://www.independent.co.uk/news/uk/home-news/police-racial-inequality-black-lives-matter-protests-a9573696.html [Retrieved July 7, 2021]

Japan Times (2020). Protesters hit Tokyo and Osaka streets with rallies against racism and police brutality. https://www.japantimes.co.jp/news/2020/06/07/national/protests-rallies-race-police-brutality-tokyo-japan/ [Retrieved August 29, 2021]

Joseph–Salisbury, R., Connelly, L. and Wangari-Jones, P. (2021), "The UK is not innocent": Black Lives Matter, policing and abolition in the UK. *Equality, Diversity and Inclusion, 40,* 1, 21-28.

Koslicki, Wendy M. and Willits, Dale (2018). The iron fist in the velvet glove? Testing the militarization/community policing paradox. *International journal of police science & management 20,* 2, 143-154.

Kraska, Peter B. (2007) Militarization and policing – its relevance to 21st century police. *Policing 1*, 4: 501–513.

Legewie, Joscha (2016). Racial profiling and use of force in police stops: How local events trigger periods of increased discrimination. *American Journal of Sociology 122*, 2: 379–424.

Lind, E. A., and Tyler, T. R. (1988). *The social psychology of procedural justice.* Springer Science & Business Media.

Maynard, Robyn. (2017). *Policing Black Lives: State violence in Canada from slavery to the present.* Fernwood Publishing.

Mishra, M. (2020). Does Denmark also need to rethink its police? https://cphpost.dk/?p=114748 [Retrieved September 16, 2021]

Munoz, Cesar (2021). From Rio, a cautionary tale on police violence. https://www.hrw.org/news/2021/08/15/rio-cautionary-tale-police-violence [Retrieved September 1, 2021].

Muvumbi, A. K. (2021). Black lives matter in Italy. *European Journal of Women's Studies,* doi: 1350506820978900. [Retrieved September 15, 2021]

Nebeling, M., and Bissenbakker, N. (2021). The white tent of grief. Racialized conditions of public mourning in Denmark, *Social & Cultural Geography 22*, 2, 170-188.

Naber, N. (2017). "The U.S. and Israel make the connections for us": Anti-imperialism and Black-Palestinian solidarity. *Critical Ethnic Studies, 3.* 2, 15-30.

New York Times (2021). As new police reform laws sweep across the U.S., some ask: Are they enough? https://www.nytimes.com/2021/04/18/us/police-reform-bills.html [Retrieved July 24, 2021].

NPR (2020). As New Zealand Police pledge to stay unarmed, Maori activists credit US protests. https://www.npr.org/sections/live-updates-protests-for-racial-justice/2020/06/11/874851593/as-new-zealand-police-pledge-to-stay-unarmed-maori-activists-credit-u-s-protests [Retrieved August 31, 2021].

Oriola, T. (2020). Why police reform won't happen without public pressure on politicians. https://theconversation.com/

why-police-reform-wont-happen-without-public-pressure-on-politicians-147453 [Retrieved August 23, 2021]

Ojedokun, U. A., Ogunleye, Y. O., and Aderinto, A. A. (2021). Mass mobilization for police accountability: The case of Nigeria's #EndSARS protest. *Policing: A Journal of Policy and Practice.* DOI: https://doi.org/10.1093/police/paab001

Parker, L. Craig (2015). *The Japanese police system today: A comparative study:* Routledge.

Penn, Everette B. (2003). On black criminology: Past, present and future. *Criminal Justice Studies 16*, 4: 317-327.

Palmiotto, Michael (1999) *Community policing: A policing strategy for the 21st century.* Jones & Bartlett Learning.

Potterf, Jebadiha E., and Jason R. Pohl. (2018). A black teen, a white cop, and a city in turmoil: Analyzing newspaper reports on Ferguson, Missouri and the death of Michael Brown. *Journal of Contemporary Criminal Justice 34*.4: 421-441. President's Task Force on 21st Century Policing (2015). Report. [https://www.justice.gov/archives/opa/blog/president-s-task-force-21st-century-policing-recommendations-print-action [Retrieved on December 2, 2020]

Ramos, P.C. and Volker, S. (2020). *Police violence against Black people is on the rise in Brazil.* Hamburg: GIGA German Institute of Global and Area Studies https://nbn-resolving.org/urn:nbn:de:0168-ssoar-68727-1

RAND (2014). *Effective policing for 21st-century Israel.* RAND Corporation

Reichel, Philip L. (1988). Southern slave patrols as a transitional police type. *American Journal of Police 7*, 51-75.

Reuters (2020). Reform, not revolution, is path to Black equality, says UK activist. https://www.reuters.com/article/us-minneapolis-police-protests-britain-idCAKBN23W19Q [Retrieved September 13, 2021]

RNZ (2020). Thousands of NZers march for Black Lives Matter. https://www.rnz.co.nz/news/national/418971/thousands-of-nzers-march-for-black-lives-matter [Retrieved September 1, 2021].

Rucht, Dieter (1999). The transnationalization of social movements: Trends, causes, problems della Porta. Donatella, Hanspeter Kriesi & Rucht, Dieter (Eds). *Social movements in a globalizing world.* (Pp 206-222). Palgrave Macmillan

Schaap, D. (2021). Police trust-building strategies. A socio-institutional, comparative approach. *Policing and Society 31,* 3, 304-320.

Shimemura, Y. (2002). Globalization vs. Americanization: Is the world being Americanized by the dominance of American culture. *Comparative Civilizations Review, 47,* 7-21.

Singh, P. (2021). One nation, one police is a reform that is long overdue. https://indianexpress.com/article/opinion/columns/one-nation-one-police-is-a-reform-that-is-long-overdue-7429149/ [Retrieved August 25, 2021].

Stanford Freeman Spogli Institute for International Studies (2020). Police reform in Brazil and Mexico: What works, what doesn't, and what the US can learn. https://fsi.stanford.edu/news/police-reform-brazil-and-mexico-what-works-what-doesn%E2%80%99t-and-what-us-can-learn [Retrieved August 22. 2020.]

The Africa Report (2021). Nigeria: Has the #EndSARS movement come to an end? https://www.theafricareport.com/85309/nigeria-has-the-endsars-movement-come-to-an-end/ [Retrieved on September 17, 2921]

The Diplomat (2020) Japan holds anti-racism rally, Protesting homegrown police brutality in solidarity with Black Lives Matter. https://thediplomat.com/2020/06/japan-holds-anti-racism-rally-protesting-homegrown-police-brutality-in-solidarity-with-black-lives-matter/ [Retrieved August 28, 2021]

The St Thomas Source (2020). As support for Black Lives Matter movement grows in Denmark, 'colonial amnesia' persists. https://stthomassource.com/content/2020/07/02/as-support-for-black-lives-matter-movement-grows-in-denmark-colonial-amnesia-persists/ [Retrieved on September 14, 2021]

The Wire (2020). Seeing India through the Black Lives Matter protests. https://thewire.in/rights/seeing-india-through-the-black-lives-matter-protests [Retrieved September 10, 2021]

Time (2020). A racial justice campaign brought new attention to Indonesia's poorest region. Will it translate to support for independence? https://time.com/5919228/west-papua-lives-matter-independence/

Toronto City News (2021). The history of Black Lives Matter Toronto and its momentous fight for change. https://toronto.citynews.ca/2021/02/04/the-history-of-black-lives-matter-toronto/ [Retrieved September 2, 2021]

UCLA Global (2021). BLM a catalyst for decolonization efforts in Belgium. https://www.international.ucla.edu/institute/article/240302 [Retrieved August 22, 2021]

Unicorn Riot (2021). Police in Brazil killed record amount of people in 2020. https://unicornriot.ninja/2021/police-in-brazil-killed-record-amount-of-people-in-2020/ [Retrieved September 13, 2021]

Unnithan, N. Prabha [Ed] (2013). *Crime and justice in India*. Sage.

Verma, Arvind and Subramanian K.S. (2009). *Understanding the police in India*. Lexis-Nexis Butterworths Wadhwa Nagpur.

Walker, Samuel and Katz, Charles M. (2022). *The police in America: An introduction*. McGraw-Hill.

Zamperini, A., Siracusa, V., and Menegatto, M. (2017). Accountability and police violence: a research on accounts to cope with excessive use of force in Italy. *Journal of police and criminal psychology*, 32, 2, 172-183.

Chapter 13

A Nigerian Youth, (2020) "Our five (5) demand", 11 October. Available at https://twitter.com/AishaYesufu/status/1318157843636387840/photo/1 (Accessed 19 July 2021)

Abati, R. (2020) "#EndSARS: Almost a revolution", *Sahara Reporters*, 13 October [Online]. Available at http://saharareporters.com/2020/10/13/endsars-almost-revolution-reuben-abati (Accessed 21 July 2021).

Adediran, I. (2020) "#EndSARS: 99 bodies deposited at Lagos morgue, three from Lekki tollgate – pathologist," *Premium Times*, 6 June. Available at "#EndSARS: 99 bodies deposited at Lagos morgue, three from Lekki tollgate – pathologist" (Accessed 20 July 2021)

Adeniran, T. (1974) "The dynamics of peasant revolt: a conceptual analysis of the Agbekoya Parapo uprising in the Western State of Nigeria," *Journal of Black Studies*, vol. 4, no.4, pp.363-375.

Ahire, P.T. (1991) *Imperial Policing: The Emergence and Role of the Police in Colonial Nigeria, 1860-1960*, Open University, Philadelphia.

Akinpelu, Y. (2020) "Despite violations, Nigeria failed to prosecute any SARS officer in three years – Amnesty," *Premium Times*, 27 June. Available at https://www.premiumtimesng.com/news/headlines/399892-despite-violations-nigeria-failed-to-prosecute-any-sars-officer-in-three-years-amnesty.html (Accessed 18 July 2021)

Alemika, E.E. (1993) "Colonialism, state and policing in Nigeria," *Crime, Law and Social Change*, vol. 20, no.3, pp.187-219.

Amnesty International, (2009) "Killing at will: extrajudicial executions and other unlawful killings by the police in Nigeria", *Amnesty International Publications* [Online]. Available at https://www.amnesty.org/download/Documents/44000/afr440382009en.pdf (Accessed 17 July 2021)

Amnesty International (2016) "You have signed your death warrant: torture and other ill-treatment by Nigeria's Special Anti-Robbery Squad (SARS)", *Amnesty International Publications* [Online]. Available at https://www.amnesty.org/download/

Documents/AFR4448682016ENGLISH.PDF (Accessed 17 July 2021)

Amnesty International (2020) "Nigeria: time to end impunity. Torture and other violations by Special Anti-Robbery Squad (SARS)," *Amnesty International Publications,* [Online]. Available at https://www.amnesty.org/download/Documents/AFR4495052020ENGLISH.PDF (Accessed 17 July 2021)

Aye, B. (2020a) "#EndSARS revolt and the bloodbath in Nigeria," *Global Labour Column* [Online]. Available at https://globallabourcolumn.org/2020/10/26/endsars-revolt-and-the-bloodbath-in-nigeria-part-2-the-missing-social-force/?fbclid=IwAR2W5yJ4PGYPYDb5zxO0G8SzijYYxkozHq7tvSSAXUz5UWeg4HPx3Hs_KNE (Accessed 1 July 2021).

Aye, B. (2020b) "#EndSARS revolt rocks Nigeria," *Labour Briefing,* November, pp. 36-7. Available at https://labourbriefing.org/blog/2020/11/11/endsars-revolt-rocks-nigeria?rq=nigeria (Accessed 4 July 2021).

Aye, B. (2020c) "Revolutionary pressures in Nigeria," *International Socialism,* Issue 169, pp. 31-8. Available at http://isj.org.uk/revolutionary-pressures-in-nigeria/ (Accessed 7 July 2021).

Aye, B. (2020d) Proteste gegen willkür in uniform, *Südlink,* pp. 12-3.

Aye, B. (2019) The actuality of #RevolutionNow1: "this act in itself will not delay their day of judgment", 7 August. Available at https://socialistworkersleague.org/2019/08/07/the-actuality-of-revolutionnow-i-this-act-in-itself-will-not-delay-their-day-of-judgment/ (Accessed 21 July 2021)

Balogun, A.S. (2013) "An Assessment of the Partisan Role of the Nigeria Police Force In The 1962 Action Group Crisis," *Journal of the Historical Society of Nigeria,* vol. 222, pp.33-62.

Beckman, B. (1984) *Bakolori: peasants versus state and capital.* University of Stockholm, Department of Political Science.

Coalition for Revolution, (2020) "CORE Charter for

Total Liberation", 1 October. Available at https://socialistworkersleague.org/2020/10/01/core-charter-for-total-liberation/ (Accessed 21 July 2021).

Cowan, L.G. (1958) "The Native Authority System in Nigeria," In *Local Government in West Africa*, pp. 12-34, Columbia University Press.

Falola T. (2009) *Colonialism and Violence in Nigeria*, Indiana University Press, Bloomington.

Feminist Coalition (2020) "In our own words: the Feminist Coalition," 18 December. Available at https://feministcoalition.medium.com/in-our-own-words-the-feminist-coalition-61bc658446dd (Accessed 19 July 2021).

Feminist Coalition, (n.d.) "Protests supported by the Feminist Coalition". Available at https://www.notion.so/80db6dfdd2 5f4277a5bc0fbcdc612857?v=027410e7a4784ceaa097e412ca610 0f7 (Accessed 19 July 2021).

Forrest, A. (2020) "End SARS protests: UK police trained 'brutal' Nigerian security forces," *Independent*, 30 October. Available at https://www.independent.co.uk/news/end-sars-nigeria-protests-security-forces-uk-police-training-b1254970.html (Accessed 31 July 2021)

Graf, W.D. (1983) "Nigerian elite consolidation and African elite theories: toward an explanation of African liberal democracy," *Verfassung und Recht in Übersee/Law and Politics in Africa, Asia and Latin America*, pp.119-138, Available at https://web.archive.org/web/20180719130157id_/https://www.nomos-elibrary.de/10.5771/0506-7286-1983-2-119.pdf (Accessed 9 July 2021)

Ikime, O. (1966) "The anti-tax riots in Warri province, 1927-1928," *Journal of the Historical Society of Nigeria*, vol.3, no.3, pp.559-73.

Jaja, S.O. (1982) "The Enugu Colliery Massacre in Retrospect: An Episode in British Administration of Nigeria," *Journal of the Historical Society of Nigeria*, vol.11, no. 3/4, pp.86-106.

Khalid, I. (2020) "Coronavirus: security forces kill more Nigerians than Covid-19," *BBC*, 16 April. Available at https://www.bbc.com/news/world-africa-52317196 (Accessed 16 July 2021)

Killingray, D. (1986) "The maintenance of law and order in British colonial Africa," *African Affairs*, vol. 85, no.340, pp.411-437.

Lakemfa, O. (2015) *Parliament of the streets: mass strikes and street protests that shook Nigeria in 2012*, Friedrich Ebert Stiftung, Abuja.

Matera, M., Bastian, M.L., and Kent S.K. (2012) *The women's war of 1929*, Palgrave Macmillan.

NBS, (2021) "Labour force statistics: unemployment and underemployment report (Q4 2020)", *National Bureau of Statistics (NBS)* [Online]. Available at https://nigerianstat.gov.ng/elibrary (Accessed 20 July 2021).

Ogun, S. (2020) "Justice for Tina Ezekwe NOW!" 2 June. Available at https://socialistworkersleague.org/2020/06/02/justice-for-tina-candlelight-rally-on-4-june/ (Accessed 19 June 2021)

Rasak, B. (2012) "Corruption, leadership and development in Nigeria," *Journal of Education and Leadership Development.*, vol. 4, no. 6, pp.1-12.

Tamuno, T.N. (1970) *The police in modern Nigeria, 1861-1965: Origins, development, and role*, Ibadan University Press, Ibadan.

Uko, N. (2004) *Romancing the gun: the press as promoter of military rule*, Africa World Press, Trenton NJ.

Yahaya, M.K. (2002) "Development and challenges of Bakolori irrigation project in Sokoto State, Nigeria", *Nordic Journal of African Studies*, vol. 11, vol. 3, pp.411-430. Available at https://njas.fi/njas/article/view/351/334 (Accessed 12 July 2021).

Chapter 14

Aguirre Beltrán Gonzalo. "La población negra en México." 3ª.

Edición. Fondo de Cultura Económica. México, 1989.

Astorga Luis. "El siglo de las drogas. Del Porfiriato al nuevo milenio." Debolsillo, Penguin Random House. México, 2016. "Drogas sin fronteras." Debolsillo, Penguin Random House. México, 2015.

Azaola Elena. "Imagen y autoimagen de la Policía de la Ciudad de México." Alter/Libros. Flasud – Ciesas – Ediciones Coyoacán. México, 2006.

Barrón Martín y Castro Laura. "La venta de oficios en el cabildo de la ciudad de México 1690 – 1700." Tesis. México, 1992.

Borah Woodrow. "El juzgado general de indios en la Nueva España." Fondo de Cultura Económica, México, 1985.

Brogden Mike. "The emergence of the police – the colonial dimension." The British Journal of Criminology , Winter 1987, Vol. 27, No. 1, Why Police?: Special Issue on Policing in Britain (Winter 1987), pp. 4-14

Chritie, Nils "A suitable amount of crime" London: Routledge, 2004

Freud Sigmund. "Psicología de las masas y análisis del "yo." En Obras completas. Vol. 19. Siglo veintiuno editotres. Buenos Aires, 2017. "La interpretación de los sueños (segunda parte)." En obras completas, Vol. 4. Siglo veintiuno editores, Buenos Aires, 2017.

Girard René. "La violencia y lo sagrado." Barcelona, Anagrama, 2005.

Harvey, David. "Breve storia del neo-liberismo. Milano, Il Saggiatore, 2007.

Inter American Court of Human Rights (corteidh.or.cr <contentious cases.Mexico> Women victims of sexual torture in Atenco VS Mexico) https://www.corteidh.or.cr/docs/casos/articulos/seriec_370_ing.pdf

Karam, Adolfo. "La unificacion de mandos de las policias federales en Mexico como strategia de seguridad publica,"

Political Publicas, Puebla, 2012.

Lafaye Jacques. "Quetzalcóatl y Guadalupe. La formación de la conciencia nacional de México." Fondo de Cultura Económica, 2ª. Reimpresión de la 2ª. Edición. México, 1992.

Melossi Dario. "La radicación (Radicamento – Embeddness) cultural del control social (o de la imposibilidad de la traducción): reflexiones a partir de la comparación de las culturas italiana y norteamericana con respecto al control social." En "Delito y sociedad." Revista de Ciencias Sociales. Año 6 número 9 – 10. Argentina, 1997.

Melossi Dario y Pavarini Massimo. "The prison and the factory. Origins of the Penitentiary System." The Macmillan Press. Inglaterra, 1981.

Merton Robert K. "Teoría y Estructura sociales." Fondo de Cultura Económica, 2ª Edición, México, 1980.

Pavarini Massimo. "Balance de la experiencia italiana en materia de reforma penitenciaria." En Alter, Revista internacional de Teoría, Filosofía y Sociología del Derecho. No. 1 enero – abril 1997. Universidad Autónoma de Campeche. México.

Paz Octavio. "México y Estados Unidos. Posiciones y contraposiciones. Pobreza y civilización." Conferencia inaugural del simposio México Today, Washington, 29 de septiembre de 1978. En: "El laberinto de la Soledad." Editorial Cátedra, España, 2003.

Rodríguez de San Miguel, Juan N. "Pandectas hispano – mexicanas." 3 volúmenes. UNAM, México, 1980.

Salazar Flora. "Los sirvientes domésticos." En: Moreno Toscano Alejandra. (Coordinadora) "Ciudad de México. Ensayo de Construcción de una Historia." Instituto Nacional de Antropología e Historia. Colección científica. México, 1978. Págs. 124 – 132.

Tavares, J. and Barrera, P., Paradoxos da seguranca cidadà, Tomo, Porto Alegre, 2016.

Tenorio Tagle Fernando. "El control social de las drogas en

México." INACIPE, México, 1991.

Universidad Autónoma Metropolitana "500 años de razones y justicia. Las memorias del ajusticiamiento." Segunda Edición, Universidad Autónoma Metropolitana – Azcapotzalco, México, 1999. Universidad Autónoma Metropolitana "Comunidad – Inmunidad. Entre los fines manifiestos de las políticas de la seguridad frente al delito y la lógica del sistema." En Alegatos No. 100, Revista del Departamento de Derecho de la Universidad Autónoma Metropolitana – Azcapotzalco. México, 2018.

Zaffaroni Raúl. "Manual de Derecho Penal Mexicano." Porrúa. México, 2013.

Zaffaroni Raúl e Dias dos Santos Ílison. "La nueva crítica criminológica. Criminología en tiempos del totalitarismo financiero." Kaos Editorial. México, 2019.

Chapter 15

Amnesty International. (2009). Greece: alleged abuses in the policing of demonstrations. London: Amnesty International Publications.

Amnesty International. (2012). Police violence in Greece: not just "isolated incidents." London: Amnesty International (in Greek).

Amnesty International. (2014). A law unto themselves: a culture of abuse and impunity in the Greek police. London: Amnesty International.

Amnesty International. (2021). Greece: freedom of assembly at risk and unlawful use of force in the era of Covid-19. London: Amnesty International.

BBC News. (2011). Greek police's strange motorbike tactic in Athens. Retrieved 30 July, 2021 from https://www.bbc.co.uk/news/av/world-europe-13957712

Christopoulos, D. (Ed.). (2014). Mapping ultra-right extremism, xenophobia and racism within the Greek state apparatus.

Brussels: Rosa Luxemburg Stiftung.

Dimou, E. (2021). Exiting democracy, entering authoritarianism: state control, policing and surveillance in Greek universities. *Crime Talk*. Retrieved from https://www.crimetalk.org.uk/index.php/library/section-list/1012-exiting-democracy-entering-authoritarianism

Kampagiannis, Th., and Human Rights 360. (2021). *The Greek police and racist crime through the proceedings of the Golden Dawn trial. Athens:* Human Rights 360 (in Greek).

Margaronis, M. (2012). Greek anti-fascist protesters "tortured by police" after Golden Dawn clash. *Guardian.co.uk*. Retrieved from http://www.guardian.co.uk/world/2012/oct/09/greek-antifascist-protesters-torture-police

Papanicolaou, G., and Rigakos, G. S. (2014). *Democratising the police in Europe with a particular emphasis on Greece*. Vienna: Transform! European Network, Nicos Poulantzas Institute and Rosa Luxemburg Foundation.

Papanicolaou, G., and Rigakos, G. S. (2021). Greece's Right-Wing Government Is Massively Expanding Police Powers. *Jacobin*. Retrieved from https://jacobinmag.com/2021/04/greece-special-forces-police-university-nd

Rigakos, G. S. (2016). *Security/Capital: a theory of pacification*. Edinburgh: Edinburgh University Press.

Rigakos, G. S., and Papanicolaou, G. (2003). The political economy of Greek policing: between neoliberalism and the sovereign State. *Policing and Society, 13*(3), 271-304.

Sakellaropoulos, S. (2019). *Greece's (un)competitive capitalism and the economic crisis: how the memoranda changed society, politics and the economy*. Cham: Palgrave Macmillan.

Vidali, S. (2007). *Crime control and state police: ruptures and continuities in crime policy*. Athens: Ant. N. Sakkoulas Publishers (in Greek).

CULTURE, SOCIETY & POLITICS

Contemporary culture has eliminated the concept and public
figure of the intellectual. A cretinous anti-intellectualism
presides, cheer-led by hacks in the pay of multinational
corporations who reassure their bored readers that there is no
need to rouse themselves from their stupor. Zer0 Books knows
that another kind of discourse - intellectual without being
academic, popular without being populist - is not only possible:
it is already flourishing. Zer0 is convinced that in the unthinking,
blandly consensual culture in which we live, critical and engaged
theoretical reflection is more important than ever before.

If you have enjoyed this book, why not tell other readers by
posting a review on your preferred book site.

You may also wish to
subscribe to our Zer0 Books YouTube Channel.

Bestsellers from Zer0 Books include:

Give Them An Argument
Logic for the Left
Ben Burgis
Many serious leftists have learned to distrust talk of logic. This is
a serious mistake.
Paperback: 978-1-78904-210-8 ebook: 978-1-78904-211-5

Poor but Sexy
Culture Clashes in Europe East and West
Agata Pyzik
How the East stayed East and the West stayed West.
Paperback: 978-1-78099-394-2 ebook: 978-1-78099-395-9

An Anthropology of Nothing in Particular
Martin Demant Frederiksen
A journey into the social lives of meaninglessness.
Paperback: 978-1-78535-699-5 ebook: 978-1-78535-700-8

In the Dust of This Planet
Horror of Philosophy vol. 1
Eugene Thacker
In the first of a series of three books on the Horror of Philosophy,
In the Dust of This Planet offers the genre of horror as a way of
thinking about the unthinkable.
Paperback: 978-1-84694-676-9 ebook: 978-1-78099-010-1

The End of Oulipo?
An Attempt to Exhaust a Movement
Lauren Elkin, Veronica Esposito
Paperback: 978-1-78099-655-4 ebook: 978-1-78099-656-1

Capitalist Realism
Is There No Alternative?
Mark Fisher
An analysis of the ways in which capitalism has presented itself
as the only realistic political-economic system.
Paperback: 978-1-84694-317-1 ebook: 978-1-78099-734-6

Rebel Rebel
Chris O'Leary
David Bowie: every single song. Everything you want to know,
everything you didn't know.
Paperback: 978-1-78099-244-0 ebook: 978-1-78099-713-1

Kill All Normies
Angela Nagle
Online culture wars from 4chan and Tumblr to Trump.
Paperback: 978-1-78535-543-1 ebook: 978-1-78535-544-8

Cartographies of the Absolute
Alberto Toscano, Jeff Kinkle
An aesthetics of the economy for the twenty-first century.
Paperback: 978-1-78099-275-4 ebook: 978-1-78279-973-3

Malign Velocities
Accelerationism and Capitalism
Benjamin Noys
Long listed for the Bread and Roses Prize 2015, *Malign Velocities*
argues against the need for speed, tracking acceleration
as the symptom of the ongoing crises of capitalism.
Paperback: 978-1-78279-300-7 ebook: 978-1-78279-299-4

Meat Market
Female Flesh under Capitalism
Laurie Penny
A feminist dissection of women's bodies as the fleshy fulcrum of capitalist cannibalism, whereby women are both consumers and consumed.
Paperback: 978-1-84694-521-2 ebook: 978-1-84694-782-7

Babbling Corpse
Vaporwave and the Commodification of Ghosts
Grafton Tanner
Paperback: 978-1-78279-759-3 ebook: 978-1-78279-760-9

New Work New Culture
Work we want and a culture that strengthens us
Frithjof Bergmann
A serious alternative for mankind and the planet.
Paperback: 978-1-78904-064-7 ebook: 978-1-78904-065-4

Romeo and Juliet in Palestine
Teaching Under Occupation
Tom Sperlinger
Life in the West Bank, the nature of pedagogy and the role of a university under occupation.
Paperback: 978-1-78279-637-4 ebook: 978-1-78279-636-7

Color, Facture, Art and Design
Iona Singh
This materialist definition of fine-art develops guidelines for architecture, design, cultural-studies and ultimately social change.
Paperback: 978-1-78099-629-5 ebook: 978-1-78099-630-1

Sweetening the Pill
or How We Got Hooked on Hormonal Birth Control
Holly Grigg-Spall
Has contraception liberated or oppressed women?
Sweetening the Pill breaks the silence on the dark side of hormonal
contraception.
Paperback: 978-1-78099-607-3 ebook: 978-1-78099-608-0

Why Are We The Good Guys?
Reclaiming Your Mind from the Delusions of Propaganda
David Cromwell
A provocative challenge to the standard ideology that Western
power is a benevolent force in the world.
Paperback: 978-1-78099-365-2 ebook: 978-1-78099-366-9

The Writing on the Wall
On the Decomposition of Capitalism and its Critics
Anselm Jappe, Alastair Hemmens
A new approach to the meaning of social emancipation.
Paperback: 978-1-78535-581-3 ebook: 978-1-78535-582-0

Enjoying It
Candy Crush and Capitalism
Alfie Bown
A study of enjoyment and of the enjoyment of studying. Bown
asks what enjoyment says about us and what we say about
enjoyment, and why.
Paperback: 978-1-78535-155-6 ebook: 978-1-78535-156-3

Ghosts of My Life
Writings on Depression, Hauntology and Lost Futures
Mark Fisher
Paperback: 978-1-78099-226-6 ebook: 978-1-78279-624-4

Neglected or Misunderstood
The Radical Feminism of Shulamith Firestone
Victoria Margree
An interrogation of issues surrounding gender, biology,
sexuality, work and technology, and the ways in which our
imaginations continue to be in thrall to ideologies of maternity
and the nuclear family.
Paperback: 978-1-78535-539-4 ebook: 978-1-78535-540-0

How to Dismantle the NHS in 10 Easy Steps (Second Edition)
Youssef El-Gingihy
The story of how your NHS was sold off and why you will have
to buy private health insurance soon. A new expanded second
edition with chapters on junior doctors' strikes and government
blueprints for US-style healthcare.
Paperback: 978-1-78904-178-1 ebook: 978-1-78904-179-8

Digesting Recipes
The Art of Culinary Notation
Susannah Worth
A recipe is an instruction, the imperative tone of the expert, but
this constraint can offer its own kind of potential. A recipe need
not be a domestic trap but might instead offer escape – something
to fantasise about or aspire to.
Paperback: 978-1-78279-860-6 ebook: 978-1-78279-859-0

Most titles are published in paperback and as an ebook.
Paperbacks are available in traditional bookshops. Both print and
ebook formats are available online.
Follow us at:
https://www.facebook.com/ZeroBooks
https://twitter.com/Zer0Books
https://www.instagram.com/zero.books